D1302004

$1.00

$1.00

Front—"Belief in God"

BY THE SAME AUTHOR

BELIEF IN CHRIST.
   (The Reconstruction of Belief Series).
THE EPISTLES OF ST. JOHN.
THE SERMON ON THE MOUNT.
THE EPISTLE TO THE EPHESIANS.
THE EPISTLE TO THE ROMANS. 2 Vols.
THE INCARNATION OF THE SON OF GOD
   (Bampton Lectures for 1891).
THE BODY OF CHRIST.
DISSERTATIONS ON SUBJECTS CONNECTED
   WITH THE INCARNATION.
THE NEW THEOLOGY AND THE OLD
   RELIGION.
THE MISSION OF THE CHURCH.
ORDERS AND UNITY.
SPIRITUAL EFFICIENCY.
THE PERMANENT CREED AND THE
   CHRISTIAN IDEA OF SIN.
THE QUESTION OF DIVORCE.

Edited by

LUX MUNDI. A series of Studies in the Religion
   of the Incarnation. By Various Writers.

BELIEF IN GOD

BELIEF IN GOD

BY CHARLES GORE, D.D.

HON. D.D. EDIN. AND DURHAM, HON. D.C.L. OXFORD, HON. LL.D. CAMBRIDGE
AND BIRMINGHAM, HON. FELLOW OF TRINITY COLLEGE, OXFORD,
FORMERLY BISHOP OF OXFORD

NEW YORK
CHARLES SCRIBNER'S SONS
1923

FIRST EDITION	.	.	*November* 1921
Reprinted	.	.	.	*November* 1921
Reprinted	.	.	.	*December* 1921
Reprinted	.	.	.	*December* 1921
Reprinted	.	.	.	*January* 1922
Reprinted	.	.	.	*March* 1922
Reprinted	.	.	.	*April* 1922
Reprinted	.	.	.	*October* 1922
Reprinted	.	.	.	*January* 1923

Printed in Great Britain by
Hazell, Watson & Viney, Ld., London and Aylesbury.

PREFACE

1. *Homme propose : Dieu dispose.* But anyway I *propose* to issue an ordered and reasoned statement of my faith as a Christian, as far as may be without assumptions, or, as I call it, a " Reconstruction of Belief," in three volumes, of which this is the first, dealing respectively with Belief in God, Belief in Jesus Christ, and Belief in the Holy Spirit and in the Church. There will be no reference to ecclesiastical authority in the first two volumes, but it will be seriously considered in the last. If the critics take notice of me and argue against my conclusions, I propose to issue a fourth supplementary volume of dissertations and discussions, in order to expand, buttress, or modify arguments or conclusions.

I endeavour to appeal to the ordinary educated reader. If any such finds the book stiff, I think he would be assisted by reading first the analysis of the argument which begins the last chapter, pp. 283–8.

2. My argument is positive. It is a statement of the reasons which seem to me convincing on behalf of a certain type of belief. It is not concerned, except incidentally, in describing, or arguing against, rival beliefs. Thus I offer no survey of the rival beliefs of current philosophers, such as is offered by Mr. W. R. Matthews in his admirable *Studies in Christian*

Philosophy (Macmillan, **1921**), but I hope I have indicated sufficiently both where I rely upon them and where they do not satisfy me.

My statement is also individual. It presents the arguments which finally, after long thinking, have seemed to satisfy my own mind. But I confess that the form of ordered argument, starting without presuppositions and proceeding from point to point, does not represent the way in which my convictions have been actually reached. I am conscious of certain strong predispositions towards certain beliefs, which seem to be inherent in me, and I will venture to be so far autobiographical as to enumerate them, so far as they are relevant.

(*a*) I have, ever since I was an undergraduate, been certain that I must be in the true sense a free thinker, and that either not to think freely about a disturbing subject, or to accept ecclesiastical authority in place of the best judgement of my own reason, would be for me an impossible treason against the light. I must go remorselessly where the argument leads me. Thus when in the early seventies I was preparing for ordination, and Ewald had seriously convinced me that the old-fashioned view of the Old Testament was impossible to hold, it never presented itself to me as possible that I could substitute the traditional view in place of the scientific in my own mind on the ground of authority or agree to teach it. There was nothing for it but to make what seemed to me fairly certain as evident as possible to my examiners for orders, and also to show how reconcilable I thought it with the Creeds. But at the same time a cordial agreement with Ruskin against the dominant Political

Economists, and other causes, prevented my ever confusing my duty to reason with any attribution of infallibility to the intellectuals of the day.

(b) I have always felt deeply, being by disposition pessimistic, the arguments against the love of God. I have always thought that the only very difficult dogma of the Church was the dogma that God is Love. But deeper than any difficulty has been the feeling that at the roots of my being I am confronted with God, from whom I cannot get away, and that the God who confronts me there is the Living God of the prophets and of Jesus Christ. Equally deep was the feeling that the Christian life was certainly " the Way," and that it was foolish to suppose that it could flourish except on its own intellectual roots and in its own proper mental soil. Also I have never been able to feel that any of the various humanitarian estimates of Christ was in any degree satisfying.

(c) Finally, though this has no bearing on the present volume or its next projected successor, I have since my childhood been what I may call a Catholic by mental constitution. I remember very well, when I was eight or nine—sixty years ago—reading a book by a Protestant author—a Presbyterian, I think—entitled *Father Clement*, about the conversion of a Catholic priest to Protestantism. I have never read it since. I had been brought up in ordinary old-fashioned English Church ways. I had only attended very Low Church services. I had never heard of the Oxford movement. I knew nothing about Catholicism, except as a strange superstition, called Popery. But the book described confession and absolution, fasting, the Real Presence, the devotion of the Three Hours, the use of incense, etc., and I felt instinctively and at once that this sort of sacramental religion was the religion for me. From that day most of the people who influenced my intellect, when I was young, were agnostics or Protestants or "outsiders" to the Catholic faith—Carlyle, Ruskin, Edward Bowen, T. H. Green—but this predisposition remained quite unaltered. My mental life has consisted in the process of confronting such predispositions with the results, so far as I have been able to see them, of philosophy and science and criticism (with a native tendency always to anticipate the worst), and to seek a unity or synthesis in which all the light I could get would be allowed its full force, without my innermost self being quenched or blinded. What I am daring to present to the public is the result of this sort of process, continued over forty and more years.

3. Like others, as I view the world and the Church—especially the Church of England—at the present day, I cannot feel hopeful about the immediate prospect. The prophets and experience alike convince me that there can be no real social recovery except through a general return to God. And of such a return I see no signs. God has smitten ; but in general we have not sought Him. Thus, taught by the prophets, I am ready to anticipate scathing judgements. But the prophets also teach us to hold with unquenchable faith to the divine purpose of progress, through all the catastrophes and judgements which widespread apostasy from God brings with it. The purpose remains, and the end is sure. No right effort is going to be lost. And the instrument through which God

works is the "faithful remnant" of those who believe Him and obey Him at all costs. Of such, I feel persuaded, there is among us as large a body, and as genuine, as at any previous period of history. What is needful for them is to think out their principles, individually and collectively : so that they shall know what they believe and why they believe. And these volumes, which I offer to God with a prayer for His blessing, are intended to help them in the task.

CHARLES GORE.

Michaelmas 1921.

CONTENTS

uncertainties tolerable or even enjoyable enough. They are content to " spend their time in nothing else but either to tell or to hear some new thing." It is enough for them that each new view is " interesting " ; they pass their life " ever learning and never coming to the knowledge of the truth." But it is not so with most men. The feeling of hopeless uncertainty breeds in them a distaste for positive creeds, and they drift away from religion altogether.

But it is ignoble to acquiesce in this sort of scepticism without at least a serious effort. It is my belief that a great deal of scepticism is due, not really to the absence of adequate grounds for conviction, but to confusion of mind, to an excessive deference to current intellectual fashions, and to the fact that a man has never thoroughly and systematically faced the problems. It seems to me that the right course for anyone who cannot accept the mere voice of authority, but feels the imperative obligation to " face the arguments " and to think freely, is to begin at the beginning and to see how far he can reconstruct his religious beliefs stage by stage on a secure foundation, as far as possible without any preliminary assumptions and with a resolute determination " to know the worst." This at least is the only course which the present writer has found himself able either to adopt in his own case or to recommend to others in a like case. It means of course an equally frank cross-questioning of traditional religious beliefs and of the current dogmas of the contemporary intellectual world. This is too often forgotten. There is a very large number of people who reject traditional religious authority with contempt, and go on even naïvely to accept, without any serious questioning, the oracles of the day.

But this is manifestly foolish. If we refuse to be frightened by one kind of authority, we must not be frightened by another. New views have frequently proved at least as misleading as old traditions.[1] The only satisfactory way for a man to save his own soul, or to become capable of helping others, is freely to use his own real judgement and accept the responsibility of decision in the fullest light that he can come by.

Deliberately to enter upon this process of reconstruction from the beginning does not, of course, mean the abandonment during the process of the religious beliefs and practices which a man holds already in use. Quite the contrary. He will make the most of the precious gift of faith, even while he is enquiring into its basis. It is part of the experience which he is to interpret. It gives him his understanding of the questions at issue. Moreover, though the process of reconstruction will be more or less different in the case of each person, according as the intellectual equipment and opportunity of individuals are different, yet it is and ought to be possible for all who have to face life for themselves and use their powers of thought. All that is really essential is sincerity and the readiness to make the necessary effort of mind.[2] And it is the aim of this volume to help especially the ordinary educated man and woman.

But I would add that there is no class for whom

---

[1] See additional note at end of the chapter.

[2] See Bernard Bosanquet, *What Religion Is* (Macmillan, 1920), p. viii. " ' As a little child . . .' ; that has been the motto, as of the saints, so of the wisest among mankind Your mind is a good instrument ; only keep it free and sincere ; keep away from selfishness, self-conceit, from the vanity of learning, and from the vanity of resentment against learning. Open it to experience, and take that as largely as you can. We know the type of man who on the whole gets nearest to truth. It is not the cleverest. It is, I think, the sincerest."

this process of fundamental reconstruction of their religious beliefs is so necessary as for those who are, or are preparing to become, ministers of the Christian Church. They are often enthusiasts for religion, who have no personal doubts, but are eagerly interested in a great many questions, doctrinal and ceremonial and social ; and their temptation is to take up the questions that interest them, which are secondary and derivative, and not really to study and test their foundations. Very likely they will themselves experience reactions and fall into fundamental doubts later in life. Certainly, if they are to be true to their high vocation, they will be constantly occupied in helping others who are in doubt. In either case they will find themselves paralysed if they have never explored their foundations. It is only those who know, from the ground upwards, what they believe and why they believe, who can help either themselves or others in the time of stress. It is only those who are felt to have a real ground for their beliefs and a real sympathy with free enquiry whose help will be sought by those who need it. And it is pitiful to see how many there are among the professed ministers of Christ who, in an hour of popular discussion of some vital truth, are proved, by their perplexity and dismay, or by their uninstructed denunciations, never to have thought at all seriously or deeply about the most momentous questions.

It is, then, the aim of this book to rehearse the process of reconstruction which has been slowly and laboriously and again and again enacted in the writer's own soul and mind, with as single an eye for the truth—from whatever source, new or old, it may come—as he has been able to win for himself. But before making a beginning it is necessary to examine the existing situation in order that we may understand what are the causes of the profound unsettlement of religious beliefs in our present society. Such an analysis must precede reconstruction by enabling us to interpret aright the breadth and the profundity of the gulf which has to be filled.

It may be said with substantial truth that in the earlier part of the nineteenth century, however much scepticism existed in special intellectual circles—and there was a great deal of it—yet on the whole popular religion in England, for all its divisions, had a substantial basis of agreement, a common doctrine which was accepted as a matter of course ; and this accepted religion, intellectually considered, had two main pillars of support. For its " Natural Religion," or belief in God, the " argument from design " was the sufficient foundation, and that in the form given it by the established scientific doctrine of the fixity of species, or "special creations." This was triumphantly used as against all atheists. " Can you look at the different orders and species which nature presents to you, each elaborately designed to fulfil certain functions, and each fixed, as science tells us, in its essential characteristics from the beginning, and doubt that they must have been created for the purposes which they fulfil by a designing mind—the almighty Creator of the universe ? " This was the argument of Paley's brilliant book on *Natural Theology*. Then for Revealed Religion—Christianity—the pillar of support was the authority of Holy Scripture, considered not merely as containing the record of the word of God, but as being in all its parts the word of God, and therefore in all its affirmations on all subjects of infallible authority. Though the teaching of the leaders of the Reformation in Germany about the authority of the Bible had been in some cases much more discriminating,[1] yet in England, at any rate, after the weakening of the authority of the Church at the Reformation, the accepted appeal had come to be simply to the infallible book. " The Bible and the Bible only " was " the religion " of Protestant Englishmen.

Now it is not too much to say that, *in their existing forms*, both those great supports of popular religion were destroyed in the estimation both of men of science and of the mass of educated people in the middle of the last century. We will take first the argument from design.

1. The fixity of species from the beginning of creation might seem to be naturally deducible from the story of the creation in Genesis, taken literally, as for example it is presented by Milton in *Paradise Lost*. But as a matter of fact the idea appears first not in Christian fathers or schoolmen, but as a scientific conclusion of the seventeenth century [2]—a conclusion drawn especially from the limits within which inter-breeding is possible. Francis Bacon plainly knows nothing of it. It is to be found first, I believe, in the writings of John Ray (1628–1705), who is called " the founder of modern zoology " ; it was affirmed by Linnaeus in his *Philosophia Botanica* (1751) as a sort of dogma : " There are as many different species as the Infinite Being originally created different forms."[3]

[1] See T. M. Lindsay's *Hist. of the Reformation* (Clark, 1907), vol. i, pp. 453 ff.

[2] See Aubrey Moore, *Science and the Faith* (Kegan Paul, 1889), p. 173

[3] He suggests elsewhere, however, an extension of view according to which all the different *species* of a *genus* were originally one *species*.

In spite of occasional doubts or protests or positive theories of evolution expressed by Buffon, Goethe, Erasmus Darwin, Treviranus, and Lamarck, this doctrine held the field in the scientific world, till Charles Darwin and Wallace destroyed it. It was then not primarily a theological, but a scientific doctrine, based on observation, no doubt incomplete ; and when Darwin speaks of its being " like confessing a murder " [1] to confess to the opinion that species are not immutable, the solid body of hostile opinion that he is thinking of is not that of the theologians, but of the scientific world.[2] But this scientific doctrine had naturally been made use of in the interests of " natural religion," and made the basis of the argument from design. It was an argument (as it appears in Paley) compact, intelligible, and incontrovertible. " Each of these kinds of plants and animals is obviously *designed* to fulfil its functions. Science on its own ground teaches you that each *kind* (i.e. each group of living things which are fertile *inter se*) has been sub-

---

[1] *Life*, ii, 23.

[2] In Paley's *Natural Theology*, chap. v (*Works*, vol. iv, p. 50). The theory of the appearance of design in nature being due to "natural selection" (as Darwin afterwards called it) acting upon the profusion of nature, which produces every kind of variation and every conceivable form—eliminating those forms which " by the defect of their constitution [were] incapable of preservation and of continuance by generation " and suffering only the fit to survive— is considered by Paley and rather contemptuously rejected. The theory was, in fact, first given reasonable consistency and plausibility by Darwin. Darwin himself denies that before he published his *Origin of Species* " the subject was in the air " or " that men's minds were prepared for it." In his intercourse with naturalists he says he " never happened to come across a single one who seemed to doubt about the permanence of species " (*Life*, i, 87). It is not necessary, however, here to review the controversy raised by Samuel Butler and renewed by Bernard Shaw as to the precise nature of the achievement of Darwin in the history of the doctrine of evolution.

stantially what it is, apart from superficial variations, from the beginning. You cannot reasonably doubt, therefore, that it was created by an original designer, the author and maker of all that is." [1] But in this form Darwin—it is not too much to say—seemed completely to overthrow the argument from design. Nature was now presented under a new aspect. Granted force and matter and law, including living matter, with its constant tendency to variation in all sorts of directions, and the whole world, with all its infinite forms, appeared as having through countless ages grown of itself, or automatically. The exact specific form of each kind of plant and animal was now represented as being due, not to the Creator having originally so made it, but to the fact that, among the infinite varieties of forms which the profusion of nature poured forth, one form at each stage proved itself the best adapted to survive, and in the struggle for existence—which is due to nature producing at each moment far more specimens of each kind than can survive—natural selection had cleared the spaces of nature by killing off all the innumerable specimens less suited to survive, and leaving the field to the one which had the best survival value. The appearance of design is thus due, not to any original creative act, but to the fact that out of innumerable hosts of things produced those only survived the struggle and successfully propagated their kind which were the best adapted to their surroundings. Of course, in the pages of Darwin the doctrine is stated with cautions and reservations and limitations which

[1] Kant's famous criticism of the argument from design hardly touched its popular use. Moreover, his chief concern is to show that the argument, if valid, would prove only a designer of great power and wisdom, not an absolute creator, almighty and all-wise.

" popular science " ignored. It is also the case that
Darwin's positions and suggestions have not in all cases
proved scientifically acceptable. But what we are now
concerned with is only the original effect on the popular
imagination of Darwin's theory. There it presented
itself as a doctrine of nature making itself—a process
which, granted the initial materials and laws,[1] seemed
to explain itself without requiring any God to design
it or " make it up." Man, moreover, appeared as, in
his physical structure, only one form of animal life,
perfected in the struggle for existence, especially in
virtue of pre-eminent mental qualities, which yet (it
was suggested) were only developments of the mental
qualities which had progressively appeared in the
animal world generally. And instead of a being
created perfect, in the full glory of intellectual and
moral power, as Milton and South, interpreting or
misinterpreting the Bible, had represented him, who
fell from his first glory and only after long ages could
be restored to it by a divine act of redemption—
man now appeared as starting from the lowest depth
among the anthropoid apes, and only slowly climbing
up from among his animal ancestry, by his own
efforts through long ages, to a dignity such as he now
enjoys. So the acceptance of Darwinism seemed in
the popular imagination to destroy not only the
argument from design, in its shortest and most

[1] All the Darwinians agreed with Clifford that " of the beginning
of the universe we know nothing at all." There is in Adolphe
Retté's account of his conversion to Catholicism, *Du diable à Dieu*,
an amusing account of how, in his agnostic days, his intellectual
conscience was scandalized by the joy expressed by some working
men, after listening to a lecture of his, that nowadays science was
able to explain the origin of things without the doctrines of religion
or the assistance of priests. This, he uneasily felt, was precisely
what science cannot do. It is concerned with process, not origin.
I am trusting to my memory for the reference.

effective form, but also the Bible doctrine of the origin
of man and of his fall, which, in its turn, lay at the
root of Christianity.

Very likely if the Darwinian doctrine of development had been formulated much earlier—let us say
in the fourth century, in the atmosphere generated
by Greek philosophical Christianity—it would have
produced no such shock. The idea that the early
chapters of Genesis are " allegory " and not history
had been widely held in the early Church, and not
only in the Alexandrian school. Augustine himself,
as is well known, following St. Gregory of Nyssa, had
propounded the view that God in the beginning
created only germs or causes of the forms of life,
which were afterwards to be developed in gradual
course.[1] And it had been repeatedly asserted by the
leaders of the Church that the first man was not
created perfect—for it is God's method to do things
gradually—but only in a fit state to advance towards
perfection.[2] Accommodation, then, between the
points of view of science and religion would probably
have been much easier then than it was in the nineteenth century. But it is in the nineteenth century
and not in the fourth that we are now interested.

We are not yet concerned with balancing and
estimating evidences and probabilities, or with dis-
tinguishing what was the real religious outcome of
the new science from its popular effect, or what was
essential Christianity from its current form. We are
simply concerned to estimate the shock to the
religious imagination which the speedy and world-

[1] Aug. de Gen. ad lit, v, 5 and 23, and St. Gregory of Nyssa in
Hexaem, P.G. xliv, 72, etc.

[2] See Lux Mundi, p. 393, n. 2 ; also that man from his creation
was naturally mortal or subject to death, p. 395.

wide acceptance of Darwin's conclusions, with whatever modifications, inevitably produced.

And this, it must be noticed, was only the last of many shocks. When Milton wrote his *Paradise Lost*, he could still—though with hesitation—present the old and comfortable view of the universe which made this world the centre of the whole system of creation. I call it comfortable, because it made mankind so obviously the central object in the divine purpose. In a few days the universe had been prepared by God for the dwelling-place of man, with the world, his home, as its centre, and the sun and the moon to give him light, and the stars to give glory to his sky and perhaps to portray his destiny ; and man had been introduced in perfection and glory into his dwelling-place, to be its earthly sovereign, all within the space of a few days a few thousand years ago. But science had aimed a series of blows at this comfortable and compact scheme. Astronomy first had shattered the geocentric theory, by disclosing the world as only a minor planet revolving round its central sun, while our whole solar system was only one of innumerable systems which stretch through infinite space . . . till the brain reels beneath the attempt to realize them ; and, on this showing, man and his dwelling become a mere speck in an unimaginable infinitude of systems. And geology had taken up the tale where astronomy left it, and rolled out its almost infinite ages while the world was in making, till man, a speck in space, became no more than a moment in time. And now, once again, biology, taking up the tale from astronomy and geology, seemed to make mankind only one phase (why more than a passing phase ?) in the evolution of life—a bubble, as it were, on the changing, flowing river. The effect of all those disclosures upon the religious imagination can hardly be exaggerated. They seemed, as represented in popular literature, almost to obliterate God behind a self-developing universe, and to reduce the position of man to insignificance, and to contradict all that view of his history which the Bible had enforced or suggested.

And before we leave this particular " shock to religion," it must not be overlooked that the imagination of each age is affected chiefly by the most successful and progressive form of intellectual work current at the time. The leading representatives of effective intellect in earlier ages had been philosophers or theologians or poets or artists. Now, beyond all question, the popular representatives of effective intelligence were the scientific men and the practical men who were using science to develop the resources of civilization. And the age—I speak of the Victorian age — was optimistic. Science and " secular " education were to be the instruments of unlimited progress and universal peace. Nothing was needed but to educate men and make them free to compete. Then universal competition would bring the best to the front, and mankind would go ahead to a glorious future. The universe was the scene of what appeared to be regarded as a necessary law of progress, of which science was the chief minister and instrument. Darwin and Huxley might shake their heads and declare that science could utter no optimistic prophesies. But the spirit of the age was not to be quenched by their warnings. And within a restricted region science responded magnificently to the task assigned to her. Material progress, of a kind, was manifest in all directions. No wonder the popular imagination worshipped " science " and " progress,"

and discarded the old-fashioned arguments for
religion, and was disposed to take reprisals on the
Church as an enfeebled tyrant which has unsuccess-
fully set itself to resist each advance of scientific
discovery, and which was, moreover, discredited by
its manifest abuses, so repellent to the Liberal
spirit. No wonder materialism or agnosticism prevailed, and Herbert Spencer became the prophet of
enlightenment.[1]

　2. And contemporaneously with the great scientific
movement, of which Darwin is the central figure,
there emerged within the horizon of the religious
world, which had been building its spiritual fabric
upon the infallibility of Scripture, the startling conclusions of literary and historical criticism. To an
extent that we do not to-day easily realize, this was
a new science [2]; and it was a real science which was
to open out vast regions of human knowledge,
especially of the earlier stages of civilization. It had

---

[1] For the present scientific position of the theory of evolution,
after seventy years of criticism, see the excellent sketch of J. A.
Thomson and P. Geddes, *Evolution* (Home University Library:
Williams & Norgate) ; and for human origins, see Prof. Wood Jones,
The Problem of Man's Ancestry (S.P.C.K.). For an estimate of the
real spiritual effect of the newer biological theories, reference may
still be made to Aubrey Moore's *Science and the Faith*, as well as to
a multitude of more recent books. But to such considerations we
shall have to return when we are occupied in reconstruction.

[2] See Gooch's *History and Historians in the XIXth Century*
(Longmans), pp. 10 ff. I think it is really suggestive to notice
Samuel Johnson's estimate of history and historians as reported by
Boswell. " Great abilities," he said, " are not requisite for an
historian ; for in historical composition all the greatest powers of
the human mind are quiescent. He has facts ready to his hand ;
so that there is no exercise of invention. Imagination is not
required in any high degree ; only about as much as is used in the
lower kinds of poetry. Some penetration, accuracy, and colouring
will fit a man for the task, if he can give the application which is
necessary " (see under the year 1763 in Boswell's *Life*, chap. vii).

applied itself in the person of Wolf to show that Homer's epics were not the work of one man at one time, but the slowly growing product of a whole epoch, however great the genius of the man or men who fixed the tradition in its final form. And it had applied itself in the person of Niebuhr to the history of Rome. In that region it had traced the emergence of history, as a trustworthy record of the facts as they occurred, out of the mythical stories and traditional lore which lie behind history; which in varying degrees contain historical material of a very important kind, but which are certainly not historical in the form in which they were handed down.

This same critical science then applied itself to the Bible records. Thus De Wette (1780–1843) and Ewald (1803–1875) and their successors led students to perceive that in the early chapters of Genesis what we are dealing with is not an historical record of human origins, revealed by God and accurately handed down from father to son in human tradition. What supplied the material of these early stories were the first efforts of the human imagination seeking, without materials to work upon, to construct a picture of the origins of the world and of man, and of sin and suffering and death. Similar stories of the Creation and the Flood existed, it appeared, among the Babylonians. No doubt what was characteristic of the Hebrew narrative was its astonishing dignity and purity of spiritual truth. That certainly suggested divine inspiration; but its subject-matter was the early product of the human imagination "making up a picture" of human origins. It was not history— neither the story of Creation, nor of the Fall, nor of the Flood, nor of the Tower of Babel; moreover, there were easily to be detected different and incompatible narratives of the Creation and the Flood interwoven in our present Book of Genesis.

Later, it appeared, we had to do with tradition in which the names of races akin to Israel appeared as individuals, and their mutual qualities and relations were reflected back into the histories of their supposed founders. Gradually from traditional history we get out upon the solid ground of real chronicle. It is the task of criticism to discriminate the character of the different portions of the Bible, whether they be like the legends of the Arthurian cycle, or like the legend of Charlemagne—a legend woven round a solidly historical person—or like the tradition of a saint among his monastic brethren, or the precise chronicle.

One special feature of ancient literature is the tendency to heap upon great founders all the gradually successive outcomes of their foundation. Thus the various codifications of the Law of Israel were traditionally ascribed to the first founder of their polity, Moses. But Moses certainly did not write the Pentateuch, nor did he do all that is there ascribed to him. Again, the Psalms as a whole were ascribed to David, but only a very small portion of them can have been actually of his authorship. Once more, a great unknown prophet at the end of the Captivity carried on the work of Isaiah in a new moment of history, and his work is incorporated with Isaiah's and called by his name.

Moreover, even in later times, the function of history is not strictly distinguished from that of edification. Thus the books of Chronicles were history written not as it was, but as in the judgement of the scribe it ought to have been and must have been. And stories with a moral, not strictly historical, like the

appeared is the same yet

think of this as incompatible our Lord's thoughts O.T.

? ? not proven

Certainly is strong for an unproven theory

narrative part of Daniel or the story of Esther, appear also among the sacred books.

Apart from questions of detail, or of more or less, all this account of the Hebrew literature appeared to be very convincing in the light of what we know of human history everywhere. It rapidly converted the scholars; but it was very revolutionary. And it presented itself to the ordinary man as the discovery that the Bible is not true—woman was not really made of a rib taken from the side of man; the Garden of Eden was a myth; mankind was not saved from a universal deluge in the persons of Noah's family in an ark; the Tower of Babel was not a true account of the origin of languages; many things written in the Bible did not actually happen—could not indeed have happened as is described: the Bible had been proved not to be true. All this was very crude. People did not ask themselves whether poetry and drama and legend and myth have not in other nations proved to be as potent vehicles of truth as historical fact. But we, in England especially, are a prosaic and unimaginative people. The credit of the Bible and with it the credit of religion was fundamentally shaken.

Meanwhile David Strauss had, in the most radical spirit, and with the most virulent animus against " priests " and churches, applied the mythical theory to the Gospels in his famous *Life of Christ* (1835); and shortly after the publication of Darwin's *Origin of Species*, Renan (1863) published his much more attractive, but hardly less destructive, *Life of Jesus*. And Ferdinand Baur, the contemporary of Strauss between 1831 and 1860, elaborated the deeply destructive view of the New Testament literature which, as developed by " the school of Tübingen," became the main subject of intellectual controversy in theological circles for many years. But it is noticeable that in England certainly the work of Strauss and Renan never produced as much effect on the popular imagination as the criticism of the Old Testament. This was no doubt partly due to the fact that our great English scholars appeared to win a decisive victory over the destructive critics of the New Testament, whose theories they seemed to show to be uncritical and unconvincing. But whatever the cause, it is worth noticing that though the traditional view of the Old Testament and of the New was subject at the same time to attacks equally thorough, equally brilliant, and equally radical, it was mainly on the field of the Old Testament that the credit of the Bible suffered in popular imagination. The Old Testament had been the stronghold of Puritan religion. It was there especially that the Bible was supposed to have been proved to be untrue. It is only recently that " Modernist " views of the New Testament have come to dominate popular and journalistic literature, and have given us the kind of view of Christian origins which may be seen in Mr. Wells's *Outline of History*.

3. To these two great shocks to established religious beliefs must be added a third—less destructive, no doubt, but still seriously imperilling the popular view of divine revelation. I refer to the rise of the science of Comparative Religion. The cause of the evangelization of the heathen had not been a popular cause in the early nineteenth century, except in the circle of the strict Evangelicals. The popular distaste for it is expressed, in ways we are familiar with, by Thackeray and Dickens. But when it told how " the heathen in their blindness bow down to wood and stone," it expressed the current view of the non-Christian

3

religions. No doubt Judaism and Mohammedanism stood on a different basis, though Judaism had decisively missed its way and Mohammed was distinctively the False Prophet. But for the rest the religions of heathenism were supposed to be rationally beneath contempt. Macaulay, though he was very far from being an evangelical Christian, expressed with his usual force the common contemptuous estimate alike of the philosophy and the religions of India. But a quite different attitude of mind was represented by the new science of Comparative Religions, of which Max Müller was in England the most prominent representative. They were now studied as examples of the various forms which had been taken in different races by the fundamental instinct of religion in man. Behind their grosser popular forms Hinduism, Buddhism, Confucianism, and even the religion of savages became the subject of a respectful study, resulting sometimes in a positive enthusiasm for what had formerly seemed a repulsive superstition. Again I say, it is not my present business to seek to estimate the exact truth of the newer views now dominant. I only note the change and the effect of the change on the common belief in Revealed Religion. Though in fact the attitude of Britons in India and Africa, whether Government officials or traders, towards the natives and their religions remained very much as it was and very far below what was to be desired in the way of sympathy,[1] the world of educated people at home began to profess an even profound respect for the non-Christian faiths. It was agreed that religion was a universal need and characteristic

[1] I ought, I think, to except Mohammedanism. The Mohammedan religion has apparently always obtained the instinctive sympathy of Englishmen.

and so Christ is not the Sole Saviour

of man, and that it had taken various forms according
to the psychologies of various races and to their varying levels of culture. All religions, it would appear,
were more or less inspired by the spirit of truth and
more or less involved in error. The conclusion
commonly suggested was that the distinctive and
absolute claim made for the religion of the Bible
would need to be very much toned down ; and that,
if there were to be a universal religion for our day or
for the future, it must be one which would negate the
exclusive claim of any one historical creed, but in
which all alike could, in their real spirit, find themselves at home. " Religion," it has been recently
said, " lives through the death of religions." [1] Thus
the claim of the historical Christian creed to be the
one divinely authorized religion which was to convert
the world—being as light to darkness and knowledge
to ignorance—came to be regarded as an old-fashioned
claim which educated people could treat with
contempt.

4. The shocks to established beliefs which I have
been enumerating arose from new discoveries or new
sciences. But hardly less important among the
causes of religious unsettlement was the revolt of the
moral conscience—which in the middle of the last
century, if it was singularly insensitive on some
points, as for instance on the cruelties and injustices
still involved in our industrial system, was acutely
sensitive and insistent on others—against certain
current doctrines of Christianity which are commonly,
if not quite accurately, described as Calvinistic. The
idea of absolute divine decrees condemning to eternal
misery masses of men even before their birth—the

[1] Kirsopp Lake's *Landmarks of Early Christianity* (Macmillan,
1920), p. 1.

so far as it can be distinguished from what prevailed a generation or two ago.

1. The atmosphere of democracy possesses the intellectual world and takes the form of an almost unlimited assertion and recognition of the right of private judgement. For reasons only too evident within the Church, whether we are thinking of the Church of England or of the wider world of Christian belief, authority is discredited. "There is nothing," it is said with some reason, " which you may not hear denied or affirmed in the pulpits of the Church." Even the Catholic movement in the Church of England, which makes its special appeal to authority, has in fact maintained itself and spread largely by an appeal to the rights of congregations to worship and believe as they please. Now, the claim to an unlimited right to believe as one pleases is indisputable as a maxim of civil society ; but there is an extraordinary lack of any balancing perception that morally the right of private judgement depends on the pains that have been taken to form the judgement by adequate and conscientious enquiry. Nevertheless, the claim prevails almost unchallenged.

2. Fifty years ago it used to be commonly held that, though there was great doubt about many established doctrines of the faith, there was, and would continue to be, almost complete agreement on the standard of Christian morality ; but any such unreasonable expectation has been indeed rudely shattered. It must have been expressed originally in sublime unconsciousness that the whole industrial system, then in its glory, had been built up on a basis of profound revolt against the central law of Christian morality, " Thou shalt love thy neighbour as thyself." There are few things in history more

astonishing than the silent acquiescence of the Christian world in the radical betrayal of its ethical foundation. But it is not only in the industrial world that there has been a rebellion against Christian moral principles. The same rebellion is evident to-day in every section of our society against the Christian standard of sexual morality, alike among the single and the married, and it is open and deliberate. Thus masses of men and women to-day are as much without any sense of a definite standard having divine authority in matters of conduct as in matters of creed.

alas !

3. This tendency to unlimited individualism, or to organized revolt from the long-accepted standards of religious and moral authority, has been accentuated by popular literature. Most people read little but novels and newspapers. Now, novels in England of recent years have been largely occupied with glorifying the revolt. Authority is represented as stupid. Passionate feeling is to have its own way. And the newspapers advertise every startling " new view," however intellectually worthless or unbalanced, simply because it is exciting and sells the newspaper, while the careful utterance of the sober thinker is passed by unreported.

4. Even the new and popular science of psychology, especially " the psychology of religious belief "— its intentions being, no doubt, misunderstood—is made to minister to the prevalent religious individualism or subjectivism. Experience, I suppose, may be properly defined to be reality as felt. The value of the feeling will thus be constantly estimated to depend upon its relation to objective reality. But psychology studies the feelings and movements of the soul without any regard to objective standards. Thus " experience " is taken to mean simply feeling, and

is valued in proportion as it is intense—often in proportion as it is abnormal and therefore specially interesting. Thus, the popular cry " Let us be our real selves " is taken to mean let us " remove inhibitions " and be our unrestrained selves. This is no doubt a parody of scientific psychology ; but it appears to be a very popular parody, and I will quote, in confirmation of what I have said, the serious words of a well-known American psychologist, Professor J. B. Pratt : [1] " Psychology studies the *idea* of God and the *idea* of the solar system, and stops there. But neither astronomy nor theology means to limit our study to our ideas. They both mean to be objective —and it is hard to see why one should be denied this privilege, if it be granted to the other. And if objectivity be denied to theology, the dangers that inevitably result are evident. Theology becomes purely subjective—a description of the way we feel ; the idea of God is substituted for God . . . and the psychology of religion, having absorbed all that was objective in religion, finds it has nothing left to study, or at best becomes a branch of abnormal psychology. ' This method,' writes Boutroux, ' if it succeed, will lead sooner or later to the abolition of the fact itself, while the dogmatic criticism of religions has striven in vain for centuries to obtain this result. . . . Contrary, then, to the other sciences which leave standing the things that they explain, the one just mentioned has this remarkable property of destroying its object in the act of describing it, and of substituting itself for the facts in proportion as it analyses them.' "

I think the language of both the above quotations

[1] The author of *The Psychology of Religious Belief* and *The Religious Consciousness* (Macmillan : New York). My quotation is from the latter work, p. 41.

is open to criticism. But their substantial meaning is plain and true.

5. In this confused world, thirsting alike for novelty and for assurance, there emerge " new religions," for instance, Christian Science, Theosophy, and (only so far as it has a special religious doctrine of its own) Spiritualism.[1] In their substance or basis they are not by any means new, but revivals of very old forms of religious belief, the first two strikingly recalling the features of ancient Gnosticism. If we examine the actual basis of their special propaganda, it appears to be extraordinarily untrustworthy and to make an inordinate claim on credulity. None the less they push their way widely amongst those who are rebels against the old-fashioned kinds of authority; they make converts, numerous, zealous, and proselytizing, and constitute a very distinctive feature in the mixed present-day world of religious opinions.

6. Finally, we must take note that the hope, widely entertained, that the trials, sacrifices, and agonies of the Great War would recall men to God—to a more vivid sense of His judgements and of their need of His mercy and protection, and so rally them to the faith of their fathers, to the old Christian Gospel, as the only really trustworthy basis for life—this hope has not apparently been fulfilled on any wide scale. On the contrary, the war and its experiences appear to have done a great deal to deepen doubts of the reality of divine love or the moral government of the world. It has weakened the Liberal faith in Progress without strengthening the faith in God. In the case of the most serious, it has left them perplexed; in

[1] I desire to distinguish spiritualism as a religious propaganda from spiritualism so far as it means a scientific enquiry into psychical phenomena.

the mass, it has weakened idealism and deepened a cynical materialism—" Let us eat and drink, for to-morrow we die." Certainly, on the whole, it has left the youth of the country widely and deeply alienated from the Church and from organized religion.

     .   .   .   .   .

It has seemed to me necessary, at starting, to attempt this sort of analysis of the causes which lie behind our present religious discontents and dis-organization. Granted that the facts are, more or less, as I have represented them, and the causes such as I have described, the question arises—What is the remedy ? When we speak of the remedy, we are apt to imagine a remedy on a large scale. But I do not think that anything like religious recovery on a large scale is likely to occur at present. I agree with Dr. Tennant, who says, " As I have repeatedly emphasized, it looks as if for the present any universally [I would say " generally "] acceptable reconstruction of funda-mental Christian doctrines is not feasible. We feel the need of it doubtless with some natural impatience ; but perhaps all we can now do in that direction is to prepare for it." [1] And the best way to prepare for it is to clarify one's own mind. It is out of a reconstruction of belief in this or that man's own mind, or in the minds of small groups of men and women, that the larger reconstruction must be based.

I ask again then, What is the remedy for religious unsettlement and intellectual dissatisfaction in the individual ? I leave for the present out of account those men and women who find it consistent with their conscience to refuse full intellectual enquiry into the difficult questions which haunt their imagination,

---

[1] F. R. Tennant, " The Present Condition of Some Fundamental Christian Doctrines," in the *Constructive Quarterly*, Sept. 1920, p. 483.

and who consult what appear to be the interests and peace of their souls by accepting passively the authority of the Church. I do not wish to criticize this procedure. But my conscience, and that of many others, will by no means admit of it. Granted the truth of the foundation doctrines of Christianity about God and about Christ and about His Spirit, and we see clearly enough that the question of authority—that is, the question of the truest or best form of the Christian religion—will become the most important question. But for me it is the foundation of all claims of Christian authority which is at stake. There is the first question. Till these foundation questions are settled, the claim of authority, especially as it actually presents itself in a divided Christendom, cannot suffice—cannot even explicitly enter. In the court of pure reason, where nothing is more sacred than free enquiry, we have heard the doubt, or more than the doubt, expressed by a long succession of serious and deep-thinking men, whether our foundations will bear investigation. We cannot put aside that claim for free enquiry, and to the limit of our power we must, for our own satisfaction, pursue it with the utmost impartiality possible.

Moreover, this is not, as has already been said, only a matter for specialized experts or professional scholars. The discussion has been left in the past too much to them. Religion, after all, is for common men. It is in the region of the common reason, at least as much as in the circles of specialized study, that it must be judged. This is, most noticeably, the assumption of the New Testament. It appeals to the common judgement. It summons each man to judge for himself. " Why even of yourselves judge ye not what is right ? " " Prove all things ; hold fast that which is good." "He that is spiritual judgeth all things, and he himself is judged of no man." [1] These words of our Lord and of St. Paul are a challenge to common men. We must brace ourselves individually and deliberately to the task of facing the intellectual questions and seeing if we cannot reach decisions, at least provisional decisions such as can be the reasonable basis, when put to account in life, of practical certainties.

And it is a quite unsatisfactory method to attack each particular problem, which happens to present itself or to be urged upon us, in isolation and at haphazard. We must train ourselves to thinking systematically.

I appeal, therefore, in this book to men and women of ordinary intelligence and education, discarding prejudices and arming themselves with nothing but the resolute determination to know and follow the truth, to begin with me at the beginning, and seek to build the fabric of a belief which they can feel in their conscience to be reasonable and convincing.

[1] Luke xii. 57 ; 1 Thess. v. 21 ; 1 Cor. ii. 15.

Additional note, see p. 3.   Mr. Bernard Shaw's Preface to his *Back to Methuselah* shows in striking and characteristic fashion how the triumphant Darwinism of the Mid-Victorian days misled the public, and how fallacious was the kind of belief in progress which it generated.   The "orthodox" and highly dogmatic political economy was equally deceptive.   Such provoking critics of the dominant intellectuals as Samuel Butler and John Ruskin have been justified.

CHAPTER II

THE CONDITIONS OF HOPEFUL RECONSTRUCTION

IF a seriously minded person is determined to emerge from the confused condition of mind on matters of religion, the causes of which I have sought to describe, he does well, for the time at least, to forget all past controversies and, like René Descartes, " the father of modern philosophy," to begin at the beginning, and freeing himself, as far as may be, from prejudices and presuppositions, to lay the foundation of reasonable certitude and build upon it stage by stage.

No doubt this is not the way in which our convictions on religion or on most other subjects actually grow upon us. The genesis of convictions appears commonly to be as little as possible the result of rational processes. And there is often no order in them. There are people who believe passionately in the Church and the Sacraments, but appear to have a very slender and meagre belief in God.[1] This lack of order or proportion in our religious convictions is, in part, the reason why they are so easily thrown into confusion. But if we are seeking to reconstruct a rational fabric of beliefs, we must begin at the

[1] I remember A. H. Mackonochie, that much-miscalled " Ritualist," saying in a sermon, somewhere about 1870, " There are people who believe in the blessed Sacrament, but do not seem to believe in Almighty God."

29

beginning; and there are certain qualities of mind which are, I think, essential.

1. We must make ourselves as free as possible from the passions bred of antagonism and disappointment.

For instance, if a man has been brought up in the Church, and, as so frequently happens, has become "offended" with the Church, because he has found it, in this or that clergyman under whose ministry he has been, or whose words have been reported, or through the records of history, obscurantist in temper, and narrow and intolerant in spirit, or if he has seen it bearing no such witness as it ought to have borne against injustice and oppression, but leaguing itself with the forces of wealth and class selfishness—if something of this kind has happened, the "offended" person is commonly embittered and quite incapable of an unprejudiced judgement. Bishop Butler, in famous words, speaks of the attitude of the fashionable world in his day towards religion. "It is come, I know not how, to be taken for granted, by many persons, that Christianity is not so much as a subject for enquiry; but that it is, now at length, discovered to be fictitious. And accordingly they treat it as if, in the present age, this were an agreed point among all persons of discernment; and nothing remained, but to set it up as a principal subject of mirth and ridicule, as it were by way of reprisals, for its having so long interrupted the pleasures of the world." [1] This demand for reprisals describes the attitude of a vast number of people in our own age. Their attitude towards the Church or towards orthodoxy is the attitude of those who would take reprisals on a weakened tyrant. In many cases it is,

---

[1] From the Advertizement to *The Analogy*.

as in Butler's day, the Church as claiming of them a
moral restraint which they have resolved to repudiate,
which is chiefly in their mind. With the nobler sort
the restraint they are repudiating is the claim laid
upon free thought and democratic aspiration. But in
either case the bitter desire to take reprisals on the
Church is totally destructive of a calm and reasonable judgement. Everything that makes against the
creed or moral standard of the Church is eagerly
welcomed. What makes for it is ignored or despised.
This is not reason, but the most deceptive of passions.
Must we be for ever in reactions? Can we not at
least recognize, as one of the most certain conclusions
of history, that the best things, liberty and equality,
no less than authority and inherited experience, are
the most capable of dangerous abuse; but that the
excesses and follies, whether of authority or liberty,
are no evidence that there is not, behind the excesses
and follies, a wisdom necessary for man? " La
vérité," said Renan, " consiste dans les nuances."
The method of " all or nothing " is of no account in
the court of reason. There is no chance of finding
truth, unless we seek calmly to estimate what is the
solid rational strength which lies behind all that
gives point and passion to the cry, " Tantum relligio
potuit suadere malorum." Those who are plainly
" out to score off " orthodoxy or, on the other hand,
eager to show up " the bankruptcy " of science or
criticism, can always do it easily enough, but the gain
for truth or for real intellectual liberty is not considerable.

2. Secondly, we ought to begin our search with a
real determination, if possible, to reach at least a
provisional decision. There are a vast number of
questions on which this is rationally impossible, and

such questions no doubt abound in theology and philosophy. For there really are no sufficient grounds for a decision. But it is impossible to doubt that the merely " critical " temper of our day, or at a lower stage the temper of mere intellectual curiosity, is sceptical in the sense that it loves the process of enquiry for its own sake and has no real desire to draw a conclusion.[1] It does not see the practical importance of decision nor feel the responsibility of making up its mind. It finds each new view interesting. It never can say a decisive " no." It miscalls its state of mental indecision openmindedness. No doubt there are a vast number of questions, besides those which, owing to the limitations of human faculty, no man can decide, on which we as individuals are without the materials for forming a judgement. They are questions for specialists. We can but read the record of this learned man's opinion and that learned man's rebutter with a certain degree of interest. We are and must be only spectators of a conflict in which we cannot share. But with regard to moral and religious matters in the deepest sense, this cannot be so. They concern us vitally. Our manhood calls out for assurance, if we can reasonably have it. The popular suggestion that " it does not really matter so much what exactly a man believes " is a fallacy. However many instances we may find of beliefs that have no influence on conduct, of atheists who live as Christians and Christians who live as atheists, yet on a broad view of human nature, in the long reaches of human life, we cannot but see

[1] There are famous instances of protests by great thinkers that the search for truth was to be preferred to the finding of it, but I believe that, at bottom, this state of mind represents a disease of the intellect.

that how men and women behave depends on what they really believe about the unseen foundations of life, about God and duty, about heaven and hell.

It does not seem to me rational to doubt that the marked differences between the various civilizations or types of human society, which have been formed under the influence of the Jewish or the Christian or the Mohammedan or the Buddhist or the Brahman religion, have been due in very large measure to the differences in the beliefs about God and human destiny which underlie them. And what is true of nations or " crowds " is true also of individuals or the smaller and more consciously formed groups. I cannot imagine a man doubting this about himself, if he will be at pains to distinguish his real from his conventional creed. And what we are seeking for is a real creed—a real intellectual decision such as is formed to be acted upon.

Of course it is a betrayal of my rational nature to make premature decisions on inadequate grounds. But with regard to what really matters for human life, I must accept the challenge of the great masters of human life and determine to seek decisions, where decisions are rationally possible, and to test their validity by putting them to account in life. It is only in this way that decisions of a provisional nature can become permanent convictions.

No doubt we may form wrong decisions, and growing experience or growing knowledge may convince us of our mistake. Then we must go through the process which James Hinton used to describe as " correcting our premises." Nevertheless, it is better to make an intellectual decision or accept a creed on what seems to be the weight of the evidence on the whole, and to use it for all it is worth, and then, if

4

need arise, revise it or even abandon it—if all this be done carefully and with all due consideration—than to remain for ever uncommitted and in suspense.

Nor must we suffer ourselves to be deluded or discouraged from thinking by what I may call the "pragmatist" argument—that it is only the "moral values" that really matter—that we can be certain about our moral duty and the conception of life which is involved in it, and that beyond this we may be indifferent to "metaphysics." For we cannot thus separate the moral from the intellectual or metaphysical question. As has already been said, the strain to-day for multitudes of men and women is especially upon the moral standard. Because it lacks the support of a clear faith, the moral standard either breaks down or becomes lowered to the level of popular opinion. To this extent certainly the mass of men are rational, that they want to know why they should pursue a difficult and, as it often appears, a solitary course of action, inconsistent equally with their apparent interests and the common opinion of their fellows. And in effect this means that they must have some sort of theology. No doubt their reason for assenting to their creed may be mainly the moral reason—the kind of reason which can be best expressed as the conviction that a belief which is necessary for a good life must be true or, as people say, "practically" true. This is an argument which we shall have to estimate later.[1] But whatever the reason which in their minds substantiates their personal creed, some sort of creed about God and their own soul individual men and women must have if they are to live by any standard better than that of public opinion; and, we may add,

[1] See pp. 111–12.

without a creed commonly accepted or at least held in reverence about God and the soul, the level of public moral opinion will be constantly degrading.

3. Thirdly, this capacity for reaching decision will need a frank recognition of the manifold grounds and methods of certainty. The methods of arriving at conclusions which is specially characteristic of science—what Darwin called "the grinding of general laws out of observed instances" [1]—is a part of the operations of the human mind in gaining truth which it would be impossible to ignore and difficult to over-estimate, but we cannot recognize in it the whole of our resources. Consider the great artists. They convey to us truth about the universe which we are maimed beings if we do not recognize, but which is apprehended and conveyed and appreciated through methods wholly different from the methods of scientific reasoning, and which scientific reasoning can neither reach nor communicate. William de Morgan [2] describes in a wonderful passage the effect of a sonata of Beethoven on a man without special musical gifts or knowledge in an hour of desolation and despair. It reasoned with him, after its manner. It conveyed to him reassurance which nothing else could convey. "I have ever since regarded the latter [Beethoven] as not so much a Composer as a Revelation." "How often have I said to myself after some perfectly convincing phrase of Beethoven, ' Of course, if *that* is so, there can be no occasion to worry.' It could not be translated, of course, into vulgar grammar or syntax ; but it left no doubt on the point, for all that." Those who have any appreciation of music,

---

[1] Of course, even the physical sciences owe very much to prophetic intuitions.

[2] *Joseph Vance*, pp. 404–7.

however deficient in musical science, must feel after long listening to Beethoven what this means. He conveys to us a temper of mind, almost a philosophy —though not such as can be made directly articulate in intellectual propositions. It is by feeling or intuition that this supreme artist gains his profound vision of experience and of God. But it seems to me quite impossible to deny that it is insight into reality, the sort of insight which at bottom involves a philosophy of rational meaning or purpose in the universe.

"The rest may reason and welcome: 'tis we musicians know."

The same claim must be made on behalf of the intuitions of the poets, the prophets, and the mystics in the most general sense—I mean the religious souls who have a clear intuition of God and live in communion with Him. All these classes of persons, who have played so vast a part in the history of mankind, are convinced of some kind of reality—some law or aspect or controlling spirit of the universe which is to them the most certain of realities; and this conviction of theirs has been reached often in utter scorn of reasoning, or at any rate not by its methods.[1]

[1] Cf. *The Sadhu*, by Canon B. H. Streeter and Mr. A. I. Appasamy. This account of a still living Indian Christian mystic is of deep interest. We may doubt his particular conclusions. I am not now concerned with these. All that I am concerned to insist is that the method of intuition is, as much as the method of scientific induction, a method of arriving at truth about the universe. We should note that the mystics differ from the prophets in this respect: that the latter tell us *about* God—they have a definite message about His will or character to deliver to men, of the truth of which we must judge; but the former, for the most part, are impressive not for what they tell us about God, but simply by the intensity with which they feel and see God in all things and all things in God.

Now it is quite obvious that such "intuitions" and "experiences" may be really quite unworthy of the names they claim. And the message of the prophets or seers may be quite contradictory. In fact they often are. We say, "They cannot all be true." For intuition means insight into reality, and experience properly means reality as felt. But the most masterful convictions reached by the power of emotion in the human soul may be pure delusions—they may correspond to nothing in the realities of the world. It would be only too easy to prove this proposition. And in these days, when every one talks about psychology, there is, as has been already said, a seriously dangerous tendency to attach so much importance to states of mind as to forget that the value of the subjective depends wholly at the last resort upon its correspondence with the objective.

It is very difficult to state precisely the tests which are to enable us to discriminate between intuition of reality and delusive imagination. Two of the most important of such tests are, no doubt, (1) that the spiritual intuition of the prophet or mystic or poet should be found in experience to give to those who accept it, and that over long periods of time and a wide range of humanity, a new power in life, as, for example, Mohammed's intuition of the One God and His will brought a startling degree of new life into the Arab races. This we believe can only have been because he had perceived some vital truth of fact, however much fanaticism or error may have been mixed up with his message. And (2) that the spiritual intuitions of the mystic, when translated, as they must be, into propositions for the intellect, should show themselves either capable of harmonization with all that, by other faculties, men have discovered about the universe in a consistent unity, or at least, if complete synthesis is beyond us, should not be in plain discrepancy with our knowledge as a whole.

I am aware that this demand for agreement, or at least absence of plain discrepancy, between the conclusions which, on different grounds, we are led to form needs to be pressed with much caution. I gather that Sir William Bragg, in his recent Boyle Lecture, has called attention within the region of physics to the discrepancy between the apparent intellectual postulate of the explosive action of electrons, suggesting something like Newton's corpuscular theory, and the "firmly established" wave theory of the transference of energy, and added these suggestive words, " We are obliged to use each theory as occasion demands and wait for further knowledge as to how it may be possible that both should be true at the same time. Toleration of opinion is a recognized virtue. The curiosity of the present situation is that opposite opinions have to be held or used by the same individual in the faith that some day the combined truth may be made plain." [1] If this is a rational attitude, as I think it is, towards discrepant theories within the region of the same science, much more may it be rational within the wide compass of the whole of our knowledge. The " doctrine of relativity," of which we hear so much to-day—the recognition that our best theories or explanations of the universe cannot express absolute truth, but only the best measure of truth attainable by us with our limited vision—makes us no doubt tolerant of apparent discrepancies between our conclusions in one depart-

[1] See *The Times* report of Sir William Bragg's recent Robert Boyle Lecture, Friday, May 13, 1921.

ment of knowledge and experience and our conclusions in another.

Nevertheless, there is a tendency in philosophy to-day, and not only among pragmatists,[1] to carry the toleration of contradictory theories to a point which seems to me to subvert rationality altogether. It is surely of the essence of reason to demand synthesis. It may be necessary to entertain contradictory theories simultaneously, at least for a time, where different classes of fact seem to force them upon us, but at least this should cause in our minds " a pressing uneasiness " and not be allowed to subvert the essential rational demand for a consistent universe.

But I am not now attempting to devise tests to discriminate the real from the delusive either in the reasonings or intuitions of mankind. All that I am now contending for is what artists and prophets and mystics have always insisted upon, and what the rising science of psychology is pressing upon us, not without perilous excess—viz. that if we want to reach the whole truth, so far as we can, concerning the world we live in, we must trust the whole of our faculties—not our powers of abstract reasoning only, or only our powers of scientific discovery higher or lower, but also the more emotional and active powers of our nature—its capacities for intuition and feeling and willing. Anyone, in fact, who examines himself must almost certainly reach the conclusion that a great proportion of the convictions of his own mind, such as he would find it impossible to repudiate without repudiating his humanity, and impossible even to doubt without

[1] The language of Dr. Bradley, for instance, surely is somewhat reckless, e.g. " Is there any need for our attempt to avoid self-contradiction ? " (*Essays on Truth and Reality*, p. 430, cf. index under heading " Consistency ").

being self-convicted of treason against the good, have
been arrived at by feeling; whether it be by a moral or
religious tradition being verified and approved in
his own conscience and experience, or by some feeling
being aroused in himself individually and acted upon,
and not by any process of reasoning. This means,
on the broadest scale, that feeling, generating an inward
vision of reality, or intuition—which is faith of a sort,
because it runs ahead of all reasoning and even resents
its interference—is a large part in our human equipment as searchers after truth and reality. It is quite
compatible with such a fundamental respect for
feeling and conscience to admit that the conclusions
of science must be allowed to correct the rashness
or crudeness of the convictions which conscience and
feeling suggest, just as, on the other hand, conscience
and feeling must be allowed to enlarge the narrowness
of the outlook of science or ratiocination. The point
is that the whole of our mental or spiritual capacities
must be trained and brought into exercise if we are
to be true to the whole of reality.

The co-operation and interaction of our different
capacities may be made clearer by two illustrations.

(1) The *Confession* of Leo Tolstoy,[1] surely among
the most moving of modern documents, though
neither our feeling nor our reason may accept all
his conclusions, yet suggests convincingly one thing
at least—how reasoning and feeling combine and
intertwine in all genuine search for the truth, feeling
insisting on reopening questions which reasoning had
sought to close, sometimes gaining the victory over
reasoning, sometimes corrected by reasoning, but
always, so to speak, intervening, if reasoning is to be
kept from losing itself in vacancy or self-despair.

[1] *A Confession*, trans. by Aylmer Maude (Oxford Univ. Press).

Finally, it appears, the ground of all sane theory seemed to Tolstoy to be the feeling for the good life, the recognition of it when we see it, and the assurance that it must be worth while to live it, and that it must turn out to be in accordance with right reason.

(2) My point could also be happily illustrated by many of us from intimacy with scientific men who are also unashamedly religious men. We must acknowledge that almost exclusive preoccupation with scientific enquiries tends to generate a disinclination for, or a distrust of, the methods of the mystic or the poet or the ordinary religious man—the methods by which religious convictions are usually arrived at and exercised. Thus it is not surprising that many scientific men are agnostics and some proclaim their agnosticism. All exclusive preoccupation with one kind of mental activity, whatever it be, is a specializing of the mind which tends to narrowness. Instances would be easy to give from many quarters. But this narrowness is not characteristic of all scientific men. Thus George Romanes bore witness that of the brilliant galaxy of mathematicians who were the glory of Cambridge about 1870–80 the majority were orthodox in religion[1]—doubtless neither because of, nor in spite of, their scientific insight, but because they were something else besides scientific men. In a somewhat later generation Pasteur, though perhaps the most eminent among scientific men who were also professing Christians, would by no means stand alone with his frank declaration of a childlike faith in the Catholic religion, again doubtless neither because of his science nor in spite of it, but by the exercise of faculties which science barely uses

[1] Romanes, *Thoughts on Religion* (Longmans), pp. 137–8.

or for its own specific purposes excludes. Once in
my life I have been privileged to know an able young
scientific man who went almost at a bound from
somewhat polemical agnosticism to a whole-hearted
faith, through an experience of mental agony which
seemed to open to him new windows to reality.
He did not find his new faith interfere with his
science or restrain it. He was free as ever to pursue
his special career. But he was more of a man. His
humanity was fuller, because he had learned that man
does not know by scientific investigation only.

In all this plea for breadth in the consideration of
the grounds of certitude I have used language about
" faculties " or " capacities "—reason and feeling and
will—in every man, such as experience, I think,
suggests or requires. We are intensely conscious of
such distinct faculties and of their conflict within us.
In one department of our life there is more claim upon
our will, in another upon our good feeling or conscience, in another upon our powers of reasoning.
Again, one person is distinguished by a vigorous will but
deficient in feeling or intelligence, and another appears
to be all intellect, and another " all heart and no
head." And in each of us heart and head, or conscience
and will, are apt to be in violent discord. Nevertheless
any deep view of personality or any sound psychology
suffices to convince us that, however mysterious the
interaction of our faculties, or however intense at times
the consciousness of distraction and conflict, yet in fact
they are but movements of the same self.[1] The

---

[1] It was the merit of Tertullian (*de Anima*, 18), at a time when
Christianity was emphasizing the unity of human personality, that
he made a strong protest against the tendency of the philosophers
to distinguish human faculties as if they were different entities—
" Non enim et sentire intelligere est et intelligere sentire est ? " etc.

root of all is the common vital movement of self-realization—the conative movement—which in man expresses itself as will and emotion and rational concept : " will " and " emotion " being distinguished from animal instinct just in proportion as they either pass into or presuppose rational concepts and theories and convictions, and thereby gain consistency and power. Our rational or argumentative powers only emerge as an element in the whole conative movement of our personality asserting itself. Thus no theory of the world can claim to be the truth for a man which either ultimately tends to paralyse his will or quench his feeling or baffle his reason. For these qualities, taken altogether and not apart, are the expression of his fundamental self.

I know that some who read this will be disposed to feel that, having begun by asking for a temper of mind freed from disturbing prejudices, I am now allowing the calm reason to be flooded with prejudices bred of will or emotion. But in fact we are bound to discriminate between " prejudice " in its etymological sense and in its popular sense. In the latter sense it means a condition of our judgement or intelligence in which we refuse to open our minds to disagreeable facts or to allow them to have weight with us. It is a fixed, unprogressive and narrow condition of mind, and it must be got rid of. But there is another sense in which we are normally born with " pre-judgements " implicit in us—as that right is better than wrong or beauty than ugliness. These implicit prejudgements appear to belong to our unconscious self in a measure, and they are strengthened by our training and our experience. It is idle to demand that we should be free of them. They are behind our coldest reasonings as evidently as behind our most emotional or wilful movements. What we can do is faithfully to bring our prejudices into the clearest light and subject them to all the corrective discipline of experience. So we can get rid of disturbing prejudices and come into the fullest possible correspondence with the large truth of things, as it appears to be. But we cannot get out of ourselves, and certain prejudgements are implicit in human personality.[1]

.   .   .   .   .

Now with this amount of preface as to the temper and method which our attempt to reconstruct belief from its foundations demands of us, let us enter upon our enquiry at its most fundamental stage—let us investigate the grounds of a belief in God.

[1] There is an admirable account of the function of education in relation to prejudice in Plato's *Republic*, book iii, 401.

CHAPTER III

WE approach the fundamental question of belief in God. It will speedily appear, I think, that the most pressing question is not whether we can believe in God, but of what sort the God is in whom we can or must believe. Atheism is very rare, and agnosticism is a question of degree.[1] In some sense we must all be agnostics, inasmuch as, on all showing, God passes our understanding. The important question is : how much can we know or rationally believe about God ? Nevertheless we must not hurry forward, but ask first whether belief in God at all is reasonable, and, if so, why.

Fundamentally to disbelieve in God—to be an atheist—means, I suppose, that we see in the world of which we form a part no signs of anything corresponding to the mind or spirit or purpose which indisputably exists in man—no signs of a universal spirit or reason with which we can hold communion, nothing but blind and unconscious force. And conversely what we mean by Theism or belief in God in its most general form is the recognition about us, within us and above us, of a universal and eternal

---

[1] See Pringle Pattison, *Idea of God*, p. 166.

reason or purpose, with which we can and ought to correspond.

This fundamental alternative was stated by the Roman Emperor Marcus Aurelius, long ago in words of which we still feel the momentous seriousness :

" The world is either a welter of alternate combination and dispersion, or a unity of order and providence.   If the former, why do I care about anything else than how I shall at last become earth ?   But on the other alternative I feel reverence, I stand steadfast, I find heart in the power that disposes all." [1]

Now, in earlier ages mankind has been found believing in many gods, or in two original spiritual principles or gods, the one good and the other evil, which are at conflict in the universe. This latter belief, which we call dualism, is so congruous with part of our experience, both within ourselves and without ourselves, that it is always reviving. Nevertheless I think that, like polytheism properly so-called, it is rationally impossible for us to-day. The science of nature has demonstrated the absolute unity of nature. Good and evil, as we know them in experience, mind and matter, the world of moral purpose and the world of material things, are not the product of two separate original forces. They are knit into one another as phases in one whole, results of one force, one system of interconnected law. The universe, material and spiritual, is, as Spinoza said, one and (in some sense) of one substance ; and God, if there be a God, in part manifest and in part concealed in nature, is one only. Long before the days of modern science

---

[1] *Meditations*, vi. 10. I take the translation, which gives the sense clearly, almost unchanged from Pringle Pattison.

in fact, and quite apart from Jewish or Christian influences, the brooding mind of man had felt the unity in things, and behind the "gods many" of popular belief, had been feeling its way to the oneness of God.[1]

Again, to-day a new dualism or pluralism is raising its head. Mr. H. G. Wells and other prophets of the day are calling us to believe in a God who is very far indeed from being the Creator of the universe or the Spirit of the universe. The Power behind the world is inscrutable. It may be cruel or merely unconscious. But we can believe in a good God who has some power, though He is very far from being almighty, and whom we, by co-operating with Him, can help to become

[1] It was, however, hampered by the prevailing dualism. In this connexion, I think, Irenaeus, the Christian Father of the second century, is an often disparaged man. If I am not mistaken, he saw deep into current controversies, and successfully emancipated the Christian mind from some of the clinging misconceptions which haunted the philosophy inherited from Greece. Thus to him we owe the first clear affirmation, as far as I know, of three important principles.

1. That no fundamental antagonism exists, or can be tolerated in idea, between spirit and matter, for the whole universe is " of one substance," as coming from one God, and " the Word has been made flesh." This principle of Christian faith and philosophy is constantly reasserted by Irenaeus, and it is one of the central certainties of modern science. It is our deliverance from Greek dualism.

2. That the method of God in creation and redemption is a method of gradual and progressive advance. Here also Irenaeus asserted again and again an important principle. He substituted the idea of progressive development from lower to higher, from the material to the spiritual, for the later Hellenic idea of emanations from the Absolute and the divine, each lower than that which preceded it.

3. He also borrowed from someone whom he does not name the assertion that the reason why all things in God's world are in measure, order, and number is because God Himself is not infinite in the sense of being indeterminate or capable of anything ; measure or order lies in the eternal being of God—the relationship of the Father to the Son—immensus Pater in Filio mensuratus : mensura enim Patris Filius (iv. 4[2]).

more powerful. Now, if this God, who is not the power behind nature, is anything more than a name for the aspirations of men—if He is declared to be a real Being, with mind and purpose—the idea seems to me to be purely mythological. The only power which holds me and all things in its grasp is the one all-pervading force of universal nature. There is no room for any other, unless it be for dependent spirits, dependent upon it. There can be no rivalry with the one and the ultimate and the all-embracing. All comes from it and must end in it. If this Power be the good God, I can have a rational religion. But any suggestion of a Being independent of it seems to me to be the language of a dream. The early Christian poet invoked God as "the persistent energy of things" —"Deus rerum tenax vigor." If this persistent energy of things be indeed God, all is well. But in any case, it is that alone in whom we live and move and have our being.

What grounds are there, for us men to-day, for believing that the Universal Power is God ? Perhaps the grounds of such belief cannot be better expressed in summary than in the verses—in this case, it must be admitted, the very blank verses—of Words-worth's Preface to the " Excursion " :

> "My voice proclaims
> How exquisitely the individual mind
> (And the progressive powers perhaps no less
> Of the whole species) to the external world
> Is fitted :—and how exquisitely too—
> Theme this but little heard of among men—
> The external world is fitted to the mind ;
> And the creation (by no lower name
> Can it be called) which they with blended might
> Accomplish."

Let us pursue this line of thinking.

1. Reason is that in us which demands sequence, regularity, and order in things. It resents mere accident and chance occurrence.[1] It could, in fact, only exist in a *cosmos*, i.e. an orderly world. And such a *cosmos* it finds from the first in sun and moon, in plant and animal, but mixed as it appears with what is incalculable and purely capricious—that is, irrational. But the more it knows, the more ground it finds for confidence that the appearance of capriciousness is due only to its ignorance. Nature, it grows to believe, is, in this sense, rational through and through, that it corresponds to this fundamental demand of reason for law and order in all things. This faith in a universal order—a faith continually more an more fully justified—is what makes science possible ; and philosophy accompanying or anticipating science finds in this response of nature to the demand of reason the irresistible evidence of a universal reason or mind, ensouling nature, of which the reason or mind in us is the offspring or outcome, participating in and co-operating with the universal reason. This belief in the universal reason, with which our reason holds communion, was the Theism or belief in God of the educated world into which Christianity came. This, it was recognized, is the divine Being in which " we live and move and are." Of this divine Being we, as rational beings, are in a special sense " the offspring." [2]

---

[1] Originally, no doubt, it was the apparently arbitrary element in experience which suggested belief in gods—powerful but capricious beings. Nevertheless some law or principle of dealing with these fearful beings must be discovered. And the sense of order and law gains upon the sense of arbitrariness.

[2] Acts xvii. 28. This is what St. Paul in his argument with the men of Athens can take for granted. So contemporary literature abundantly witnesses.

5

This argument (if it is to be called an argument, or this almost irresistible impression made upon us by the world) is the more popular form of what is called the epistemological argument—the argument, that is, from the analysis of knowledge. If we are at pains to analyse the most elementary kind of knowledge, our knowledge of external objects, trees and houses, chairs and tables, we discover, to our surprise and perhaps annoyance, that it is not the case, as we had supposed, that the world of objects is presented to us through our senses of touch and taste and sight and hearing, as it were, ready made. To constitute an object in a world of objects there is needed a mind to hold together in permanent relation the materials of colour, pressure, sound, and smell which come to us through our senses. Only for such a perceiving, relating, remembering mind can a concrete object or world of objects exist. Mind, it appears, is necessary for its constitution. What sort of world a dog or a dragon-fly sees we cannot tell. But whatever it sees is, we must suppose, what its special soul or mind constitutes for it out of the materials which its senses supply to it.

This fact (for such it appears to be) has sometimes been represented by " subjective idealists " as if it meant that my mind is the maker of my world. But this is plainly contradictory to the ultimate certainty of common sense, which assures me that the world is presented to me, not made by me. The very suggestion of the opposite has made philosophy ridiculous. Also it is not what the analysis of the rudimentary act of knowledge would really suggest. Whatever the mind in me does, it does in absolute dependence upon and subordination to what is supplied to it in sensations—not only the sensations as isolated

facts, but their impact upon us in a certain regularity
of succession or simultaneity. The constructive work
of my mind is absolutely dependent upon what it
receives—the subjective process upon the data
supplied. Thus I need have no fear that philosophy
is so absurd as to suggest a doubt that the external
world is independent of me or the myriad other
individual minds. But what it does suggest to me,
or even force upon me, is that the reality of an ordered
world can exist only for mind and in terms of mind.
There seems to be no way of escaping this conclusion.
The real world of a fly or a dog—whatever it may be—
requires the mind of a fly or a dog for its existence.
The man's world of fuller reality requires the man's
mind. The whole of the world-reality in all its
fullness and complexity postulates a universal and
perfect mind, which (whether it is to be represented
as its Creator or as its soul) would be instinctively
called divine. And it is this divine mind which
is communicating with me through all the process
of sensitive experience. In knowing more about the
world I am learning about God.

At least since the great days of Greece the philosophers and the poets of the human race have been, on
the whole, constantly engaged in reinforcing this conviction, that you must interpret the material world in
terms of mind or spirit, and not mind or spirit in terms
of matter or physical force. Mind has the making of
things, and without creative mind they could not be.

In reasserting this old idealist argument, I know
that I am challenging the New Realists. Thus Dr.
Alexander says in his Gifford Lectures [1]:

" The effect of the empirical method in metaphysics is

[1] *Space, Time, and Deity* (Macmillan, 1920), vol. i, p. 6.

seriously and persistently to treat finite minds as one among the many forms of finite existence, having no privilege among them except such as it claims from its greater perfection of development. Should enquiry prove that the cognitive faculty is unique, improbable as such a result might seem, it would have to be accepted faithfully and harmonized with the remainder of the scheme. But *prima facie* there is no warrant for the assumption, still less for the dogma, that because all experience implies a mind, that which is experienced owes its being and its qualities to mind. Minds are but the most gifted members known to us in a democracy of things."

This attempt to treat minds as simply things seems to me blankly impossible. It is not, I think, an assumption or a dogma that " things," that is, an ordered world, involve and presuppose mind. It is the inevitable conclusion of the first analysis of common experience.[1] I must profess that the epistemological argument does seem to me irresistible, when it claims our recognition of Mind as necessary for a world; and when it bids us feel ourselves in the mere act of perceiving a world of ordered objects brought into some sort of communion with this Mind which is in all things.

2. To some of us the form in which this kind of argument presents itself with the greatest force is what we may call the argument from beauty. Evolutionists have attempted to show that beauty in animals can be accounted for without the assumption of any " intention " of being beautiful in nature simply by the fact that beautiful beings—especially the males—have an advantage in the struggle for existence, and that beauty has thus a survival value,

---

[1] The new realists are involved, I think, in a further difficulty when they postulate the existence of universals independently of minds : see Haldane, *Reign of Relativity* (Murray), pp. 133, 265, etc.

because the qualities which give beauty to males
attract the other sex. Among all the occurring
varieties the more beautiful would, therefore, without
any intention on the part of nature, tend to propagate
their species, and the less beautiful to perish. I
believe that the biologists are using this argument
to-day with much more hesitation than Charles
Darwin. Sexual selection on account of beauty has
a measure of truth, it seems, but there is fair certainty
that Darwin gave it far too great an extension.
Moreover, how are we to account for the basis of this
theory, viz. the existence in the universal female of
a consistent æsthetic standard ? But I do not want
to pause over an argument with which I have not
the exact knowledge to deal. Because, in any case,
it has no application to inorganic nature, and that is
enough for me. How shall we account for the beauty
of inorganic nature—for the glory of the sea, for the
majesty of mountains, for the exquisite beauty of
nature's lines, for the splendour and delicacy of sunsets,
for the loveliness of clouds, for the music of sounds,
for the fascination of motions and colours and shapes ?
On the largest scale we must confess that " nature all
the time that it is working as a machine is also
sleeping as a picture." [1] All this has no connexion
with utility or survival value. And certainly, if any
other quality in things is objective—in whatever sense
the reality and qualities of natural objects are prior
to the perceiving mind in man—beauty is so. It
forces itself and impresses itself upon us. And we
cannot conceive it to be accidental. Our reason
insists that there is in nature an intention of being
beautiful—we cannot call it anything else—long prior

[1] From Mozley's *University Sermons*—the wonderful sermon on
nature which everyone ought to read.

dark animal or tribal origins of this majestic faculty, lies its real meaning and interpretation. It is incontestable that the glory and dignity of humanity depend upon, and are bound up with, the recognition of the supremacy of the moral ideal or law at a point where it has risen above, or distinguished itself from, social exigencies or personal advantages. Here, first, and here alone, where conscience recognizes its spiritual subordination to an eternal righteousness, claiming its glad obedience and co-operation, is the home of the moral freedom in which we recognize our true being. Such a belief in an Absolute Right is consistent, history shows us, with a very inadequate recognition (or none at all) of a personal God. It may, and sometimes does in fact consist (illogically as it would appear) with explicit atheism. But it cannot be given fair expression except by the recognition that right and wrong is no mere outgrowth of human interests or the necessities of human society. If it emerges out of these, it gains its true character only so far as it transcends them. It involves the recognition of the morally right as a quality of absolute value, which imposes itself on man absolutely because he is rational and spiritual. It cannot be interpreted as a merely human quality. Thus we are bound to conclude that the ordered world, of which man is only a part, contains or involves this quality of eternal righteousness. Like reason itself, of which it is an aspect, like beauty, so righteousness belongs to the universal and eternal Being, and, because this is so, men have called this Being God, and worshipped it.[1]

[1] The above argument, in its three divisions, here very summarily treated, may be found, underlying their many differences, in most of

Here, in the moral region, very much more than in the region of beauty, we are encompassed with the sense of what *ought* to be. Moral goodness exists, but under conditions of continual and sometimes desperate struggle, and in each individual with more or less of manifest imperfection. But whatever its struggles and imperfections, goodness, we are convinced, is what ought to be. It represents the purpose of the world for free personalities. Whatever else the world may be, it is, in the region covered by the existence of persons, a " vale of soul-making," as Keats called it, a scene for the making of character and goodness under conditions of severest trial. And we find ourselves, in spite of appearances, impelled to believe that the moral purpose of the world, in general and in particular persons, is *intended to* gain the victory. This is the ground of the strong conviction of our moral consciousness that our best aspirations are not kindled in us only to be baffled and defeated. The great world-force, which over vast areas of the universe appears so wholly indifferent to moral considerations, here seems unmistakably to disclose a mind and purpose making for righteousness, though it must be admitted that the disclosure seems often in experience painfully ambiguous and embarrassed.

So far we are taken by the general trend of contemporary philosophy, and we feel the ground secure under our feet. But of course it will be said, we have reached here no more than " the higher pan-

our recent philosophers. Perhaps the best recent books to which to refer a would-be student are Dr. Pringle Pattison's *Idea of God* (Oxford, 1917), and Dr. Sorley's *Moral Values and the Idea of God* (Cambridge, 1918)—an extraordinarily impressive book—also Lord Haldane's *Reign of Relativity* (Murray, 1921).

theism " [1]—the recognition in the world, of which we are a part, of spiritual qualities and values, and what we cannot but call spiritual purpose, with which as spiritual beings, rational, beauty-loving, and moral, we are called to co-operate, and which as eternal and universal spirit we are moved to worship. This is the immanent God—God in all things and in us.

Well, if this belief and accompanying worship is no more than pantheism, let us be at least pantheists. And let us recognize that, to this spiritual interpretation of nature, the scientific view of the world, which since the days of Darwin has become approximately universal, offers no sort of hindrance. Science bids us contemplate an age-long process by which, out of some original elements and conditions, to us but dimly imaginable, there was evolved a universal order, and out of the inorganic order life and the forms of life, vegetable and animal, and out of the animal creation rational man. We shall not, if we are wise, lay stress on the gaps in the scientific story of creation, or build on the conviction that living matter could not have been evolved out of what had no life, or rationality out of animal mind. But what we shall claim is that the fact that living beings and spiritual beings emerged in an age-long process out of a world which was lifeless and without any spiritual consciousness in itself, does not mean

[1] Dr. Inge (*Personal Idealism*, p. 43) would restrict the name Pantheist to "those who hold that God is present *equally* in every part of His creation," equally in rational man and in the clods, and thereby abolish all sense of " values "—all sense of higher and lower, or of an ascending scale in nature as God is more fully revealed. But it is more in accordance with general usage and with the facts of the case to speak of Pantheism higher and lower, and to reckon as Pantheists all who recognize a spirit immanent and operative in nature, but not, as far as they can see, independent of it or transcending it.

that life and spirit can be interpreted in terms of material force and chemical change, as if they were nothing more. The opposite is the case. Rather it is the flower and fruit of nature which interpret the seed from which it springs. When mind in man emerges in the process of creative evolution, then, and only then, does the secret of nature begin to be recognized. "Man is organic to nature."[1] The reason in man discovers the rational in nature; the sense of beauty in man finds itself in presence of the universal beauty; the conscience in man finds itself in presence of an eternal righteousness. The conclusion is forced upon us that instead of interpreting mind in terms of matter, you must interpret the whole process of physical evolution in terms of that in which it culminates, that is, mind. Here first we see what it all meant and whither it was all tending. Thus are we led to see the quality of spirit, that is, mind and purpose, in the first beginnings of the material world. That is, in some sense, we are led to believe in God.

M. Henri Bergson is no doubt at many points open to criticism. But he seems to me to have given effective expression to a set of ideas which are destined to dominate. "I see in the whole evolution of life on our planet a crossing of matter by a creative consciousness, an effort to set free, by force of ingenuity and invention, something which in the animal still remains imprisoned, and is only finally released when we reach man."[2]

I think it must be said that in the fundamental

[1] The argument will be found in Pringle Pattison's book just referred to, cap. viii, and in many other recent thinkers.
[2] See *Mind Energy* (*L'Energie Spirituelle*), by H. Bergson, trans. by Prof. H. Wildon Carr (Macmillan, 1920), p. 18, cf. p. 25.

conflict between materialism—which would explain spirit in terms of matter, because the material appears before the spiritual and the spiritual emerges out of it—and the spiritual interpretation of nature—which insists that the orderly evolution which ends in spiritual beings also presupposes spirit and spiritual purpose—in that philosophical conflict materialism has been shown to be untenable. I think it is true to say further that in the two generations full of constant discussion which have now passed since Darwin's *Origin of Species* appeared, the idea that the world of organized life can be accounted for by nothing but "natural selection" and "sexual selection" acting upon the material supplied by chance variations has become less and less probable.[1] Grant to these agencies all the force they can be allowed to have had, it seems impossible to account for progressive evolution of living forms unless some sort of direction, some sort of organic tendency to become this or that, is assumed in nature—which suggests irresistibly a progressive purpose in the world of living things, which has found for the present its culmination and interpretation in man. In fact, we are driven back for our interpretation of nature upon the principle first clearly enunciated by Aristotle that the essence of anything, or its real meaning, is only manifest when it has reached its full growth. We are to interpret the beginning in the light of the end; not the end in the light of the beginning.[2]

[1] For an account of the present standing of the doctrine of evolution, see Thomson and Geddes's admirable little volume *Evolution* in the Home University Library.

[2] Cf. Haldane's *Reign of Relativity*, p. 254. "The higher is the explanation of the lower, and not the lower of the higher." He is speaking of the Greek philosophers.

Moreover, it does not appear to be at all the case that the scientific doctrine of the world—for all the length of its vast epochs and all the extension of its infinite spaces in which man appears but as a moment and a speck—has in any way really dethroned man from his position of supremacy in the visible order as the climax and consummation (so far) of creation.[1] What intelligent beings there may be in other worlds or spheres of being, into which we cannot penetrate, and how much superior to man—" thrones, dominations, virtues, princedoms, powers "—our science cannot tell. It must frame its conceptions on what it knows. And within that sphere of possible knowledge it is in man first and in man only that vast nature finds its interpretation, because here only can its large meaning and content be understood, here only can its general law and tendency be appreciated, here only is one who can co-operate with it by intelligence and will, and by co-operation fashion it in a measure to his purpose.

But this " natural religion "—the vision of God in nature to which the poets and philosophers and artists and moralists open our eyes, and which, with their help, we can make our own—is to most of us a very unsatisfying religion. It suggests to those who have lived in the Christian tradition some urgent questions. Thus, (1) this God who is " the wisdom and spirit of the universe," the Truth and Beauty and Righteousness which I can contemplate and with which I can, in a measure, enter into communion, is

[1] Cf. Pringle Pattison, *The Idea of God*, pp. 28, 82–3, 110–11. He points out that if Kant depreciated the old argument from design in the sphere of physical nature, he also restored the argument from design by his recognition of moral values as supreme, and his theory of the universe as " a realm of ends."

He (if I may speak of "He" and "Him") personal?
While I seek to know Him, does He know me and
love me and respond to me? Ought I to tremble
before Him as my personal Sovereign and Judge,
awful in His righteousness? And through such fear
of the Lord can I learn to love Him and trust Him as
my Father?

Can He hear my prayers and help me in my
troubles? Can He take specific and positive action
on my behalf and on behalf of humanity? Or is
it really only certain gracious aspects of nature which
I am abstracting from the whole and calling God,
while all the time the Absolute, the whole, the
ultimate force and energy of all things, remains
inscrutable and ambiguous?

Again, (2) I call God "the wisdom and spirit of
the universe," but does He only gradually realize
Himself in the world and (if the words have any
meaning) come to the knowledge of Himself in man?
Is He thus as dependent on the world for expression
of Himself as the world is on Him? Is He simply
the world, as it were, viewed from within? Or, on
the other hand, does He transcend the world, free
and perfect in Himself, before ever the world was,
its Creator and its Lord?

Once again, (3) if He is the ground and source of
all things, evil as well as good, the ground and source
of the whole universe which in its main bulk seems
so morally indifferent, can He be Himself pure
goodness? Is it possible to believe that the spirit of
the whole is righteousness and love?

Then when we turn from God to ourselves, other
urgent questions arise. We find ourselves intensely
conscious of moral freedom only in part realized, but
conscious also of being bound as links in endless

chains of cause and effect, in soul as well as in body, with the whole of nature. Thus (4) is my sense of freedom a reality, or is it at the last analysis an illusion? And is the God whom I seek and seem to find in nature, a really free creative spirit, or simply a name for certain aspects of an endless necessary process? Again, (5) I am conscious of personality and freedom in myself, such as the experience of my present life stimulates but also oppresses. Is this spiritual consciousness, so thwarted here, the pledge and assurance of an immortal life in God and with God where it can find its realization?

These are momentous questions indeed. We know in a measure the answer which the Christian Faith gives to them, on the ground of a personal revelation of Himself believed to have been given by God through His prophets and His Son. But apart from any postulate of divine self-revelation, what answer can the brooding mind of man, by its eager search, discover to such questions? Now, it must be admitted that the answers of our philosophers and wise men and poets—apart from those who have believed the Christian revelation and built boldly upon it—have been extraordinarily vacillating and ambiguous. For instance, the great Greek masters seem hardly to have asked themselves the question about divine personality which seems to us so important. It was indeed the spirit of Christianity which first made the question of personality in God and in man real and urgent [1]; and it was Christian philo-

---

[1] Cf. Haldane, *Reign of Relativity*, p. 260, "Where Hellenistic reflection remained least complete, etc. . . . It did not take sufficient account of the infinite value belonging to human personality, humble as well as great. That was where it laid itself open to the criticism of Christianity, a criticism which subsequent reflection by degrees assimilated and found justified."

sophy which first found it necessary to devise a special word to signify it. The greatest philosophers, on the whole, are content to think of God as an object of intellectual contemplation rather than as a person who knows us, loves us, and helps us. Certainly, again, we shall find no satisfaction, but rather definite discouragement, if we address such urgent questions as our religious needs suggest to the wisdom of the remoter East. In Europe, after the decadence of Greek philosophy, there is a period of a thousand years when the philosophers of the Catholic world accepted among their premises the doctrines of the Christian faith and philosophized on the assumption of their truth. But since modern philosophy began its course with Descartes and Spinoza, on a basis of free thinking without regard to the authority of any Church, there has been indeed an intense application of the deepest thinking to these problems, but, so far as the answer to these questions of ours is concerned, with singularly vacillating and ambiguous result. Thus Descartes still, like a scholastic, " proves " the existence of God as the eternal, perfect, and personal Creator, distinct from all His creatures ; but for his greater successor, Spinoza, God is simply the one eternal substance, indistinguishable from nature, whom indeed it is our highest intellectual joy to love, but whom we cannot conceive of as loving us, or as willing and doing particular things, or as in any respect what we call personal, without His ceasing to be God, the universal substance. Thus while Spinoza has been called the God-intoxicated thinker, he was excommunicated by the Jewish community to which he belonged, and, not without some excuse, spoken of as an atheist. Indeed indecision about questions, which to minds coloured by the Christian tradition seem vital, haunts modern philosophy. Mr. Clement Webb, who himself argues strongly for personality in God, admits [1] the general reluctance of philosophers to affirm it. They seem always falling back to a position akin to that of the Greeks. Even so strong a contemporary theist as Dr. Pringle Pattison, though he labours to assert the divine transcendence, does not really succeed in doing so,[2] and he seems to think, with Spinoza, that divine perfection excludes all choice of particular things or persons.[3]

Then, as regards the character of God, philosophy seems to leave us with a perpetual and insoluble contradiction between the postulate of a perfect good God, made by the healthy moral consciousness of mankind, and the sort of conception which this mixed world of good and evil seems to suggest of a spirit in whom (or in which) good and evil can lie together as simply necessary modes of being; which line of thought again suggests or coincides with the philosophy which, at the last resort, makes human freedom and responsibility an illusion. Nor again do our philosophers give us any clear answer to the question of personal immortality.

No doubt this or that man of vigorous and confident intellect may seem to see his way through these tremendous questions to a solution. He may be able to proclaim the verdict of reason in favour of divine personality, divine goodness, and human freedom and immortality. But for most of us, if we rigorously try to shut out from our minds all

---

[1] Webb's *God and Personality*, p. 110.

[2] See appendix at the end of the chapter.

[3] See his essay on " Transcendence and Immanence," p. 14 in the volume entitled *The Spirit* (Macmillan, 1919).

6

the light which can only be ours as believers in the divine revelation of which the Bible is the record, it must be confessed that great nature, for all its divine qualities, remains an impenetrable mystery—a sphinx who gives no answers to importunate questions which we cannot but continue to ask.

We shall have to return later from another point of view upon these momentous questions and consider them more at leisure. But it is concerning this other point of view—that is, the point of view of divine revelation —that I want now to speak. St. Paul assures us that the nations of men were put into the world "that they should seek God, if haply they might feel after him, and find him," [1] and that "the living God left not himself without witness," [2] and that His invisible attributes, "His everlasting power and divinity," are since the creation of the world "clearly seen, being perceived through the things that are made." [3] This is substantiated in experience. The universe warrants or compels, as we have seen, belief in God, in some sort. But St. Paul also assures us that "in the wise providence of God, the world through its philosophy was not able to know God," and that it was God's good pleasure, in consequence, to disclose His real mind and purpose through the message of the preacher which the philosophers ridicule [4]—that is, by a real and effective self-revelation. Elsewhere the Bible tells us, in memorable phrases which haunt our memory when we are wearied with philosophical argument, that we "cannot by searching find out God." [5] These two kinds

---

[1] Acts xvii. 27.   [2] Acts xiv. 17.   [3] Romans i. 20.
[4] This is, I think, a fair paraphrase of 1 Cor. i. 21.
[5] Job xi. 7.

of statements seem to me to correspond with the facts. We are bound to search for God with all the energy of our reason, and in a measure we find Him ; but at the same time He baffles our search. It carries us a certain way, and then leaves us, disappointed and disheartened. We discover *that* God is, but not *what* He is. But both the eager search and the discovery, and, on the other hand, the disappointment and the failure, may, we feel, both be parts of a movement of God in us which is to be met by a corresponding movement of God, if I may so speak, from without or from above, to reveal Himself in much more satisfying fullness.

Now, no doubt this idea of positive divine revelation has often been so presented, both in its relation to reason and in its relation to natural religions, as to be very difficult of acceptance. Faith in divine revelation has been set in opposition to reason. The merit of faith has been represented as if it lay in triumphing over reason. But this kind of represen-tation may be simply a misrepresentation. It may be the case that revelation supplements but in no way contradicts the conclusions and intimations of " unassisted " reason. Perhaps there is no real justification for setting revelation and reason in opposition at all. What I think is amazing is how little the modern intellectual world, which claims to be, and appears to be, seeking God with all seriousness —how little it faces the question of the reality of positive divine self-revelation. We are bound to think of a self-revealing God in some sense—self-revealing in nature as a whole—in its law, in its order, in its beauty—self-revealing with extraordinary intensity in conscience, and moreover with extra-ordinarily different degrees of intensity. It is face to face with this universal self-revelation of God that there has arisen that general consciousness of God which we have been considering, with all its occasional clearness of vision and also with all its profound and disturbing uncertainties. Why, then, should not this process of self-disclosure on God's part have been along one particular line intensified and clarified so as to become a real illumination ? Why, moreover, should not one race of men have been the channel of this fuller self-disclosure of God to the whole world, as other races have been of other good things which, when matured, have become universal in application ? [1] Of course all this involves a conscious providence in history—a real personality in God. But we do not, for the most part, feel that we have any *a priori* reason justifying the exclusion of the possibility of a particular providence and a personal God. Is it not our duty at least to examine the question of the reality of a divine revelation which certain religions press upon us ? Our memories are haunted by Plato's pathetic words, put into the mouth of Simmias in the *Phaedo*, where the question of the immortality of the soul is under discussion. "It seems to me, Socrates, as to you also, I fancy, that it is very difficult, if not impossible, in this present life to have clear knowledge concerning such subjects ; but that, on the other hand, it is the mark of a faint-hearted spirit to desist from examining all that is said about them in every way, or to abandon

---

[1] More is said later on the point, and on the whole relation of special revelation to the general reason. See also Dr. William Temple's *Mens Creatrix* (Macmillan), the prologue. The contrasted ideas of struggling reason and illuminating revelation is put with extraordinary impressiveness at the end of James Mozley's essay on Blanco White: see his collected Essays (Rivingtons), vol. ii.

the search so long as there is any chance of
light anywhere. For on such subjects one ought
to secure one of two things, either to learn or
discover the truth, or, if this is impossible, at least
to get the best of human argument (words) and
the hardest to refute, and relying on this as on a
raft, to sail the perilous sea of life, unless one were
able, more securely and less perilously, to make
one's journey upon a safer vessel—upon some divine
word." [1]

Let us, then, at least contemplate the possibility
of a particular divine self-disclosure, gradually
maturing, and finally becoming universal. Let us
consent at least to face the evidence and " to go
where the argument leads us."

Appendix on Dr. A. Seth Pringle Pattison's article
entitled " Immanence or Transcendence," in *The Spirit*—a
volume of essays edited by Canon Streeter (Macmillan,
1919).

It is a very interesting question whether—quite apart
from the acceptance of a positive self-disclosure of God,
such as the Christian Church believes to have been given
through the prophets and by Christ the Son of God—it is
possible to arrive at any secure intellectual hold upon a
transcendent God—upon a God, that is, who, in some
sense prior to the slowly developing universe, existed and
exists eternally, self-conscious and self-determined,
holding in His eternal being and mind the law and
purpose and power of all the slow development. It is
quite plain that this is the God whom the Christian
Church has believed in. It has believed in God the
eternal, who before the world was, was alive, ' the living
God,' self-complete and perfect, and who freely of His
goodwill created all that is.

There is, of course, profound intellectual difficulty—

---

[1] Plato, *Phaedo*, 85 C.D.

amounting, I think, to impossibility—in conceiving of such an eternal, living, personal God as a solitary monad, seeing that all the elements of conscious life, whether will or knowledge or love, involve relationship—an object of will, an object of knowledge, an object of love—and an eternal and perfect Spirit therefore involves an eternal and perfect object. But when, long after Biblical times, the Church became conscious of this intellectual problem, it had already been long familiar with the idea of the trinity of persons in the unity of God and found in this belief the solution of the intellectual difficulty. We must be careful to note that the idea or doctrine of the Trinity had not been originally formulated with any reference to the intellectual problem. It had been formulated as an attempt to put into words the Church's new experience of the Son, Jesus Christ, and of the Holy Spirit as persons in some sense to be ranked with God, the Father, without violation of His unity. But later it found in this trinitarian creed the solution of the intellectual problem in this manner—God could be conceived of as eternally alive, with the full life of will and knowledge and love, prior to and apart from creation, because His own eternal being contained in itself the necessary relationships—the fellowship of the Father with the Eternal Word or Son and with the Holy Spirit. In this eternal fellowship the full activity of life was possible. All that was to be created in time—" whatever has come into being "—already existed in eternal counterpart in the Word or Son [1]; and whatever life there be in the world was already active and conscious in the Eternal Spirit.

But all this conception which is due to the belief in a positive revelation must at present be ignored, whether we hold it for true or no. At any rate its grounds are not yet within our purview in this enquiry. The question now is : Can the unassisted intellect of man attain by speculation on the universe or out of its own resources any secure hold upon the transcendent God ? Let it be granted

[1] This is the interpretation given in early days to St. John i. 3–4, R.V. marg., " Without him was not anything made. That which hath been made was life in him." But I doubt the punctuation and interpretation of the particular passage.

that it can attain to the secure conviction that in some real sense God exists as " the spirit of the universe " or " the soul of the world." But the world, as we know, is not static. It is a world of gradual process and evolution. In it we see first force, then life, then, first fully in man, self-conscious mind and will. This suggests to us the conception of Henri Bergson (apparently lying in his mind side by side with another conception) of an unconscious spirit of life striving to express itself in the material world and finally becoming conscious of itself in man. Is this the only idea of God which nature suggests—an unconscious mind or purpose (if the words have any intelligible meaning), gradually gaining consciousness and self-expression in man ? But the difficulty of such a conception is enormous.[1] The unity of the world is so close-knit that there is no room for two principles, matter and life, such as Bergson's language might sometimes suggest. It is one force (or God), and one only, which there expresses itself alike in things material and spiritual. And order, which presupposes mind, belongs to the material universe prior to the emergence there of life or mind. Can we then conceive of a cosmic Mind or Spirit, which is unconscious or semi-conscious till it becomes conscious of itself in man ? I cannot give reality to the conception. And the question I am now asking is, Does Dr. Pringle Pattison help us in this difficulty ? Does he succeed in giving reality to the idea of the transcendent God ?

1. No doubt he seeks to affirm the transcendence of God. He is plainly not satisfied with the idea, appearing first in Spinoza, of a God (*natura naturans*) who has no will or consciousness in Himself, but only in the finite spirits who are parts of created nature (*natura naturata*): see *Idea of God*, p. 255, and the Essay on which we are commenting.

2. Yet he plainly and constantly denies any such idea of personal self-completence in God as would present Him as independent of His creation, or prior to creation, as He is presented in the Christian view. On the contrary, he insists that the creation is necessary to God and co-eternal. It is only in creation that God realizes Himself (*Essay*, p. 13 ; *Idea of God*, lect. xvi).

[1] See further, pp. 148–53.

3. Moreover he quite clearly can attach no meaning to the existence of material things apart from conscious beings (*Essay*, p. 16). Consequently " there is in strictness no creation—no finite universe at all—till spirits are created " (or " begotten ") (p. 17). It is only, therefore, in finite spirits that God can realize Himself. This, again, he makes quite clear.

4. But finite spirits appear first, in the world as we know it, in man and as the last stage of an age-long development. How then does Dr. Pringle Pattison escape the conclusion that first in man does God become conscious of Himself or alive with the life of will and knowledge and love ? In what sense can he talk of an eternal or transcendent life or consciousness of God ? In no sense, so far as I can see. I suppose it is because he feels the difficulty that he throws out the suggestion of finite spirits other than man ; " multitudes of self-conscious spirits may exist " in other worlds (p. 21), and they " may vastly surpass mankind as we know it." Well, the Christian, through the assurance of Christ, may have grounds for believing this to be true, and may reasonably take it as a fact into his calculations. But—apart from the belief in a positive and supernatural disclosure through Christ of spiritual facts which would be otherwise unknown to man, which Dr. Pringle Pattison does not, I gather, find an acceptable idea, and which at any rate is not at present in question—this suggestion of unseen hosts of spirits is purely mythological and hypothetical. Certainly it cannot be relied upon. The eternal must somehow, he tells us, find room for the time series. It must include it. Does it not, in Dr. Pringle Pattison's philosophy, depend upon it ? Is his eternal anything more than the idea of creation viewed as completed ? I do not see how he can substantiate his transcendent God. I think he remains in effect with Spinoza.

Moreover, if his hypothesis be granted, these hosts of conscious spirits either emerged, like men, at a certain stage in a long development—in which case the problem is simply duplicated and not solved—or they are co-eternal with God and co-essential—in which case we appear to have the foundation of a pluralism or polytheism capable of strange developments and utterly alien to Dr. Pringle Pattison's monotheism.

Apart then from this speculation in the unknowable, where for Dr. Pringle Pattison is there ground for belief in any transcendent God eternally conscious and alive ?

CHAPTER IV

THE QUESTION OF REVELATION

THIS, then, is the question : Has the Divine Mind or
Spirit whom we discern by the light of reason hidden
in the world—hidden in that its nature and character
are involved in such obscurity—has it, or has He,
taken action, like a person, on His side to disclose or
reveal Himself to those " who are seeking after God,
if haply they may feel after Him and find Him " ?
No doubt the basal assumption or fundamental
faith on which alone any scientific or philosophical or
religious view of the universe can be built up is the
assumption that our reason can be trusted ; and therefore any alleged self-revelation of God which should
prove to be inconsistent with the requirements of
reason could only increase the bewilderment of mind
in which we already find ourselves in view of the
obscurity of nature. But on all showing the human
reason is partial and imperfect ; and a self-disclosure
of God is easily conceived which should not violate
but augment the light of reason—should supplement
it and supply some satisfaction and response to its
urgent questions and ignorant prayers. There is
to-day in most men's minds a profound and easily
justified scepticism on all abstract dogmas of philosophers as to what is or is not possible or believable.

In this our temper contrasts markedly with the temper
of the scholastic period or the period of Descartes and
Spinoza. Science has proved so many things true
which in the abstract appeared inconceivable, and the
abstract dogmatists have proved themselves singularly fallible. Thus we may peremptorily refuse to
decide *a priori* that the supreme reason or God cannot
directly communicate His mind and purpose to the
reason and conscience of men. The opposite anticipation is at least as tenable. Moreover, the facts of
the moral conscience among men—to which the
Right appears regularly, especially in the noblest of
our race, as the divine will and purpose, enjoining
obedience and correspondence on our part, and in a
measure self-revealing—and the nearly universal
popular belief that certain individuals are in a special
sense inspired by God or by a God—these facts of
common experience show us human nature in the
broad ready to recognize divine self-revelation.

Unhindered therefore by any prohibitory dogma
of the reason, we may approach the real question, which
is one of fact. The religion of Israel, on which
Christianity and, in a different degree, Mohammedanism are based, claims that such a revelation has been
given. It has persuaded the whole Western, and in
a sense the Mohammedan, world over long centuries
of the truth of its claim. And, what is much more
important, the strength of our morality has been
drawn from the belief in a self-revealing God. The
belief has obvious power. It has apparently put man
in touch with reality. Thus the claim deserves at
least the attention of every rational man. What the
admission of this claim involves will be matter for
further consideration. Let us first of all, as simply
and objectively as possible, consider the claim of

positive revelation made by the Hebrew religion, and the grounds on which it rests for us to-day.

What, then, precisely is the point to be considered? To restrict the area of enquiry, and to remove it from the region of doubtful questions, let us take the period of the prophets of Israel whose writings remain to us, beginning with Amos, about 760 B.C. or earlier, and ending some three hundred years or more later with Malachi.

A word must be said in explanation of these limits. No one can read the earliest prophet whose writings remain to us, Amos, without seeing that the foundation of the prophetic teaching had already been laid before his day. He can apparently take for granted that the God of Israel—Jahweh—is the one and only God, the Creator of heaven and earth,[1] the just Judge of all mankind, perfect in righteousness. He and all the prophets would repudiate the idea that they were innovators. They would no doubt refer themselves back to the time of God's first redemption of His people from Egypt, and to the covenant given through Moses, or to an earlier period still. I believe that we must take it to be true that the essential features of the prophetic doctrine do date from Moses, and that the popular Jahweh-worship, against which the prophets of our period protest, was really a corruption and degradation—a falling away from what had been delivered to the fathers of Israel. Nevertheless the question of what exactly the religion of Abraham was, or what the original Mosaic deposit was, is a very complicated question involved in all the uncertainties which surround documents whose date cannot be put near to the events which they describe. Whereas

[1] Amos v. 8–9.

from Amos to Malachi we are on the clear ground of history, and we shall be assuming nothing that is doubtful in considering the plain facts of their doctrine. Also the date when the supposed divine communications began makes no real difference to the argument. Whether it began with Moses or whether with Amos, the question of its source remains substantially the same.

As to the later limit which I have chosen, it is probable that some written prophecies, such as Joel and the later part of Zechariah, date some hundred years later than Malachi, and it is certain (in my judgement) that the book of Daniel dates some three centuries later than Malachi. And the prophetic spirit is conspicuously to be found not only in the Prophets, but in Psalms and Wisdom literature and later apocalypses. These again contain fresh elements of teaching, which are incorporated in the Jewish authoritative tradition as it was received and perpetuated in the primitive Christian Church, e.g. the doctrine of the Wisdom of God immanent in nature, the fuller doctrine of the angels, and the clear assertion of the resurrection. But I am not prepared to argue that these elements of the Jewish tradition cannot be accounted for partly as inevitable developments and partly as incorporations from Greek and Persian sources, once granted the fundamental basis of prophetic doctrine.

These considerations have led to the choice of the limits Amos to Malachi. All that I want is to be found there and nothing that is fairly disputable.

During these 300 years, then, there was a continuous succession of prophets whose writings are preserved to us. There are obscure passages in these books which for our present purpose we can wholly ignore,

and there are passages assigned, perhaps rightly, to
a later date with which we are not concerned. What
is important is undisputed and is plain, so that he
that runs may read. It makes its impression only if
we read it continuously.[1]

Here, then, we find a succession of wonderful men,
mostly conscious of profound unpopularity in their
contemporary world, who nevertheless, even in the
face of the most determined hostility of courts and
people, delivered a message which we feel to be self-
consistent and to involve the same great principles
throughout, about God—His nature, His will, His
purposes—and about human nature—its dignity, its
responsibility, and its sin; a message which they
declare, with the fullest conviction, to be derived not
from their own reasoning or speculation, nor from
tradition[2] (though they would have indignantly
repudiated the idea that they were its first recipients),
nor from any external source at all, but from God,
the God of Israel, speaking in their own souls, so
intensely and clearly that there could be no mistake
about it. Let us listen to some typical utterances :

" I was no prophet, neither was I a prophet's son ;
but I was an herdman, and a dresser of sycomore
trees : and the Lord took me from following the flock,
and the Lord said unto me, Go, prophesy unto my
people Israel. Now therefore hear the word of the
Lord." [3]

---

[1] The best assistance in doing this is *The Hebrew Prophets*, by
Woods and Powell (Oxford Press)—four handy little volumes with
introduction, text, and very brief but sufficient notes.

[2] Their relation to earlier revelation may be compared to that of
St. Paul. St. Paul was not the first recipient of " the truth as it is in
Jesus," but he held it, and his commission to teach it, " neither
from men nor through men."

[3] Amos vii. 14.

" But I truly am full of power by the spirit of the Lord, and of judgement, and of might, to declare unto Jacob his transgression, and to Israel his sin." [1]

" Mine heart within me is broken, all my bones shake ; I am like a drunken man, and like a man whom wine hath overcome ; because of the Lord, and because of His holy words. . . . Is not my word like as fire ? saith the Lord ; and like a hammer that breaketh the rock in pieces ? " [2]

We notice that they are acutely conscious of the contrast between their own feelings and ideas on the one hand, and on the other the purpose and mind of God who constrains them. This is vividly presented where the prophet holds conversations with God, represents to God his own feelings, questions and complains, and is answered.[3] These prophets are clearly conscious of two distinct currents or forces within them—the current of their own feelings, and the overmastering pressure of God who possesses them, making His mind and will articulate to them.

Such passages recur constantly. The prophets, then, because they are conscious of being thus even violently dealt with and possessed, claimed to utter with supreme authority a word or message from God to man. The content of this message is, on the whole, quite clear in its final outcome. It is a message which proclaims God as intensely personal and moral, as the one and only God, the absolute creator and sustainer and judge of all that is, almighty in the sense that no other God or external power exists to restrain Him. It proclaims Him in unmistakable terms for

[1] Micah iii. 8.   [2] Jer. xxiii. 9–29.
[3] See Amos vii. 2–9 and 15, viii. 1–2 ; Isa. vi. 5–12, xxi. 2–10, xxii. 4–14 ; Jer. i. 6–14, iv. 10, xiv. 7 to end, xv. 10–21, etc. Cf. Sanday, *Inspiration* (Longmans, 1893), p. 148.

a practical purpose, not, that is, with a view to the
satisfaction of metaphysical enquiries, but for the
sole purpose of making His people understand that
there is no manner of fellowship with Him possible
except by conformity to His character, that is, by
goodness, social and individual, by " doing justly,
and loving mercy, and walking humbly with God."[1]
It proclaims the responsibility of man as a free being
and his awful power to thwart God by his pride and
wilfulness, and to throw His world into confusion, in
Isaiah's tremendous phrase, " to make God serve with
his sins." [2] It assumes that God does not over the
long course of this world's history intend to remove
man's liberty thus to thwart His purpose ; but it
declares God's intention to judge and overthrow one
by one every structure and device of human pride
and wilfulness, and finally to vindicate Himself in
His whole creation.   That is " the day of the Lord."
Meanwhile, His prophets are His mouthpiece to make
His character and will and purpose known, and to
call on those who have ears to hear to correspond
and co-operate with Him, that is, to stand for
righteousness and truth in evil days.

And it was upon this revelation of God, given through
the prophets, that in later days Jesus unmistakably
took His stand.   After a long period of what in one
sense was the victory of the prophetic teaching since
the Captivity, and in other sense turned out to be its
eclipse [3]—after a long period during which there were

---

[1] Micah vi. 8.   [2] Isa. xliii. 24.

[3] By the victory of the prophets after the Captivity I mean that
their whole teaching was formally accepted. There was no more
idolatry or tendency to idolatry on the part of the people. And
the whole ceremonial *cultus* was reorganized—following the teaching
of Ezekiel—so as to express the ethical principles of the prophets.
This was a great victory as the result of a divine judgement. On the

no prophets—Jesus of Nazareth, following on John the Baptist, renewed the prophetic message, infinitely deepening and broadening it, but in no respect altering its fundamental character. About the relation of Jesus to the prophets, however, more will have to be said later. Here it is enough to call attention to what is indisputable, that no representation of the teaching of Jesus Christ can make any pretence to truth which fails to recognize that He stood upon the foundation of the prophets, and that the civilization of Christendom, in its whole moral and religious fabric, stands with Jesus Christ upon that basis.

The message of the prophets made, and still makes, a profound difference to mankind. It impinged upon the human soul and conscience in a quite new way, with new motives, new fears, new hopes, new aspirations, new possibilities. This monotheism of the prophets created a new type of character. Judged by its effect, it is markedly different from the religion of the philosophers, whether ancient or modern. And that because its ideas are different. It claims, in fact, to introduce into human experience a new source of information about God of the most important kind, such as never could have been derived from the consideration of nature. If the claim of the prophets to speak the word of the Lord is a true claim, the philosopher (as well as the ordinary man) has got

---

other hand, prophecy gave way to law, and law tended to formalism. So the later Judaism tended to "make the word of God of none effect by its tradition." Any one of the old prophets who had been "raised up" to visit earth again when John the Baptist began his mission would have been profoundly disappointed with the results of the victory of the prophetic teaching four hundred years before. He would have joined John in his denunciation of "the offspring of vipers." He would have seen a new idolatry in their misunderstanding of the character of God.

the material with which he has to deal immensely
enlarged.   Athanasius, in a striking phrase, described
the Hebrew prophets as " the sacred school of the
knowledge of God and of the spiritual life for all
mankind." [1]   If there really was such a divine education of mankind of which the Hebrew prophets were
the instruments, we must put them, with regard to
religion, in a position analogous to that which we
commonly assign to the Greeks in philosophy or art,
and to the Romans in administration and law, but
profoundly different in respect of the source of their
authority and the method by which they gained their
assurance—the method of positive revelation, given
and received.

It seems to me that the intellectual world of to-day
is studiously refusing to face exactly this question.
But the peremptory form in which the question
presents itself can be realized by any man who likes
to read the prophets—to read and to ponder the vivid
accounts which the prophets give us of their commis-
sions,[2] and in general their intense experiences of
the dealings of God with them—experiences from
which it is not too much to say the world gained a
new spiritual life and a wholly new moral power.
Were these real experiences—that is, experiences
which brought them into contact with reality, external
to and independent of themselves, experiences of God
forcing Himself upon them with a message which could
be made articulate in human words and intelligible
to human hearts and minds ?

Some of the ways in which an attempt is made to
explain or explain away the prophetic experiences so

---

[1] *De Incarnatione*, 12 ; cf. the noble preface to Ewald's *History of Israel*.
[2] Isa. vi. ; Jerem. i. ; Ezek. ii.-iii.   Amos vii. 14.

that they shall not bear the conclusions which they appear to bear, if taken as veridical, we must with all anxious impartiality seek to examine. But to obviate in advance certain current misconceptions, we must first take special note of some facts concerning the origin, nature, and progressive character of the prophetic teaching.

1. It had its origin amidst phenomena familiar to all religions and especially to the Semitic religions around it. St. Chrysostom [1] boldly declared that all the elements of the Jewish ceremonial law—" the sacrifices and the cleansings and the new moons and the ark and the temple itself had their origin from heathen grossness." The same thing is true about prophecy in its external aspects. Almost all nations, and in particular the nations with whom the Hebrews were acquainted and to whom they were akin, had a special class of " professionals," priests or seers or diviners, whose supposed science enabled them, by various methods, to ascertain the will of the god of the nation and to claim his guidance. A certain ethical effect may be found in some of these religious institutions, as, for instance, in the Greek oracles, and we need not stay to discuss whether there was by their means a really divine influence at work. Let us grant it. But in the main the influence of these " natural religions " was not ethical. Especially the religions which surrounded Israel, whether the religion of the local Canaanite Baalim and Ashtoreths, or the religions of the national gods, such as Chemosh the Moabite god, were not ethical. They

[1] St. Chrys., *Hom. in Matt.* vi. 3, *P.G.* lvii. col. 66. The patristic recognition of the earthly origin of the religion of the Jews in its material elements has been generally ignored in the orthodox tradition.

were at their root nature worships, and often worships of the productive and reproductive powers of nature. Thus as nature seems to be indifferent to morality, so nature worships are non-moral or immoral. It is surprising to most of us to discover to how great an extent we of the Western world owe the intimate association of religion with morality to the direct or indirect influence of the special class of Hebrew prophets whom we are considering Among the people great and small with whom Israel was brought in contact, religion was profoundly popular. The gods were taken for granted. The god belonged to his people and the people to their god. He was not conceived of as asking of them anything contrary to their customs. They were to give him his proper *cultus*—his sacrifices and rites—and to avoid all that annoyed and irritated him. But character and morality were not among his attributes or his claims. On the other hand, he belonged to his people and could be expected to help them, and there existed the class of professionals who knew how to find out his will and disclose it, and who could more or less foretell what was to happen. So they were to be consulted by the peoples and their rulers in their difficulties. Doubtless in some such way by the help of the priests Mesha King of Moab, contemporary with Omri King of Israel, whose inscription remains for us, ascertained the will of Chemosh.

" I am Mesha King of Moab. . . . I made this high place to Chemosh because he has helped me against all them that attacked me, and has caused me to see my desire upon all my enemies. Omri King of Israel oppressed Moab long, because Chemosh was angry against his land. . . . And the King of Israel had built Ataroth. I attacked the town and took it, and I exterminated all the men of the town—a pleasing spectacle for Chemosh and Moab, . . . and I dragged [some others] before the face of Chemosh. And Chemosh said to me : Go and take Nebo from Israel. And I set out by night, and I besieged that town . . . and I took it and killed all things . . . for I had vowed them to Ashtar Chemosh. And there I took the altar hearths [?] of Jehovah and dragged them before the face of Chemosh. The King of Israel built Jahash and fortified himself there against me, and Chemosh drove him before his face . . . and Chemosh said to me : Go down and fight against Haronaim." [1]

Obviously this narrative and its religious tone recall familiar features in the Hebrew books. In fact it is impossible to read attentively some of the narratives of the book of Judges, or the books of Samuel, or the denunciations of the popular religion from the lips of the prophets, as they saw it in being, and not to own that the popular religion of Israel was much the same as the religion of the people round about them. This religion, the religion of Jahweh, as the people understood it, was popular and universal. The people trampled Jahweh's courts in crowds ; they spent lavishly on the worship, the sacrifices, and the incense ; they loved the festivals ; but plainly they entertained no idea of any connexion between their religion and what we call morality, individual and social. Religion in their sense was quite compatible both with sexual immorality and drunkenness and with social oppression and fraud and cruelty. It is on this ground only that the earlier prophets denounce so utterly the ceremonial *cultus* as worthless in the sight of God.[2] Also the people of Israel, through prophets

---

[1] See Hastings's *D. of B.*, art. Moabite Stone, vol. iii, p. 407.

[2] It is hardly necessary to refer to the famous passages Isa. i. 10–17, Hos. vi. 6, Amos iv. 4–6, v. 21–7, Micah vi. 6–8, Ps. l. 8–15, etc. Such denunciations cease with the Captivity. The tone of the prophets after the Captivity is quite different.

and seers, by Urim and Thummim, by sacred pillars, by ephods, and by the sacred ark, ascertained the word of Jahweh, much as Mesha, the king of Moab, ascertained the will of Chemosh—that is to say, the directions which He was believed to give His people in their practical concerns, military and personal. The existence of this sort of Jahweh-religion in Israel is unmistakable through the period of the Judges and the early kingdom. It is the religion and the religious worship which the later prophets denounce.[1] In the main it was Jahweh-worship, for the Hebrews had on the whole no desire to forsake their national God, as they understood the matter, either in Israel or in Judah. They did indeed lapse into the worship of other gods, and more and more as the fierce teaching of the prophets identified the name of Jahweh with a tremendous moral claim which they were not prepared to accede to. This idolatry the prophets alternately denounce and ridicule. But in the earlier days, before the continuous succession of the prophets, the people in general probably felt very little essential difference between Chemosh and Jahweh, or the religions of Chemosh and Jahweh, or between one Baal

---

[1] See, for a conception of Jahweh as in some sense limited to His own land and peoples, like Chemosh to Moab, Judg. xi. 23-4, 1 Sam. xxvi. 19. For seers and prophets as paid professionals see 1 Sam. ix. 7-8. For music and violent motion and mental disturbance as the accompaniment of prophecy see 1 Sam. x. 5-6, 10-13, xix. 24, Num. xxiv. 4, 2 Kings iii. 15. For divination by Urim and Thummim, 1 Sam. xiv. 41, [restoring the text according to the indication of the LXX: " If on me and my son, Jehovah give Urim, but, if on the people, give Thummim,] 1 Sam. xxviii. 6. By teraphim and ephod and ark, Judg. xvii. 5, 6, 1 Sam. xxiii. 9-12, xxx. 7-8, 2 Sam. v. 19-23, Josh. xviii. 6-10, Hos. iv. 12 (by stock and staff), Zech. x. 2. Cf. among the heathen Gen. xliv. 5 (by goblet), Ezek. xxi. 21 (by arrows and teraphim and liver). By dreams, 1 Sam. xxviii. 6, Jer. xxiii. 25 ; by wizards, Lev. xix. 31, Isa. viii. 19. See list of prohibited methods in Deut. xviii. 10-12, with Driver's notes.

and another.   Such, as we read the earlier records and
the sweeping denunciations of the prophets, we discern to have been the popular religion of Israel.

It was in this kind of atmosphere and out of this
tradition that the great moral prophets, whose writings remain to us, emerged.   They were few among
many.   The mass of the prophets all along, until after
the Captivity the whole prophetic office fell into dis-
repute,[1] retained the old low idea of religion, mixed
with mere fraud and avarice.   The " true " prophets
habitually denounce them as a corrupt class, misleading the people.[2]   They themselves retain some of
the characteristics of the " natural " prophets—they
perform symbolic acts for a sign, they see visions, and
one of them (Ezekiel) is notable for going into conditions of trance.[3]   Nevertheless, as compared with the

---

[1] See Zech. xiii. 3–6.

[2] Elijah's adversaries appear clearly as prophets of a false and rival
God (1 Kings xviii. 19).   But Micaiah's adversaries claim apparently
to be prophets of Jehovah : 1 Kings xxii., see ver. 24.   For denunciations of the prophets as a class see Hos. ix. 7–8, Micah iii. 5–11,
Zeph. iii. 4, Isa. xxviii. 7, xxix. 10, Jer. ii. 26, v. 31, xxiii. 15–40 (a
very illuminating passage), Ezek. xiii. 15–16.   All these passages
imply that the prophets as a class were abandoned men.

[3] I feel that I have not the qualifications for writing on the psychical
condition of the prophets.   I do not see signs of *trance* conditions
in any of the prophets whom we reckon as the true prophets except
Ezekiel.   Job iv. 12–17 and Dan. viii. 18 perhaps suggest that in
the later period of Jewish literature a trance condition was regarded
as the natural condition for the prophet.   All that I would insist
upon is that, whatever the physical condition of the prophets when
they received their communications, their minds were intensely
alert and conscious and rational.   What possessed them did not
annihilate or override their own mental faculties.   No one can
read their prophecies and fail to see this.   The early Christian
Church (in the Montanist controversy) was clearly right in asserting
that in the true succession of prophets the inspiring Spirit did not
destroy but intensified the natural rational faculty of its human
organs.   They retain their full personality with its individual characteristics.   See *The Church and the Ministry*, Appendix H and I,
and references to Bonwetsch there given.

popular prophets, they are something wholly different. Their aim is wholly different. Their message is associated with the clearest mental vision and fullest consciousness. It speaks out of the moral reason of the prophet to the moral reason of the people. If the prophets were what they claimed to be, it must be recognized that God was doing through them a new thing, but that the new thing sprang out of what was natural and racial. And it is, as we have already recognized, a most false method to imagine that, because some new thing emerged out of something lower, therefore the lower thing explains the new birth. It does this in the case of prophecy no more than physics can explain life or irrational nature reason. Rather in the new thing we see the explanation of that lower thing out of which it had its origin, as man explains nature rather than nature man.

2. In what sense is it the special function of the prophets to foretell the future ? In a sense this had been the characteristic function of the Semitic prophets. They were the men who were believed to be able, by vision or dream or mechanical instrument, to declare the will of God not yet evident—to say for instance, like Ahab's prophets, whether a certain expedition was going to be successful. " Shall I go against Ramoth-gilead to battle, or shall I forbear ? " " If I pursue after this troop, shall I overtake them ? " [1] was the kind of question they were expected to answer. But this was not the special characteristic of the prophets whom we call the true prophets, few among many, whose writings remain to us. Their special characteristic was that they knew the character and purpose of Jehovah and His moral claim on their contemporaries. But for this very

[1] 1 Kings xxii. 6; 1 Sam. xxx. 8.

reason, because they saw so clearly into the nature and will and purpose of God, so they saw in large measure what He would do. " Surely the Lord God will do nothing," cries Amos, " but He revealeth His secret unto His servants the prophets." [1] Thus Amos proclaims with certainty the imminent doom of the Northern Kingdom, and, less distinctly, the judgement on Judah. Later Micah is found announcing the doom of Jerusalem, as certainly as Jeremiah a hundred years later, or our Lord again seven hundred years later, under circumstances of renewed apostasy.

Again, the instrument of these dooms or judgements is sometimes, but not always, clear to the prophet's mind. Thus it is clear to Jeremiah that Babylon is to be the instrument of divine chastisement on Jerusalem; but it appears that Hosea had, in an earlier age, no certainty whether the instrument of chastisement on the Northern Kingdom was to be Egypt or Assyria. On the other hand, in the days of the righteous King Hezekiah, Isaiah foresees distinctly that the apparently resistless might of the Assyrian monarch is to be baffled and Jerusalem is to be saved ; and all the prophets, those most clearly who were occupied in proclaiming immediate doom on God's people, proclaimed also that His purpose in calling Israel would not ultimately fail, but that through chastisement would come restoration and a vast enhancement of spiritual glory—the Kingdom of the Messiah.

But the divine instruments of chastisement, whether Assyria or Babylon, though they are used by God for the purposes of divine justice, are not themselves just. They are cruel and monstrous tyrannies. Thus on them in turn judgement must come, as it is certain to come on all the institutions which represent

[1] Amos iii. 7.

human insolence and cruelty and lust. Thus a large
part of the prophetic message consists in the announce-
ment of "oracles of Jehovah" upon contemporary
kingdoms or empires or civilizations. It cannot be
said that these forecasts are infallible in detail.
Ezekiel pronounced distinctly a doom on Tyre at the
hand of Nebuchadnezzar King of Babylon which
was not by that hand or at that time fulfilled.[1] But on
the whole these prophecies were remarkably fulfilled.
For instance, one of the miracles of history is the fact
that Israel, the divinely appointed instrument of the
true religion (as it is contended), though it was again
and again apparently absorbed, or on the way to be
absorbed, in the great nations which trampled it down,
such as Babylon or the empire of Alexander, was in
fact preserved to fulfil its separate function. There
is force in the famous answer which is said to have
been given to Frederick the Great's question, " What
is the best argument for the truth of the Christian
religion ? " " The Jews, your Majesty." But all
these announcements of what was to happen were
forecasts—mainly of the immediate future—uttered
by the prophets for the warning or encouragement of
their contemporaries, forecasts arising out of the
circumstances of the present and (this is the most
important point) involved in the proclamation of the
righteousness and righteous government of God. This
—and not future events, except so far as they were
bound up with this—it was the prophet's business to
declare. It is true that, inasmuch as the reign of the
righteous God is declared to be universal, it is necessary that God should vindicate Himself finally in the
whole universe : thus we have the magnificent prophecies of the day of the Lord—that is, the world-wide

---

[1] Ezek. xxvi. 7-14 ; cf. xxix. 18.

judgement upon all that resist God, and the world-wide
establishment of the kingdom or reign of God. And
the definite prophecies of particular judgements upon
particular nations are thrown upon the background of
this vast and vague vision of final and cosmic catastrophe and salvation by the prophets of the Old
Testament, as later by our Lord, when He announced
the coming doom upon Jerusalem. But such forecasts—though, if God be God, they *must* be fulfilled—
though the " end of the world " must lie in God coming into His own in the whole of His own creation—
involve no detailed knowledge of the future outside
the horizon of the prophet's own time.[1] There is
no map of the future spread before his eyes. Prophecy is not in any such sense " history written
beforehand." [2]

The foretelling of the future was, then, a real function
of the prophets of Israel, and it was part of the
Semitic tradition that they should foretell. In the
case of the true prophets their anticipations of the
future were intimately bound up with their moral
message : they foretold what God must do because
He is just. On the whole their anticipations have
been indeed wonderfully fulfilled. But it is not in
predictions fulfilled that their chief function is to be
sought ; it is in their message about God and His
nature, His character, and His purpose—and about

[1] Thus Micah (v. 5) anticipates the Messiah in time to deliver
Judah from the Assyrian. And Haggai and Zechariah in like manner
anticipate immediately the glory for recovered Israel. And in the
book of Daniel there is a detailed sketch of the actual history, but
only up to the time of Antiochus Epiphanes (when the author
certainly lived), and after that only the quite vaguely conceived
picture of the immediate glory of the holy nation.

[2] Butler's most unfortunate phrase did mischief proportioned
to his extraordinary merits and greatness.

man's capacity, responsibility, and true hope. I am
going to argue that their claim to speak the word of
the Lord was a true claim ; and it was necessary,
therefore, that I should describe and more or less limit
their function, because the conception of it has, no
doubt, been distorted in tradition.

3. In this age we like to place all history in the
category of development. We receive great encouragement to do this in the Bible. But we are slowly
learning that the dogma of development must be
moulded to the facts, frankly observed and fairly
interpreted ; and that historical development has been
something quite different from orderly and necessary
progress. Now, when the author of the Epistle to the
Hebrews contends for a progressive revelation " in
many parts and many manners " through the line of
prophets culminating in Jesus Christ, he is so far at
least justified that there was an undoubted advance,
as all are agreed, in the conception of God and of
human life, say from the Judges downward to the New
Testament.[1] Certain steps in advance, from which
there was no withdrawal, are easily noted. It was a
step forward when Jahweh, the God of Israel, was
realized to be the one and only God, the Creator of all
that is, in such sense that there could be no other god.
It was a step when Amos proclaimed that God, because
He is God, must deal impartial judgement upon all

---

[1] The Christian Fathers are full of this conception of gradualness
in God's creation and in the education of man. They solve in this
manner the moral difficulties of the Old Testament. The sign of
the success of the divine method, they argue, is that commands which
could be given to Abraham or Samuel could not be given to Christians. See passages cited in *Lux Mundi*, pp. 240-2. An interesting instance of advance is Hosea's judgement on Jehu's massacres
at Jezreel : see Hos. i. 4, compared to the judgement of the book of
Kings.

nations, including Israel and Judah.[1]   It was another
step when Ezekiel first clearly proclaimed the great
principle that God does not merely deal with nations
or mankind in social groups, but deals in His absolute
justice with each individual.[2]   It was again a step when
the same Ezekiel overcame the crude antagonism
which appears in the earlier prophets between the
cultus or external and traditional worship on the one
hand, and the moral spirit of prophecy on the other,
and proceeded to outline a synthesis of spirit and
cultus by remodelling the traditional worship to
be the centre of the social life of the new Israel
which he foresaw.[3]

On the other hand, there is retrogression. Thus
the visions of Isaiah and of others of a converted
world in which Egypt and Assyria shall be included
in God's people,[4] gave way on the whole to the visions
of apocalyptic judgement in which the adversaries of
Israel were to be not converted but overwhelmed in
final ruin.   And on the whole it has to be said that
the prophets who stand at the head of our succession
in point of time, Amos and Hosea, Micah and Isaiah,
show the prophetic spirit at the full.   No presentation
of the one God, creator of all that is and righteous
judge of all the world, can exceed that of Amos in
startling clearness.   No picture of the passionate love
of God for His people can exceed in fullness and
poignancy the teaching of Hosea.   And though later
prophets show much more clearly the influence of
their predecessors—though they " borrow " more
plainly—yet none of them show such dependence
as to weaken their personal consciousness of divine
commission and direct inspiration.   But especially

[1] Amos ii. 4, 6, iii. 2.   [3] Ezek. xl. ff.
[2] Ezek. xviii.   [4] Isa. xix. 19 ff.

is this true of all the prophets down to the restoration.
Though now and again they may quote an earlier
prophecy, yet unmistakably on the whole each one
speaks no borrowed or inherited message, but one
which he is entirely convinced is given to him
personally by the supreme God.

Thus we have in these prophets of Israel something
which is not correctly described as a " development "
or " evolution " of spiritual truth, if, as is commonly
the case, we mean by these words the natural expansion or unfolding of truth, by its own force, from
thinker to thinker. What we see is much more
accurately described, supposing that the prophets
gave a trustworthy account of their experiences, as a
process of divine education, which is more or less
progressive, but by way of successive lessons or
disclosures from above, adapted to the circumstances
and capacities of the pupil, not by way of gradual
discovery from below.

4. I must insist—and with somewhat more precise
definition of the point—that Jesus Christ, whom we
consider now without any reference to the question
of supernatural personality, simply as a prophet
following on John the Baptist, unmistakably took
his stand on the prophetic message, both as delivered
by the prophets and as embodied in the law, as being
truly the word of God. Thus He corrected in its light
the tradition of scribes and Pharisees as being " the
commandments of men " by contrast to " the word
of God "—that is to say, He appealed back behind
the ecclesiastical traditions to its fount in the divine
revelation of the Old Testament.[1] Not, of course, that
He was merely dependent on the Law and the prophets.
No: He claimed the right to supersede, on His own

[1] Mark vii. 1–14.

authority, the teaching of the Law. " It was said to them of old time . . . but I say unto you." [1]   Again, He recognizes elements of higher and lower in the Mosaic Law, appealing in the case of the Sabbath to its moral purpose behind specific enactments,[2] and in the case of marriage recognizing the moral imperfection of the Mosaic provisions and appealing back to a word of God more original and fundamental.[3]   Moreover, in regard to the prophetic teaching about God, He infinitely intensified the idea of God which it conveyed on the side of His personal love to individuals, and He universalized it so that it should apply to man as man and not only to Israel.   But when we have given full weight to all these considerations and recognized to the full the personal authority of Jesus as derived from no tradition (" No man knoweth the Father save the Son and he to whomsoever the Son willeth to reveal Him "), there can be no question that He took His stand on the Old Testament revelation as the real utterance of God, and preserved it. In respect of God's personality and His righteousness, His almightiness, His omnipresence, His claim on man—in respect of the responsibility of man and his sinfulness—in respect of the divine purpose of redemption—in respect of the day of judgement and the final reign of God, Jesus Christ takes the Old Testament revelation for granted as God-given.

And it must be noted that our Lord lays no stress upon one important element in the later Jewish tradition—which was perhaps a reflection of Greek philosophy—the doctrine of the divine wisdom or

---

[1] Matt. v. 21-2.   [2] Mark ii. 23 ff., iii. 1-6.
[3] Mark x. 1-12.

word immanent in nature.[1] This was already established in a measure in the Jewish tradition, and it is
welcomed, as by Philo, so also by St. Paul and St.
John and the whole Christian Church. But in our
Lord's teaching all the stress is on the transcendence
and absoluteness of God the Father. And God's
relations to the world and to men are described in
the most naïvely personal terms.

I have thought it necessary to enter into these
preliminary explanations in order, if possible, to
prevent a "red herring" being drawn across the path
of our argument at a subsequent stage (1) by the
suggestion that the very earthly origins of Hebrew
prophecy discredit it ; or (2) by a mistaken estimate of
the prophets as primarily foretellers of the future ; or
(3) by the inspiration of the prophets being assimilated
in a way the facts will not warrant to the natural
development of thought from thinker to thinker ;
or (4) by forgetfulness that in the succession of the
Hebrew prophets we must reckon not only John the
Baptist but also Jesus of Nazareth.

Now, having so far cleared the ground, we find ourselves again confronting the main question : Are these
prophetic conceptions of God and man on which our
Christian life is founded—the conception of God as
intensely personal, the creator and sustainer of all
that exists, the Father and the judge of all created
spirits, eternal and unchangeable in His power, His
righteousness, and His love, and the accompanying
conception of man—his spiritual capacity, his
freedom and responsibility, his appalling sinfulness,
his opportunity for recovery through the redemptive

---

[1] He does, however, fully accept the later tradition concerning
spirits good and bad, and concerning personal survival of death, which
He declares to be implied in God's relation with the patriarchs.

action of God, his outlook into an immortal life and a reign of God to come,—are these allied conceptions true ?   Is it true that the prophets, and Jesus Christ the successor of the prophets, were, as they claimed to be, in such close contact with the eternal Reality that they could, in speaking as they did of God and communicating His word to men, " speak that they did know and testify that they had seen " or " heard " ? For my own part, having studied the prophets and the Gospels all my life long and asked myself this crucial question more times than I could enumerate, I can give but one answer. I believe their claim is true. It is a momentous decision morally, and it is momentous no less intellectually, because, if I mistake not, it dominates the intellectual situation. What precisely it involves, intellectually considered, and whether it brings us into any real conflict with the fairly certain conclusions of the philosophical reason or of science, we shall be considering shortly with all seriousness. But first of all we have to ask ourselves what other estimates of the prophetic message can be suggested and whether they ought to satisfy us.[1]

1. It cannot be even plausibly suggested that we are dealing in the prophets' utterances with intellectual conclusions reached, like the conclusions of the Greek philosophers, by process of reasoning or observation of nature, and liable, like the conclusions of philosophers, to revision by themselves and their successors in the light of subsequent reflection. The Hebrews showed almost no tendency towards philosophical speculation, and the prophets are not like philosophers. They assume the reality of God, the

[1] In what follows I am following Hamilton's *People of God* (Oxford Press), or rather I am conscious of the impression the argument of his first volume made upon me when he first issued the book.

God of Israel, and that He can communicate with them if He will, and they are convinced that He has done so—in such a manner as leaves quite unsolved a number of questions which profoundly interest philosophers, but apparently have no interest for the prophets ; but also in such a manner as supplies them with all the knowledge of God required for practical life, and in such a manner as admits of being rendered into clear propositions about God and His will such as men can understand and must accept or reject. No doubt God may reveal more to those who come after. But they know that what has been given to them so far must be true as God is true.

2. It is also plain that their dominant conviction that God governs the world in justice cannot be what we should call a deduction from experience—the experience of Israel as a nation or of the individual. It is quite true that the Bible is full of assurances, given on divine authority to Israel, that if they will be obedient to God they will be prosperous, and that, on the other hand, disaster will follow disobedience. And we commonly forget how true it is that any nation which as a whole should set itself to obey a lofty moral and social law like that of the Hebrews would indeed be prosperous. But it is the constant testimony of the prophets that Israel has been since the days of the Exodus almost uniformly rebellious, and that the crowning mercies of Jehovah have been bestowed on them not in accordance with their deserts but in spite of them. According to the prophets, at no period has God had a chance of showing what He would do for an obedient people.[1] There are indeed in the

---

[1] This is the tone of the prophetic history as a whole : cf. Hos. i., iii., Isa v., Ezek. xvi., xx. 6 ff., xxxvi. 17 f., cf. Ps. lxxviii. 17 ff.

prophets a few appeals to happier experiences like that
of Jeremiah to " Shallum the son of Josiah King of
Judah "—" Did not thy father eat and drink, and
do judgement and justice ? then it was well with
him.   He judged the cause of the poor and needy ;
then it was well." [1]   But on the other hand the earlier
prophets who were contemporary with Jeroboam II
witnessed the highest point of Israel's prosperity
coinciding with the gross moral degradation which
they denounce ; and Jeremiah, just before the Captivity, heard the lamentations of those who attributed
their disaster to their desertion of the Queen of
Heaven, and looked back on their past prosperity as
due to her favour when they were faithful to her.[2]
And the prophets show no signs of being taken in by
evidences of prosperity accompanying moral faithless-
ness to Jehovah.   The fact is that their conviction that
national prosperity would always follow obedience to
God, and disaster always follow rebellion, is not a
conclusion based upon experience, but a conviction
that so it must be, if God is God, or a conviction that
God has so promised to order national life.   And as
regards individuals, it was the frequent experience of
the righteous man in undeserved affliction, which in
part forced the Hebrews forward to the vision of a
future life in which God's justice should have room to
vindicate itself.   Certainly their doctrine of God's
justice, though in part it can appeal to experiences,
does not vary with their experiences and is not based
upon them.   It is a conviction established in their
souls by what they believed to be the voice of God
bearing witness concerning Himself.

3. It used to be more the fashion than it is to-day

---

[1] Jer. xxii. 15.   [2] Jer. xliv. 17–18—a vivid passage.

to talk about "the Semitic genius for monotheism,"
and to treat the Hebrew monotheism as if it were the
natural development of the religious tendencies of a
certain large group of the human family to which
the Israelites belonged. But we know, or can
conjecture with a certain measure of certainty, what
the religion of Canaan and Moab and Ammon and
Edom was. We know how much there was in the
instincts and the tradition of Israel inclining them
to assimilate and to retain this type of religion, and
that the religion of the prophets—their ethical monotheism—only established itself by violent conflict
with this "Semitic genius." On a wide view of
Semitic religions, a great scholar [1] has described their
characteristic on the whole as not "monotheism,"
but "sexual dualism." Certainly there is nothing
in the religion of the races which touched Israel
between the Exodus and the Captivity which could
in any way account for the prophetic teaching. Again,
it is as far as possible from being a reflection, through
Moses, of the Egyptian religion. It is markedly
contrary to it in all its chief features—its polytheism,
its idolatry, its preoccupation with the dead and the
world of the dead. Attention has recently been
directed to the heretical Egyptian King Akhnaton, and
the noble expression which, in his psalm to the Sun's
Disk, the only god whom he worshipped, he gives to
the idea of the One Lord and Giver of Life. This is
indeed a noble utterance, worthy to be set beside
the 104th Psalm in the Bible; and it may rightly
be used as evidence that divine inspiration was not
limited to Israel. But the religion of Akhnaton was
killed almost at its birth, and was buried, and so

---

[1] Nöldeke ; see Wellhausen's *Prolegomena to the Hist. of Israel*
(English trans., Black, 1885), p. 440.

remained till quite recently it was disinterred. It did not affect the Egyptian tradition at all, and no one has supposed that it affected Israel. Once more, there were noble Babylonian hymns in which a certain unique majesty and high moral attributes are ascribed to one God, considered for the time apart from all others.[1] But these, again, were probably individual utterances which did not affect the popular polytheism and idolatry, and also no one would suggest that Hebrew prophets before the Exile had any knowledge of them.[2] What elements in their tradition the Jews shared with their neighbours, like the stories of creation and the flood, which were at their root common to them with the Babylonians, were wholly transmuted, in their religious or theological meaning, in the process of being adopted. Of course, in this paragraph I cannot attempt to argue the matter at any length, nor have I the requisite knowledge or authority. But I seem to see a growing disinclination in scholars to question the complete originality of the distinctive prophetic religion, and there is no source which can be plausibly suggested before the Exile from which it could have been either consciously borrowed or unconsciously derived.

It must, then, be admitted, I think, that the ethical monotheism of the prophets neither was derived from any foreign source nor was anything

---

[1] This is called " henotheism," as distinct from " monotheism," i.e. exclusive concentration on one God, without denial of the existence of others.

[2] For the Babylonian hymns see Hastings's *Dict. of the Bible*, vol. v, pp. 563 ff. For Akhnaton see Weigall's *Akhnaton, Pharaoh of Egypt* (Blackwood); see also on both subjects, Sanday, *Divine Overruling* (Clark), pp. 36 ff.

which the natural genius of the Semitic peoples would be likely to generate.

4. But there is one other " explanation " of the voice of God to the prophets, which is more likely to commend itself to our generation—it is the psychological. " Does the experience of controlling force which the prophet feels really come from some external influence, or is it merely his consciousness of ordinarily unknown depths in his own nature ? It is obvious that a theory of prophecy could be made on lines rendered familiar by psychologists, by suggesting that what happens in a prophetic experience is the sudden ' coming up ' of what is ordinarily subliminal." [1] Something of this sort is constantly being suggested to us in the name of psychology— that what prophets and seers and religious people have taken for divine voices or influences are really only the occasional " uprushes," whether in a state of trance or without any such suppression of normal consciousness, of what is ordinarily kept outside consciousness, buried in the region of the unconscious mind—a vaster region than that of our consciousness —assuming the form of an independent consciousness or a different person from ourselves communicating with us.

Now, there can be no doubt that this unconscious or subconscious or subliminal region of mind is a very important fact, which psychology to-day is fulfilling an exceedingly important function in investigating. My mind is, it appears, much wider than my present consciousness. Thus it is quite certain that we retain the record of much more of our experiences than we consciously remember at any

[1] Kirsopp Lake, *Landmarks of the Early Church* (Macmillan, 1920), p. 43.

moment, whether we interpret this fact in physio-
logical terms (as in Dr. Carpenter's theory of " unconscious cerebration ") or more purely pyschologic-
ally.   Perhaps everything that has happened to us,
or been willed or imagined or done by us, is somewhere unconsciously remembered and may be one
day consciously disclosed.   Uprushes   from   the
unconscious memory occur to all of us.[1]   And besides
being a storing-place for our personal experiences, it
appears to be certain that the unconscious mind is
also what Bergson terms a " racial memory "—that
therein are stored hereditary instincts, tendencies,
and capacities, such as are not merely individual,
and yet constitute the background, the deeply
influential background, of our individual and conscious
life.   So it must be that there subsist in us, with
varying degrees of force, ancient savage and animal
tendencies and instincts, such as conscious reason has
tended to submerge and exclude (more and more
completely the more rational and self-conscious our
life becomes), but which are never quite extinguished.
Here may lie normally disused faculties of telepathy
and intuition into natural forces, which some animals

[1] I suppose that the two forms in which the existence of the unconscious mind is most vividly brought to our notice are : (1) the
uprushes of memory from a region outside one's present consciousness, which in part we can and in part we cannot control.   Thus, if
I struggle to remember a name and fail to do so, I am powerless.
But when I have ceased to struggle, it often presents itself un-
expectedly after a time, as from a hidden field of memory.   (2) When
I have struggled with some intellectual problem and brought my
mind to a state where the solution seems to be appearing and yet
disappears in confusion, if I can get a night's rest, the chances are
that the tangle disappears in a measure, and order appears with the
morning.   In such ways we become conscious that our mind is
larger than our field of consciousness.   But there is no tendency
in these normal experiences for the subliminal mind to appear as a
co-consciousness or another person.

and savages appear to possess, and which certain individuals among us appear to recover or exercise in normal or abnormal states. It is also the case that in certain abnormal individuals the uprushes from the unconscious take the form of a " co-consciousness," that is, the appearance of being another person different from ourselves, though " the co-conscious, so far as the evidence goes, is either non-existent or practically negligible in normal persons ; while in pathological subjects, though sometimes, indeed, the source of valuable ideas and useful actions, it is always limited and inferior to the waking self, and likely to be very far from beautiful or sublime." [1]

Now, granted all this, it is obvious how much in spiritism, and in the lower forms of prophecy and divination, such as those familiar in and around early Israel, may be explained in terms of the sub-conscious.[2] It is obvious also how vast an influence the subconscious exercises upon all our religious tendencies.[3] But so far the subconscious or uncon-scious region appears as containing only what our personal experiences or the age-long experiences of our race or its animal progenitors have stored within it. But when I set myself to consider the message

[1] Pratt's *The Religious Consciousness* (Macmillan Co., New York, 1920), pp. 59–60.

[2] I think, for instance, that the " word of the Lord " commanding Israel to destroy Amalek, and Jehu to destroy the whole house of Ahab, would, if the supposed divine communications had reached no higher level, have been of a piece with the " word of Chemosh " to Mesha King of Moab, and would have admitted of a very natural " explanation." It is only because of what Israel's religion was to become under the leadership of the great prophets that we are naturally disposed to see a higher meaning and purpose even in its lower stages.

[3] Pratt, *op. cit.*, pp. 61–3.

of the Biblical prophets, which they believe to have been directly inspired into them by God, it seems to me absurd to seek to interpret this as the echo of tradition or instinct stored in the unconscious. We need not discuss whether the new voice was first heard by Moses or by Amos, at any rate the racial tradition knew it not, and it never succeeded in becoming the tradition till after the Captivity, when the succession of the prophets ceased. And the message of each prophet in the succession of prophets, such as Amos, Hosea, Isaiah, Micah, Jeremiah, or Ezekiel, gains its power not only from its intense individuality, but also from the obvious elements of novelty in each. In each case the voice was intensely individual, and the message in some respects markedly new—something which the human race had not heard before. Moreover, the communication between the prophet's consciousness and the mysterious Power which addresses itself to him is carried on in the highest region of clear consciousness and will. Thus, as the communication claims to be, so also on close enquiry it appears to be, from above—from what is higher than the personal consciousness of the prophets, not from what is lower. A great deal too much is made of the fact that Ezekiel [1] and St. Paul—the one more often than the other—fell into trances, during which, in some manner, their spirits were awake while their bodies were not. This did not apparently occur in the case of most of the prophets ; and the message which Ezekiel and St. Paul delivered was a message addressed to their will and conscious intelligence, and by their will and conscious intelligence received and

[1] In Ezekiel we appear to have extraordinarily interesting instances of telepathy—perception in the remote region by the river Chebar of scenes occurring in Jerusalem.

delivered. I see, therefore, no evidence at all making
it plausible to suggest that what presented itself to
them was really—though they mistook its nature—
their unconscious mind. Whence did the unconscious
mind get this astonishing series of messages? It
does not lie within the compass of the materials out
of which, as far as we can judge, it is and must be
formed.[1] In other words, it seems infinitely more
probable that it was " a downrush from the super-
conscious "—the voice of the Spirit of God, as the
prophets themselves so imperiously insist.

.   .   .   .   .

Every man must draw his own conclusion as to the
nature or source of the prophets' inspiration. It can
be done only by a reverent and continuous reading of
at least some large portions of their writings, passing
lightly over the obscure passages and paying the
deepest attention to what we can easily understand,
which is incomparably the most important and largest
part of their message. We have to take note both
of the individuality and distinctiveness of the message
of each of the prophets and of the continuity of the
teaching through their whole succession. We have to
pay regard to the resumption of the prophetic message
by John the Baptist and its consummation in Jesus

---

[1] See Pratt, p. 64. What is highest " in the religious genius is
to be sought in his conscious states rather than in some form of
insensibility. . . . It is difficult to see why God should choose to
communicate with a split-off complex . . . rather than with the
man himself." . . . " Hence the emphasis I have put on the
absurdity of looking to the subconscious as nobler and purer than
the conscious self." Of course we must recognize that the forms or
scenery of the prophet's vision come from their traditions and their
experiences. What I am speaking of is not the form of the visions,
but their moral and spiritual content.

Christ. Then we have to ask ourselves the great question : Can we ascribe the message to any lower source than that to which the prophets themselves ascribe it ? I do not think we can.

As to the psychological method of the divine communication, we may be as ignorant as we generally are of the psychological conditions under which artists and poets and mystics attain their intuitions. But of the source of the communications, as coming really and directly from God, I dare to feel certain. And I am bound to go on to consider the intellectual consequences of this momentous conclusion. For the communications to the prophets had the sort of vivid reality which required them to state what they " heard " in the form of propositions or messages appealing to the intellect as well as to the will. That is to say, they carry inevitably intellectual conclusions.

And I am sure that in the consideration of the truth of the prophetic testimony we must not leave out of account the effect of their teaching on those who accepted it, and that on the widest and most permanent field. It is impossible not to feel that men who exhibit a quite new power in life are thereby proved to have got into closer touch with reality. And if this new power appears as a direct consequence of a theological belief, the new power so far accredits the belief. Buddhism and Mohammedanism and Stoicism liberated new human power to deal with life, and doubtless in proportion to the truth which was in them. But I believe that the spirit of Jewish prophecy and that towards which it led—the spirit of Christianity in its most genuine form all down the ages, the spirit of sonship in Christ—exhibits human nature at its best and richest. Something has

CHAPTER V

THE CONTENTS OF THE PROPHETIC FAITH

WE find ourselves now in this position—that we have deliberately, even if still provisionally,[1] accepted the reality of God's disclosure of Himself through the Hebrew prophets and Jesus Christ. Thus we assent (so far) to the statement with which the Epistle to the Hebrews begins, that " God in many parts and many manners spake in old times unto the fathers by the prophets and in these last times by His Son," though no question concerning the person of Jesus Christ—as to whether He differs from the prophets in being the Divine Son—has yet been raised.

This self-disclosure of God was given, through the prophets and Jesus Christ, for a practical purpose—as a " word of life," that men might know how to live if they would be in fellowship with God. Thus there are many questions which have always troubled speculative philosophers of which the prophets appear to be quite unconscious. But life and thought cannot be separated in a rational being, such as man is. If he must live in a certain way in order to please God or be at peace with Him, that must be, he feels, because God Himself has a certain character or nature.

[1] Because we have still to consider whether any irreconcilable conflict, such as would throw into confusion our whole conception of truth, is going to appear between the substance of the professed self-disclosure of God and the rest of our rational knowledge.

And, in fact, the divine self-disclosure assumes constantly this form—" Be thou holy, for I am holy." There may be many things concerning God which are not disclosed because they have no practical bearing on life, or because they pass human comprehension. This is what St. Paul suggests when he says, "We know in part." Again, the expression given of the being and nature of God may be naïvely given and not in the way of precise intellectual definition, or it may be presented in figure and metaphor, because it can be so more effectively presented as guidance to the plain man. And this involves perplexities from the point of view of the speculative understanding. This is what St. Paul means when he says "we see through a glass darkly," that is "like a reflection in a mirror, in dark sayings." Nevertheless, in St. Paul's view, all is not dark. Far from it. Our life is to be lived in the light. It is to be based on the luminous convictions that God is one; that everything that exists He made and controls; that He is awfully and inexorably righteous, but nevertheless ungrudging, self-sacrificing, love; that He takes constant care of each man and loves each with an individual love; that His purpose at the last resort for each and all is redemption and salvation; that there is a Kingdom of God already in being and still to come in full perfection. These are practical truths, but they are only practical—that is, practically effective—so long as they are believed to be true; and they can only be believed to be true if they can be taken as propositions for the intellect, propositions dealing with reality, like the propositions we frame about nature, of course with due regard to their limits in each particular case.

In recognizing this we are deliberately traversing

certain tendencies in contemporary philosophy. There are schools of philosophy [1] which bid religion take all it needs in the way of truths about God for granted. They are " facts for faith." They are the presuppositions of religious experience. They can be assumed as true. But they must not be translated into philosophical or historical or scientific propositions. There is to be no connexion between the truths of religious faith on the one hand and historical science or physical science or metaphysical philosophy on the other. But this is impossible. Religious experience, like every kind of experience, if it is not a delusion, is experience of reality, it is reality as felt.[2] If what religion feels it does not at the same time know to belong to the world of reality, with which the man of science and the historian and the philosopher are also dealing, it must cease to feel it. It is only the consciousness of objective reality which can keep the feeling in being. And our religious nature cannot be secluded in a water-tight compartment from our scientific or rational nature. Thus our present task is twofold. We must first (1) discover what are the

[1] I am referring of course to the Ritschlian school of theologians and the philosophical pragmatists : no doubt they have done good service in vindicating the right of religion and morality to make the postulates necessary for their maintenance and development. Cf. Dr. Bradley : " The ideas which best express our highest religious needs and their satisfaction, must certainly be true " (*Essays on Truth and Reality,* p. 431). But it is idle to tell us to make the necessary postulates if we are told that these necessary assumptions are destitute of reality from the point of view of science or history or metaphysics. It cannot, we feel, be done. I should like to refer my readers to *Faith and Facts, a Study of Ritschlianism,* by Ernest Edghill (Macmillan, 1910), a young scholar whose loss we have every reason to deplore.

[2] As to the question of grades of reality something is said below (pp. 176, 292). I am here thinking, not of Dr. Bradley or Lord Haldane, but of the pragmatists.

intellectual propositions about God and man which the prophetic revelation plainly and unmistakably postulates as real and valid. And secondly (2) we must consider whether these propositions are in harmony with the conclusions of philosophy and science, that is to say, whether there is a synthesis either attained or attainable between faith and knowledge. The former of these enquiries will occupy this chapter.

1. *The Personality of God.*—What we mean by this term lies at the very heart of all that the prophets taught. Their God is not an abstract quality to contemplate, such as beauty, justice, truth ; but a being of deliberate will and energetic action, approving and disapproving, loving and hating, judging and blessing ; who not only can respond to man's advances and prayers, but who from the beginning has been, and always is, taking the initiative in willing and acting ; whose will is to be discerned behind everything that happens and working through everything that happens, yet who also appears as acting more intensely here than there, in the execution of particular, individual purposes. There can be no question about the truth of this conception of God if, in any real sense, the experience of the prophets is an experience of reality. For it is its very heart and substance.

Of course we may say—nay, we must say—that the human personality is an inadequate image of the divine personality. We may prefer to call Him supra-personal. We may lay stress upon the necessary element of metaphor in all human language about Him. But we are bound to recognize the fundamental intellectual implication of the whole experience of the prophets—that God is, in some supreme and transcendent sense, all that we mean when we speak

9

of a person. The Old Testament, as is well known, used " anthropomorphic " terms about God freely— that is, it runs the risk of lowering the conception of God sooner than suffer Him to be thought of as an abstraction or an idea.

There was a tendency, no doubt, in later Judaism, from an excessive sense of the transcendence of God, to shrink from the use of the personal name Jahweh, and to speak rather of " the heavens " or " the Blessed One " ; but it is noticeable that our Lord, by His habitual use of the term " Father " for God, and the associations He attached to it, brought back the emphasis upon His personality. The Father is one who wills and does, not merely all things in general, but particular things, who goes out to seek and save individual souls—in short, who is a person.

Mr. Clement Webb has recently said that " it was in connexion with the doctrine of the Trinity that the words ' person ' and ' personality ' came to be used of the Divine Being," and that though person-ality *in* God is the orthodox Christian doctrine, to speak of the personality *of* God has a suggestion of the unitarian heresy.[1] Now, it is true that the *terms* for personality, whether in Greek or Latin, were only elaborated in this connexion. But Christianity felt the importance of personality, both in man and in God, before it found a term to express the idea. And the personality of the one God was surely a central idea of the prophetic religion which Chris-tianity inherited long before any question was raised about personal distinction in the Godhead.[2]

2. *God (Jehovah) as the Absolute Being.*—Whatever

[1] *God and Personality* (Allen & Unwin, 1918), p. 61, etc.
[2] Indeed, Mr. Webb admits this (p. 85) : " Few would hesitate to describe Judaism as a religion with a personal God."

exists, according to the message of the prophets, is
from God as its author, and in Him as its sustainer,
and in some sense expresses Him. Everything
depends on God so that ultimately there is no
power but God's power. There is no rival power,
external to Him. In some sense He is the doer of
all that is done. " I am Jehovah and there is none
else ; beside me there is no god ; I will gird thee
[King Cyrus], though thou hast not known me ; that
they may know from the rising of the sun, and from
the west, that there is none beside me ; I am the
Lord, and there is none else. I form the light and
create darkness ; I make peace and create evil [1] ; I
am the Lord that doeth all these things." [2] " The
whole earth is full of his glory." " Whither shall I
go then from thy spirit ? Or whither shall I flee
from thy presence ? " [3] This absoluteness of God is
the jubilant proclamation of all the prophets ; and
the New Testament reiterates it. " Without him (the
Word who is God) was not anything made." " All
things have been created through him and unto him,
and in him all things consist." [4] "In him we live
and move and have our being." [5] It is only to say
this in other words to say that the constant assumption of the prophets of the Old and New Testaments
is the divine omnipotence—that is, the summary
power of God over and in all things that exist.

But to this teaching of the divine absoluteness
there are two qualifications. (*a*) The first, which
will be dealt with later from another point of view,
but must be referred to here, is that, in willing to
create hosts of free beings, God has willed to submit

[1] I.e. cause calamity ; see below.   [3] Isa. vi. 3 ; Ps. cxxxix. 7.
[2] Isa. xlv. 5–7.   [4] John i. 3 ; Col. i. 16–17.
                    [5] Acts xvii. 28.

Himself to a most important limitation of His omnipotence. The free beings may rebel, and in fact have rebelled, against God, and ignored God, and their wilfulness and insolence and consequent ignorance of God have on the vastest scale disordered God's world, in which they were appointed His vicegerents. And God has not overruled their liberty because it was misused, but submits Himself to their misuse of their powers, which are at bottom His, so that in Isaiah's tremendous phrase already referred to, He is made to serve by their sins.[1] Thus He appears in the world's history as one weak and defeated: "He delivers his strength into captivity, and his glory into the enemies' hand."[2] He appears as contending for His own cause under every kind of disadvantage, and suffering in the sufferings of His faithful people—a "limited" God indeed, though self-limited by His own choice in creating free beings, not limited by any external power; a suffering God even in the Old Testament. "In all the afflictions of his people, he was afflicted."[3] Also He is represented as a God who, because He has made men His vicegerents, must appeal to His people for their help: "Whom shall I send, and who will go for us?"[4] No doubt the conception throughout the Bible is that there can be no final failure of God or of His cause. Because God is God, He must "come into His own" in the whole of His universe; and each insolent power in turn must be overwhelmed. These epiphanies of divine power are the "days of the Lord," and there is to be a final "day."

---

[1] Isa. xliii. 24.

[2] Ps. lxxviii. 61. The words in the Prayer Book version, "*their* power . . . *their* beauty," are a mere mistake.

[3] Isa. lxiii. 9.   [4] Isa. vi. 8.

The Bible never allows us to forget that. Nevertheless God's long-continued meekness, or self-submission to be defeated and to suffer at the hands of His own creatures, constitutes an even startling limitation upon the conception of His absoluteness. And it ought to be remarked that increasingly after the Captivity and in the New Testament the universe is conceived of as the dwelling-place of hosts of free spirits other than men, some of whom have misused their freedom at least as fully and disastrously as men ; so that the struggle for right must be regarded as universal—far beyond the limits of human activity. "We wrestle [and God wrestles in us] against the principalities, against the powers, against the world-rulers of this darkness, against the spiritual hosts of wickedness in the heavenly places." [1]

(b) And there is another limitation of the divine absoluteness as represented in the Old Testament to which we need to give careful attention. Absoluteness, involving omnipotence, may be represented as arbitrariness. If God is personally the doer of everything at every moment, there might be imagined to be no limit to what might happen— nothing that we could calculate upon. But that God's will is the law of nature, and God's will is constant and covenanted, was affirmed in the prophetic religion throughout. "He has made a decree [for

---

[1] Eph. vi. 12. The conception of Satan and his angels as rebels, like men but before men, misusing their legitimate powers, becomes dominant in later Judaism. It is the assumption of the New Testament, it being inconceivable that God could have created spirits to be evil. If the devils are what they are, that must be because they, like man, are sinners (1 John iii. 8, John viii. 44). In the Biblical view there can be no essentially evil nature. The morally evil things can be only good things misused ; and the morally evil spirits only good spirits become rebellious.

nature] which shall not pass away." [1] This sense of
the inherent order of nature—"laws of nature"
in the modern sense—grew in the later period of
Israel's history, perhaps under Greek influence.
Thus in the Wisdom literature,[2] the order of nature
is represented as the influence of the Divine Wisdom
(personified) "reaching from one end of all things
unto the other, mightily and sweetly ordering all
things." The idea suggested is that the principle
of order lies in the Divine Being Himself, and inasmuch as "the being of God is a kind of law to His
working,"[3] so God can do nothing arbitrarily or
foolishly, any more than He could "deny Himself"
by doing wrongly. Thus the sense of the divine
absoluteness and omnipotence is conditioned by the
sense that God is self-limited by His own being, and
that we can know for certain that neither unrighteous-
ness nor disorder is possible to Him.[4]

Thus man, as made in God's image, both rational
and moral, has within himself a certain standard by
which to judge of God. In magnificent passages of
the prophets God is represented as appealing to man
to recognize and vindicate the justice of His actions.[5]
The Bible, we may say, justifies John Stuart Mill
in his famous refusal to call God righteous if His
action did not respond to the ultimate demand of the
human conscience. It is true that at moments the
awful sense of the divine greatness and the pettiness
and short-sightedness of man overwhelms the feelings

[1] Ps. cxlviii. 6; cf. Gen. viii. 22, ix. 16.

[2] See, e.g., Prov. viii. 22–30, Wisdom vii. 17–viii. 1.

[3] Hooker, *E. P.*, bk. i, ii, 2.

[4] In Isa. xxviii. 23–4 there is a very subtle appreciation of the
divine wisdom, both in its unity of purpose and variety of application, as illustrated in the parable of the husbandman.

[5] Isa. v. 3–4, Micah vi. 2 ff., Ezek. xviii. 25; cf. Ps. li. 4.

of the Biblical writers, so as to make all human criticism seem foolish and blasphemous. Thus the great answer of God out of the whirlwind to Job seems to be a mere appeal to His transcendent power. But this is not the only or the chief impression the book of Job leaves on us. The chief impression is of the unconquerable strength of the appeal for justice on the part of the innocent and helpless sufferer ; and even after the overwhelming appeal to the divine omnipotence, the great dramatist cannot draw to his conclusion without making God satisfy the requirement of human justice, in the most naïve fashion, by restoring to Job more than his former prosperity.

Or, again, we find St. Paul in the New Testament sharply rebuking the Jew who dared to criticize the justice of God, if He really had, as St. Paul said He had, disinherited in its main bulk His own chosen race—" Who art thou that repliest against God ? . . . Hath not the potter a right over the clay ? " But we must pay attention to the main point of St. Paul's argument. What St. Paul is refuting is a claim on the part of the Jew really destructive of all morality, viz. that God had so tied Himself to one race as to be bound to show it preference, however it might behave. St. Paul, then, is asserting God's absolute liberty, not to override moral distinctions, but to ignore a merely racial claim ; and the end of his argument is a vindication of the justice and graciousness of God's world-wide purpose.[1]

On the whole we must recognize that the omnipotence of God is in the prophetic teaching the opposite of arbitrary. It must correspond with certain principles

[1] See Rom. ix.-xi. I have worked this point out in an *Exposition* of the Romans (Murray), vol. ii. pp. 1-14.

of order and justice which have their seat in the being of God Himself.

3. *The Moral Perfection of God.*—In the pagan religions it was common to represent a God as formidable in an arbitrary or irrational sense : so that he should be carefully provided with all that he is accustomed to require, without asking why, and be hedged about with tabus lest he should "break out" upon his worshipping people, like a physical plague. It cannot be denied that this sort of conception appears in the earlier stages of Israel's religion.[1] But in the prophetic religion the sense of the divine holiness is purged from such unworthy physical associations and has become absolutely spiritual. The fear of the Lord is no irrational fear of something unaccountable, but a rational awe in the presence of one whose character is known. God is absolutely righteous— of purer eyes than to behold iniquity : inexorably and impartially just. If clouds and darkness are still round about Him, yet there is no doubt about the quality of His will, " righteousness and judgement are the habitation of his seat." And there is with Him no respect of persons, no favouritism of His own people such as could lead Him to ignore their sins ; and no possibility of error in His judgements, for He sees men's hearts and knows their most secret thoughts. But though He is thus awful in His holiness, there is an equal emphasis upon His love. This appears in the intensest form in the manner in which Hosea is bidden to symbolize the love of God for His own people,[2] and there is no need to dwell long on what everyone would admit, that at the climax of the self-disclosure of God, Jesus Christ represents Him—

---

[1] See Exod. xix. 22, 24 ; 2 Sam. vi. 8.
[2] In his relations to his adulterous wife; see Hos. i., ii.

not less than before as unalterably righteous and
tremendous in His holiness, for the Gospels are very
severe books, but as unquestionably love—self-
sacrificing love—love that goes out to every individual
to seek him and to save him.[1] The limitations and
the imperfections of the Old Testament conception of
divine love, which are conspicuous in its earlier stages,
are here quite obliterated. The love of God is active
and universal. Its " jealousy " remains, because
God cannot endure to see men wasting themselves
on things that cannot profit, but it has in it no element
of grudging, and covers with its sanction and blessing
all uses of life which are within the wide purpose of
God. The final summary expression of the character
of God is St. John's phrase, " God is love." Where
God is, love is : and where love is, God is : and the
end of all things is to be the victory of love.

There are profound difficulties in the way of re-
ceiving this comforting doctrine of the goodness of
God which some of us in our day feel acutely. Some
of these modern difficulties—such as that which arises
from the vast amount of animal pain in the world—
the believers of the Old and New Testaments hardly
seem to have felt at all. With others—such as the
sufferings of innocent men—they obviously wrestled.
When we are considering [2] whether the doctrine of
divine love can be accepted without violence to

[1] Not long before our Lord's time the love of God for every individual was beautifully expressed in the Book of Wisdom xi. 23:
"For thou hast mercy on all men, because thou hast power to do all
things, and thou overlookest the sins of men to the end they may
repent. For thou lovest all things that are, and abhorrest none of the
things that thou didst make ; for never wouldest thou have formed
anything if thou didst hate it. . . . But thou sparest all things
because they are thine, O sovereign Lord, thou lover of souls."

[2] See below, pp. 156 ff.

reason, we shall naturally ask whether the Bible, Old Testament and New, assists us to a solution of our difficulties. But for the present we are only considering what the Biblical doctrine of God affirms. Certainly, then, it affirms that the absolute and supreme Being is perfect righteousness and ungrudging love. And certainly this doctrine is presented not as an argument to convince us, but as a word of God Himself to be believed and realized in the responsive experience of faith.

4. *God the Creator.*—As has been already noticed, the prophetic conception of God insisted upon His presence everywhere, as the spirit of life and order in all things. Hence it coalesced easily with the philosophic doctrine of the divine reason immanent in the world, which occupied the minds of thinking men when the Christian religion began its course. But this popular philosophy got no farther than this recognition of a rational soul or spirit of the world ; or if it did conceive of God as transcendent, He was so transcendent as to be inaccessible, abstract, and indifferent to men. But the God who reveals Himself to the prophets is indeed intimately concerned in all things that are, but in Himself is absolutely distinct from them as their Creator.

Indeed, the intensely personal and moral conception of God which possessed the prophets made impossible to them any confusion of God with nature. It lifted Him into absolute distinctness or transcendence.

This idea is vividly expressed in the prophetic horror of idolatry. The prophets almost weary us by their alternate denunciation and ridicule of idolatry. Philosophy has been generally able to make terms with idolatry. God is in all things—that is the farthest point to which it can get. Therefore, though the popular myths about the gods are childish and foolish, it can sympathize with the tendency to see God in this and that. Only in this and that can the vulgar worship the All in all. This philosophic tendency to tolerate idolatry is familiar in ancient times, and it is obvious in the sympathetic attitude towards idolatry of a great many moderns.[1]

They show themselves restive under the denunciations of idolatry alike of the ancient prophets and the modern missionaries. But such denunciations are inseparable from the prophetic belief which will tolerate no confusion of the creature with the Creator, of nature with God. However true it be that God is everywhere, yet the first thought of Him must be as absolutely distinct from everything. Whatever be the grades of creation, yet these distinctions of higher and lower are as nothing compared with the absolute distinction between the Creator and the works of His hands. What inspires the prophetic denunciation of idolatry is the feeling that it involves a senseless insult to the Creator by confusing Him with His creatures.

So also the idea of God as Creator lies at the heart of their claim for humility in man, and their denunciation of pride. If, as pantheistic philosophy conceived, a man, in respect of his reason, is a part of the universal reason or God, destined ultimately, after all the defilements and hindrances due to his temporary incarceration in the body, to return to the Divine Being, humility might seem a grovelling quality unworthy

[1] See Pratt's *Religious Consciousness*, p. 276: " Much more may thus be said in defence of the practice of ' idolatry ' than most of us have been brought up to suppose. It is based upon a perfectly sound psychological principle, and it appeals to a widely felt human need."

of a rational being, and pride a legitimate expression of his true nature, God and man being essentially one interdependent being. But all this mode of conceiving the relation of man to God is by the prophets rendered impossible. Man is not a part of God, but the creature of God. His relation to God is one of absolute dependence, as for the beginning of his existence so moment by moment for its continuance. This is the ground of humility. This is what makes all pride or boasting preposterous. And if humility is in effect nothing less than a servile spirit, that is because God has been pleased to make man in His own image and likeness, to admit him to His friendship, and to make him His vicegerent in the world which he inhabits.[1]

Once more, the transcendence of God the Creator involves His unconditional spirituality. He is present in all things but unconfused. Implicated in no conditions of time and space, and essentially tied to no requirements of any special sanctuary, " God is spirit ; and they that worship him must worship in spirit and truth." [2] And again we must notice that if the Jewish thought of God is gradually lifted to this highest level, it is not by the process of reasoned reflection, but by the way of inspired utterances. " Thus saith the high and holy one that inhabiteth eternity." [3]

5. *The Freedom of Man.*—But how, then, if God is the Creator, responsible for the existence of all that is, is His character for goodness to be maintained in view of the evil and misery of the world ? The answer of the prophets to this portentous question

---

[1] Cf. the mixture of humility with exultation in Ps. viii. or in the Magnificat of Mary.

[2] John iv. 24.   [3] Isa. lvii. 15.

is, if not complete, yet simple, and, as has been said, it is expressed or implied everywhere. It attributes the mass of evil in the world to the lawlessness of rebel wills—to pride, greediness, ambition, cruelty, selfishness, jealousy, lust ; and to the judgements which those things bring upon individuals and upon the world, whether as their natural results or (what is perhaps only their natural results viewed from a different angle) as the punishment for sin which God inflicts.

There can be no question that this is the general account which the prophetic scriptures give of the presence of evil in the world.   St. James, who speaks in the New Testament in the prophetic spirit, describes how the ungoverned human tongue, though it be a little member, yet can disorder a whole world, setting on fire the divinely-ordered course of nature.[1] The sins which inspire the tongue are jealousy and rivalry.   But what James says so truly of these particular sins acting through human speech, generalized so as to apply to all sin, expresses the common mind of the prophets.   And when St. James further speaks of the fire of the tongue as kindled from hell or " devilish " he is, again, representing the common belief of later Judaism which, as confirmed by Jesus Christ, the New Testament writers share, that the source and home of evil is to be found beyond the circle of human nature in an unseen world of free spirits.

We should note that the insistence of the prophets, and of the scriptures inspired by their teaching, upon the reality of human freedom is unhesitating, and is allowed to condition their doctrine, not only of

[1] James iii. 6; see Hort's suggestive notes.

God's omnipotence (as already pointed out), but in a measure also of His omniscience.

Everyone who thinks at all feels the acuteness of the question : If God knows to-day, and indeed from all eternity, what I am going to do to-morrow, how can I be really free ? To me it seems that in this sense belief in divine foreknowledge really is incompatible, according to any standard of thinking possible to us in our present state, with belief in human freedom. I can recognize that the whole conception of absolute and eternal knowledge is totally outside our present faculties. But within the region of our present capacities for thinking, the two beliefs are incompatible, and it is to our present thinking that the word of God in the Bible is directed. The Bible, then, does not concern itself with the metaphysical question. It contents itself with saying, " At any rate, you are free and responsible." That God is powerful over all and in all, and does not for a moment allow the world or any single man to escape out of His control, that He knows everything that is or can be, and discerns infallibly the thoughts of men's hearts and their tendencies—all this it would be easy to " prove from Scripture." Also that individual men like Judas, or classes of men, may have so fundamentally chosen evil that they have no longer ears to hear or wills to choose freely, and that their actions are foreknown and predetermined—this also appears as true but as abnormal. On the whole God is represented as waiting on man, pleading with man, being disappointed in man (" I looked that my vineyard should bring forth grapes, and it brought forth wild grapes ") ; and it is impossible to " prove from Scripture " that God knows generally how the individual man is going to choose on each particular occasion. I repeat, the overruling of God is always maintained. No will or action passes out of His hands. All the disorder that wilful men or spirits can cause is, as we may say, superficial. Under it and over it and beyond it is the everlasting power and wisdom. Nevertheless, within the scope of the universal providence room is left for free spirits to act. And God, so to speak, keeps far enough aloof to let them act freely. And at least His word never lets them suppose that He knows beforehand what they will do.

Whether philosophy or science can raise any valid objection to the doctrine of real human freedom is another question which we shall shortly have to face. Here our sole object is to ask what is the intellectual presentation involved in the Bible.[1]

6. *The Day of the Lord and the World to Come.*—As has been said already, though the prophets recognize so frankly the lawless liberty of men to thwart God's purpose and disorder His world, there is no doubt of the sovereignty of God—that He allows no fragment of His world to pass out of His control ; and, because He is God, He must vindicate Himself at last. Thus the prophets contemplate unmoved the vast structures raised by human insolence—" the giant forms of empires "—and speak against them, and against every rebellious individual, the oracles of God which announce their inevitable doom. And in the later stages of prophecy, as on the lips of Christ and in the New Testament as a whole, the whole vista of history is represented as closing in the Day of the Lord when God is to come into His own in His whole universe. This is a Day of judgment and doom on all that has refused God, and a day of realization—the perfect

[1] On St. Paul's doctrine of divine " foreknowledge," see my *Ephesians*, p. 66.

kingdom or reign of God—for all that responds to Him. In the earlier stages of Israel's history, they were taught to look for the vindication of God's purpose here and now in this world. There was no glimpse of a life beyond. But as the sense of individuality and of the worth of the individual soul developed in Israel, and the accompanying sense of personal fellowship with God, such as appears in so intense a form in the Psalms, a wider horizon than this world became a necessity. If God was just, then there must be a life beyond in which He would vindicate the justice which was plainly not vindicated in "the wild and irregular scene" of this world. Again, if the soul of man was admitted here and now to the fellowship of God, then this divine fellowship, in part gained here, must be realized hereafter. So before the close of the Jewish canon the doctrine of the resurrection and of the world to come has taken possession of the Jewish conscience, and it gains consistency and definiteness in the New Testament. We shall have to return to the matter at a later stage, when we come to consider the full Christian faith. Here all that is needed is the recognition that the message of the prophets about divine justice and "the day of the Lord" was found to involve the belief in a resurrection of the dead and of a world to come, and that Jesus Christ in His teaching gave to these already established doctrines His explicit and solemn confirmation.

.   .   .   .   .

Let it be said again, the whole teaching of the prophets was given for a practical and not a speculative purpose. It was a "word of life," a message as to how men must live. So also Christianity came out into the world as "the way." It was a life before it was a doctrine. But it was a life which involved a whole body of truths about God and man : and though these are affirmed for a practical purpose, they are none the less affirmed as true. They must be true in fact—and therefore truths for the intellect—or the life proposed becomes impossible.

Now, we have been asking what are the intellectual propositions which the prophets insist upon as the word of God, and we have found them to be especially these : that Jehovah, the God of Israel, is personal ; that He is the absolute Being, beside whom there can be none other ; that He is in character perfect holiness and love ; that He is absolutely distinct from all His creatures as their Creator ; that He has given to His creature man, and to other orders of spirits dimly perceived, such moral freedom and responsibility as admit of their co-operation with God or of their resisting and thwarting Him on the widest scale ; but that as God is God He must fully vindicate Himself over and in all His creation, if not in this world, then in the world to come.

Now, it cannot be denied that if these propositions, which the prophets reiterate as being the word of God, are really the legitimate expression in human language of God's own self-disclosure—that is, of impressions, convictions, images, and communications really wrought by God into the prophets' souls and minds—a whole new body of facts and data is added to the material on which philosophy must work. The " word of God " must plainly be received in faith. It is not the product of human reasoning. But so accepted as true, it can be and must be the basis of a fresh philosophy. So the Christian Church—which inherited the prophetic teaching, as it was renewed and deepened in Christ—showed itself at home in the highly intellectual and philosophical world of the

10

Graeco-Roman Empire. It showed itself a body as well able to think philosophically as to live and die nobly. Among its men of greater intellect it had no one equal to the greatest of the Greeks—Plato or Aristotle or, perhaps, Plotinus—but it had, especially among its Greek Fathers, men capable of acute intellectual and philosophical discrimination. It was able to assimilate and also to revise, add to and correct the ideas of current philosophy. Thus out of the treasures of its faith it enriched philosophy with a deeply enhanced sense of personality as the most ultimate and important of categories ; it assimilated the conception of divine immanence in nature, but also it contended strenuously for the conception of the transcendent Creator independent and complete in Himself ; it used the conception of the Trinity in God to make rational and intelligible the thought of a God eternally alive and complete in Himself without dependence upon His creation for self-expression ; it emphasized the idea of human freedom ; it firmly fixed in the will and not in the flesh the source and ground of sin ; it introduced among men the pregnant thought of the world as a scene in which a divine purpose is slowly and progressively realized ; it showed Greek philosophy a way of escape from the embarrassing dualism of matter and spirit. Thus it enriched and stimulated philosophy while it used it to gain intellectual coherence and expression for its faith. And if it made mistakes which proved dangers and hindrances to the later Church, that was largely because at times it was more subservient to Greek philosophy than to the conceptions of the prophets and of Christ.[1] I must not now stop to dwell on these

[1] Thus I feel sure that it was a false subservience to Greek philosophy which caused the Greek theologians to emphasize the im-

points. All that I want now to suggest is that Christianity showed itself from the first conscious that the materials of its faith, simply because its faith was true, required of it to enter into the field of human philosophy, as well as of human life, and there, too, to test all things and to show that it believed in human reason as the gift of God.

Once again, in the thirteenth century, in the dawn of the renaissance of humanity after the really dark ages, the schoolmen, headed by the great Thomas Aquinas, showed the Christian faith to be capable of supplying a synthesis in which all available knowledge could find a place. Never since then has such a complete synthesis, nor anything approaching to it, been accomplished. For any such synthesis to be again accomplished and accepted by a whole civilization, as the scholastic synthesis, taken as a whole, was accepted, would be only possible if mankind or Christendom were again to realize such an ordered unity of life and faith as that common ideas or doctrines could really prevail and become the current coin of life.[1] From any such state of things we are far indeed. But what cannot at present be done for a whole society

passibility of God in a sense which evacuates in great measure the meaning of the Bible. Also it derived surely from Greek philosophy, and not from the Bible, the idea of the essential *indestructibility* of the human soul or consciousness.

[1] Since the Renaissance there has been in certain regions, and within our own country more than once, such a degree of unity as has rendered possible the wide and common acceptance of constructive intellectual work—expressing some sort of intellectual synthesis. Thus Hooker's *Ecclesiastical Polity*, Butler's *Analogy of Religion, Natural and Revealed, to the Constitution and Course of Nature*, and on a lower plane Archdeacon Paley's *Natural Theology* and *Evidences of Christianity*, became classics, i.e. adequate expressions in a book of the best common mind of a whole community. But it would be impossible to-day to conceive such a book appearing. The " common mind " is lacking, except in groups.

or civilization can be done for individuals and groups. That is the only possible preparation for something wider. Any individual or group of to-day, which accepts the revelation of the prophets as a true disclosure of the ultimate realities of the universe, must ask himself how, on the basis of his faith, he can face the whole sum of scientific and philosophic knowledge of his time, and whether he can see his own way to an adequate synthesis. Perhaps, as was suggested earlier, the greatest reassurance that this is possible is to be found in the fact that great scientific men and capable philosophers, if they are also believers in God, as Christendom has believed in Him, are not in experience found to be hampered in their scientific or philosophical thinking. They bear witness that in their faith they have retained or found their intellectual freedom. But this is not enough. We cannot be content with the witness of others. We need to be able to realize our intellectual freedom in some sort of intellectual synthesis, or at least to see the way opening towards such a synthesis. Thus we must approach the task of relating what we have gained from the prophets and Christ to the whole of our knowledge.[1]

[1] The Italian philosopher Croce gives an interesting appreciation of the mediaeval historians, to whom he gives the preference over their Graeco-Roman predecessors, in spite of their immense inferiority to them in culture and ability, in this respect—that they first viewed history as progress towards a goal, and that their pessimism was thus irradiated with hope. They saw a divine purpose working through scathing judgements to an assured end : see *Teoria e storia della storiagraphia* (Bari, 1917), p. 188. But, in fact, it is the Hebrew prophets, especially Ezekiel, who should have the credit of having been pioneers.

CHAPTER VI

REVELATION AND REASON

Now we come back to the field in which we made our first efforts in the reconstruction of belief, unassisted by any idea of positive revelation—that is, to the world of natural knowledge, of the sciences and of philosophy. In this field we had found ourselves up to a certain point enlightened and reassured. We had found that reason and beauty and goodness cannot be regarded as merely qualities of our minds. They belong to the universe of things. There is an " eternal, not ourselves," which is at once reason and beauty and goodness, with which we can hold communion and co-operate. And this eternal being we can call God and in a sense worship. And a belief of this kind has at different periods and in different countries been the basis of what may be called a natural religion for educated men. But we had also found ourselves speedily dissatisfied and baffled. This God of nature could be so dimly descried. His personality, His character, His purpose, on the whole appeared to be so ambiguous that the question was forced upon us—If there is a God, is it not at least conceivable that He may have (so to speak) taken action on His side, and disclosed Himself in a more satisfying manner in response to the anxious quests and prayers of our groping and thirsty minds and spirits?

viously current presentations of the revealed religion
on a very wide scale. And we are bound to claim
the fullest liberty for science, and for reason in
all its legitimate activities, because reason is at the
last resort our only instrument of truth. Thus we
cannot play false to our reason, or be content with any
crude antithesis between faith and reason, faith, we
find, being only reason in the making. If then, on a
fresh review, we find the data of revelation, as they
stand out so clearly before our minds, bringing us into
positive and apparently irreconcilable conflict with
what seems to be solidly grounded knowledge, we shall
be indeed bewildered and thrown back baffled again.
Can we find a synthesis, or a way towards a synthesis,
between these data to faith and the conclusions—more
or less definitive—of the sciences or of philosophy ?
Or where such conclusions are precisely what is lacking,
can our faith contribute to the solving of otherwise
insoluble questions ?

Probably the greatest difficulty which will emerge
for most of us will concern the belief in the absolute
goodness of God, if He is also to be believed to be the
Creator of all that is. This problem we will face
under the head of philosophy. But first of all we will
enquire whether, with our recently won faith in the
God of revelation, we stand free in the world of the
physical sciences.

I

It has already been pointed out that exclusive
preoccupation with the methods of the sciences has
tended inevitably to a materialistic interpretation of
the world. But such an interpretation we have
claimed, with the encouragement of most of our

contemporary philosophers, to set aside as quite one-sided and untenable. It is our reason which compels us to see spiritual meaning and purpose in the world. It is our reason which forces us to interpret the material in terms of mind and not mind in terms of the material. But the current spiritual interpretation of the world by the philosophers is a sort of pantheism. The question now is whether the distinctively Christian theism—the religion of the prophets and of Christ —raises any fresh difficulty from the point of view of the sciences.

On the whole, the answer is in the negative. Science is increasingly disposed to recognize its abstract character—which means that for its own purposes it makes abstraction from the world as a whole of certain departments or functions or aspects of the world, and studies them apart from the residue which is irrelevant to the purpose in hand.[1] In particular it is not concerned with origins. It neither affirms nor denies anything about the source of being and life. As far as I can see, there are only two points at which conflict threatens between the claims of science and the postulates of revealed religion—(1) as to whether the Biblical account of creation is not in such marked conflict with the scientific account of the origin of the universe as to discredit itself ; and (2) as to whether the universe scientifically viewed can make room for free will.[2]

1. Science, then, presents us with the universe, and

[1] See Haldane's *Relativity*, p. 40, and *passim*.

[2] Perhaps the appearance of conflict between Religion and Science to-day is most serious on the question of the Fall of Man. But we had better postpone that question till we are in a position to consider it in connexion with St. Paul's doctrine of Christ and His functions —that is in the next volume.

particularly that part of it which we know more or
less intimately, as the scene of an age-long evolution
of matter and life, out of which, only at its last stage
and through infinite struggles, emerges rational and
spiritual life in man ; which again only through long
ages, and that very imperfectly and intermittently,
has succeeded in asserting itself and realizing itself
in the world.   But as regards material nature confessedly the revelation contained in the Bible gives
no hint of such an age-long process.   It gives a
picture only of sudden creations.   " God spake, and
they were made : he commanded, and they were
created."   What are we to say of this broad contrast ?
I think a believer in the reality of Biblical inspiration
must admit in the widest sense that this inspiration of
certain men by the Spirit of God does not appear to
have carried with it any special enlightenment on
those subjects on which man has proved able, though
with infinite labour, to enlighten himself.   In the
broadest sense " the Bible was not given to teach us
science," and does in fact speak only in terms of the
science of its times.   Its only concern with nature is
to affirm that all that exists is the creation of the one
God, and that His will is its law.   But in the region
of human nature, with which the revelation is particularly concerned, it does present us with a picture
of evolution—that is, of a divine purpose only very
slowly and gradually, and after vast catastrophes and
infinite struggles, and as yet very imperfectly, realized
—nay, only beginning to be realized, though thousands of years have intervened between Abraham
and us.[1]   Plainly, then, though the revelation did not

[1] The Biblical expression " the ages of the ages " or " all the
generations of the age of the ages " (Eph. iii. 21) represents profoundly the idea of slow process towards a conclusion.

do anything to teach men about an age-long process of physical creation, yet it did give them a conception of God's method in dealing with man which is in agreement with the method which science now discloses to us in nature as a whole. Science, we may say with truth, has only brought our notion of the creation of nature broadly into harmony with the conception of the making and remaking of man which we find in the Bible.[1]

To put this in other words—the Bible in its account of God's dealings with man—and this is the only field of its professed inspiration—suggests a God as unlike as possible to the " Great Emperor enthroned somewhere outside the world, ordering it by absolute fiats to be accomplished in a moment."

2. But can science make room in its universe for the Biblical emphasis on human freedom, which means that, wherever human wills occur, there are points of spontaneity and contingency ; and which also involves the actual occurrence in the world on the largest scale of much that ought not to have been and need not have been, for this the prophetic religion plainly requires ? Or can it claim the right to declare free will at the last analysis an illusion ?

Now, it may well be the case that neither our science nor our philosophy nor our theology will ever arrive at an adequate theory of the relation of the elements of determination from beyond and spontaneity from within in human conduct. But for the sake of simplifying theory we must not deny facts. And I contend that freedom of will is a fact and reality. It is a fact of which we have direct consciousness

[1] We must remind ourselves that the Miltonic idea that man was created perfect and in full development is not suggested by Scripture and is repudiated by the Fathers. See above, p. 10.

that within the world of physical sequences there are points—viz. human wills—where the direction in which the energy accumulated in the human organism is liberated, as in this or that kind of action, is in part determined by free choice.

We need not pause to ask how widely this element of freedom exists in the universe. Among our more imaginative philosophers and men of science there are those who treat it as highly improbable that men should be the only free spirits, and postulate a universe full of them. But we need not concern ourselves with what at this stage is purely hypothetical. Nor need we seek to determine how much truth lies in Henri Bergson's view that only in dead matter do we find the dominion of physical necessity, and that wherever life is, from its earliest stages, there also is something indeterminate and free. We must, I think, at any rate confess that the theory of determination gained its strength when the characteristic sciences were mathematics and physics ; and that, since biology became dominant, it has never proved adequate to express the movements of life. Also, seeing that life develops so gradually and, as it seems, continuously into conscious mind and freedom, it is hard to resist the impression that mind and freedom belong to it in a measure from the beginning.

But leaving all these questions concerning the range of free will in the universe aside, let us concentrate our attention on the point in nature where moral freedom becomes part of direct human experience. At least in man there is something which the sequence of physical determination cannot account for, something totally different in kind to physical determination.

The action of any mechanically determined object is

the resultant of the forces acting upon it in combination, as a billiard-ball touched by two cues moves in a line representing the combination of the two forces. Obviously such mechanical formulas do not avail to interpret vital movements. Yet though the movements perhaps of plants and certainly of animals appear to involve selection and choice, we cannot know what happens as from within. But in the region of the human consciousness the process of that portion of our activities which is deliberate and voluntary discloses its nature quite clearly, and especially clearly in the worthiest and noblest of our race. There we have a scene in which what we call (by the use of a physical metaphor) motives appear as appealing to the sovereign will, and the will by choosing between motives gives preponderance to one, and the others are neutralized, and the resultant action is what it would have been if they had been exercising no pressure. Nay, as we often know, the fact that we were under strong temptation to yield to some lust or appetite, but rejected the suggestion as unworthy, seems to give increased energy to the action which contradicts the unworthy impulses, or, on the other hand, if we yield to temptation, the remembrance of duty deserted causes us to plunge all the more violently into the unworthy course we have chosen. Here, then, in the region of human choice we claim to know that the energy stored in the human organism is liberated in movements the direction of which is determined by the choice of the will—the movements involved in doing right or doing wrong respectively. Of the conviction that this is so we may say what Zeno the Stoic said of sense impressions, that it " takes hold of us by the hair and drags us to assent." If I am not certain of free choice, I am certain of nothing ; and I mean by this that if I have done wrong, if I have given my consent to the " lower " motive against the " higher," I have done what need not have been done and ought not to have been done. We may restrict as anxiously as we can the limit of freedom ; we may point out that whatever we do we can only surrender ourselves to some impulse from beyond—either, in religious language, to the Spirit of God, whose service is perfect freedom, or to the lusts of the flesh, to obey which is to become the slaves of sin—but that in neither case is there pure initiative in the will. We may make the most of all the influences of heredity and character. Nevertheless at the last analysis you cannot rob the will of the sane man of responsibility for the choice by which it surrenders to one motive or another, and thereby determines action in this direction or that, so as either to promote the divine order or to add to the moral confusion and lawlessness of the world. And God Himself, in the disclosure of Himself which we have been considering, does not bid us think that even He foreknows which way we are going to choose.

This conviction I could not surrender under any pressure from science. For if I know anything, I know it is true. But, in fact, it does not really affect science. Science can only take account of the fact that the energy first stored in the human organism is then liberated in action. That it might have been liberated in some other kind of action it is not its business to affirm and it cannot deny. It cannot pretend, whether in man or in an animal, to answer the question, What is the place of the will in the liberation of the energy ? That can be known only from within by direct experience in the soul of man.

Without fear of discord, then, with legitimate science, we must hold to the conviction that God has created beings with the responsibility of freedom— that within the scope of His universal presence and energy He has so far limited Himself as to leave room for their free activity, with all its disordering effects upon His creation, when it is misused; and in each act of our moral choice, however largely determined by conditions over which we have no control, such as circumstances, heredity, and the character generated by our whole past, we must recognize that the determination is not complete—there remains a spontaneous element in each choice which constitutes, according as it is exercised, our moral worth or our sin, our moral liberty or our moral servitude.

This doctrine of freedom and responsibility rests on an assurance than which nothing can be more sure, because there is nothing I know so surely as what I myself am. Objects I can only know as they are presented to me from outside. The definition of them for me must be in terms of such external knowledge. But I know myself from within. It is from inside that I discover the definition of self-hood, though, of course, what I seem to know for certain of myself is confirmed by the consent of other selves. I know that amidst all the forces, physical and social, acting upon me, I am a largely self-determining being, responsible for the making of my own soul. I am therefore constrained to believe that the power which brought me into being, brought me into being that I might freely realize the ideal of human life which presents itself to my conscience. Here, in its freedom and its duty, lies the worth of personality. The more I trust this consciousness the more it proves itself by my moral progress. If I doubt or ignore it,

I sink in the scale of being. It is nothing less than intellectual blindness to prefer to this direct consciousness of myself from within, the conclusions which I might draw, if *per impossibile* I could view the world and form my estimate of it, without any such knowledge from within.[1]

II

But how do we find ourselves when, with our recovered confidence in God's real disclosure of Himself through the Hebrew prophets and in Christ, we start again face to face with contemporary philosophy? We have found philosophy on the whole affirming the spiritual interpretation of the universe, and in some sense the existence of God, but very much divided in judgement and doubtful in mind as to (1) whether we are justified in speaking of God as personal; (2) whether we are entitled to think of God as an eternal and perfect consciousness, or only as gaining self-consciousness in man and other rational beings, if such exist; (3) whether He can be thought of as the Absolute Being or as only one element or aspect of a whole that is more than He; (4) whether we can entertain the thought of God as the Creator, prior to, independent of, and the absolute author of all that

---

[1] It appears as if philosophical intellectualism was always at work to *depersonalize* the universe: see Pratt's *Religious Consciousness*, p. 17, quoting Von Hügel: " The intellectual and speculative faculty seems habitually, instinctively to labour at depersonalizing all it touches." Cf. an interesting article by F. C. S. Schiller on William James (*Quarterly Review*, July 1921, pp. 31, 35): " Ever since Plato the treatment of personality has been involved in inextricable difficulties, because the accepted theory of knowledge has found no room for it." ... " The academic attempts at dehumanizing personality." Cf. also an interesting article by Dr. Relton in *Theology* (S.P.C.K.), August 1921, on " The Meaning and Value of Finite Individuality." See also note p. 170.

exists in the universe of things. We found it again (5) giving a very uncertain sound, not only on the question of the reality of human freedom, with which we are not going to deal further at present, but also on the question of the personal immortality of human souls. Finally, though not so much on the ground of philosophy, perhaps, as of common sense, we find ourselves confronted with (6) a deep and widespread protest against the doctrine that the God who made the universe of our experience can be a God of love.

Now, confessedly, the religion of the prophets claims to assure to us the solution of all these difficulties. It brings down the balancing scales certainly on the side of the personal God, who is the only absolute being and the Creator of all that is, who has made man a free being, destined for personal immortality, and who, in spite of all appearances to the contrary, is perfect goodness, perfect love. What we have to do now is to seek in all sincerity to see how our provisional faith in the revealed religion stands towards the conclusions which our reasoning powers, working on the basis of our experience, suggest to us. And we must be honest with ourselves—that is to say, if we must decline to yield our reason into the keeping of ecclesiastical authority, we must equally decline to be terrorized by the authority of the intellectuals. History is full of the record of their profound mistakes. We have already declined to be satisfied with their apparent refusal *a priori* even to consider the evidences of God's positive self-revelation of Himself in an historical process, of which the Bible gives the record. As a result of this refusal, we have been profoundly impressed with the grounds for believing

11

in the reality of this revelation. Now again we must claim to use our reason to the full with regard to their *a priori* determination of what kind of God is rationally conceivable; and history seems to warrant in many directions a profound scepticism as to the power of *a priori* determination which the human reason possesses.

1. It is not, however, in any distrust of abstract reason, but by making the fullest use of it that I am capable of, that I, for my part, declare that I find the conception of an impersonal God—an impersonal mind or righteousness in nature—which is the conception of the higher pantheism, really far less intelligible and far less rational than the conception of a personal God. I cannot hold the conception of mind or of truth or of purpose or of righteousness except on the background of personality. In experience I only know these things as functions or qualities of persons. No doubt the personality of God must be something much greater and more comprehensive than human personality. We may prefer to call God super-personal. No doubt also, if at a later stage of enquiry I find reason to believe that the divine personality is complex and social, as the doctrine of the Trinity represents it, I shall experience a certain intellectual relief and enlightenment. But at least my reason welcomes the assurance that God is what the human person is—conscious of Himself and of His relationship to all things that in any sense exist, capable of determinate will and judgement and action, and self-determined by essential spiritual character; in other words, that the human personality is at least a better image of God than mechanical force or merely vital movement or merely abstract idea. This, I suppose, is the substance of the Psalmist's

argument—"He that made the eye, shall He not see?" If personality is the highest known thing, must not God be at least that highest thing?

2. Again, I must profess that I cannot attach any meaning to the idea, presented to us by so many philosophers, of a God who is eternal reason, order, and purpose in the universe, but who only attains to self-consciousness after long ages in man. I can understand, on the one hand, the idea of a slowly realized purpose in the world, and of a world in which finite persons, endowed with the rational power to correspond freely with this purpose, appear only late in its history, if behind the world and prior to it there is the conscious mind of God. I can understand, on the other hand, what is meant by a universe which, through all its main bulk, shows no signs of mind or purpose, though I find decisive reasons for rejecting this opinion. But this idea of unconscious mind and purpose I find very difficult. If I see in the whole universe a rational order, if I see a purpose of beauty in the world prior in time to man's appearance, and a purpose of fellowship and love becoming dominant in the animal world before man, the conclusion which my reason welcomes coincides with what the prophets proclaim as God's word—that His conscious purpose is behind all, the background of all development and all progress, and the security of their final goal.

3. The revealed religion undoubtedly postulates a God who is the absolute; not, of course, that the universe is identical with God its Creator, but that the God of the prophets, or the Father of our Lord Jesus Christ, is the one and only ultimate source of whatsoever force, power, quality, or kind of being exists in the universe, and that He contains and

sustains in being all that is, and guides it to its goal, and shall finally be "all things in all." This absoluteness of God must, as we have seen, be qualified so as to admit of the existence, by the creative will of God, within the scope of His universal activity, of free spirits who, though they draw all they are from God, yet are granted such spontaneity of choice as involves the power of disordering over long ages, though not in the final issue, the world as God would have had it be—God, so to speak, standing far enough aloof from such free spirits to allow for their dependent but spontaneous action. But the revealed religion strenuously contradicts the idea of any ultimate dualism or pluralism in the universe—the idea of any original "matter" [1] or force or will outside God or other than God. And in this it seems to me to be in harmony with reason. I think that in the fullest sense it is the postulate of both philosophy and science that the ultimate reality is one ; and that the only difficulty suggested by either experience or reflection on experience is—what we must be considering directly—the profound difficulty of believing that the one ultimate force and law behind the world and in the world of our experience is absolute goodness and love.

4. There is no doubt a revolt among philosophers against the Biblical doctrine of God the Creator, and a demand that we shall recognize that God and nature are correlative in such sense that we must hold " creation " to be co-eternal with God, inasmuch as God only realizes Himself in nature, and cannot be conceived of as existing prior to and independently of nature.

---

[1] See further below, p. 150.

Thus Dr. Pringle Pattison [1] states the conception which must be rejected in these words :

" According to this conception, God existed in all His perfection and blessedness before the creation of the world. He chose to create a world, but He might equally have foreborne to create, and this abstention would have made no difference to His self-sufficient being. The world, in other words, is in no way *organic* to the divine life. . . . It cannot be deduced from the essential nature of God."

This position is rejected, and the ground of the rejection is stated thus :

" To perfect knowledge and perfect goodness there can be no choice, in our sense of the word, as dubiety between alternatives and a making up of our minds for one or the other . . . His action is simply the realization of His nature."

Now, we must be profoundly conscious that in this discussion of what might conceivably have been, or, in other words, of the nature of divine choice, we are moving in worlds too high for us. But we have seen reason to believe that a self-disclosure of God has been granted to us " from above," not as a conclusion of human reasoning, but yet through human minds, and in such a manner as has necessitated its expression in intellectual propositions ; and these propositions, if they are necessarily inadequate to eternal realities, must be the best image of the truth possible under our present conditions of knowledge. And there is no doubt that this revelation has both by its first recipients, the prophets, and by its exponents, both Jewish and Christian, been held to involve the self-complete and independent existence of God " before the world was."

[1] In the volume entitled *Spirit*, edited by Canon Streeter, pp. 13-14.

As has been said before, when Christianity makes its historical appearance in the world of the Roman Empire, it is found contending vigorously for its own specific theism against the current philosophic pantheism, and especially contending for the conception of God the absolute Creator, perfect and self-complete and free. On this it clearly felt that its whole moral attitude to God reposed.

The formulas for which the Church contended were (a) that God created all that came into being " out of nothing," as against the current Greek idea that God was eternally confronted with a co-eternal " matter " upon which all He could do was to super-induce " form." Now that matter appears to be resolvable into force, and force for a believer in God appears to be simply the putting out of His will, it is perhaps true to say that the danger from the idea of a formless matter co-eternal with God no longer exists. The limitations on the omnipotence of God in creation which we are now called upon to recognize are not those of an external and more or less intractable material, but those which appear to inhere necessarily in the production of a gradually evolving universe, the very idea of which involves imperfection at each stage and mutual limitation by its parts or elements. But (b) the Church also contended for a distinction between the being of God on the one hand, which alone is absolutely necessary and could not have been other-wise, and on the other hand everything which belongs to the created universe, which is not eternal nor necessary but contingent upon the divine will. It exists (so the formula ran) " not by nature, but by will." Philosophically it was soon found that such a conception of God as self-sufficient, prior to and apart from all creation, was facilitated by the doctrine of

the Trinity, which had been already accepted by the
Church on quite other than philosophical grounds.
This doctrine enabled the Church to think of God as
containing within Himself the full conditions of life
and self-realization—the Father eternally expressing
Himself in His Word or Son and Spirit, and in that
eternal fellowship realizing the full life of will and
knowledge and love ; and enabled it also to think of
creation as the expression on a lower plane of what
existed already in eternal counterpart in God.[1] But
this doctrine we cannot yet entertain. Its grounds
are quite beyond us. All that can be urged at this
stage is that no idea of God can be satisfactory to
our reason which at the last resort makes God dependent for self-expression upon creation—that is,
represents God as immanent in nature and not
transcendent. And He cannot be spoken of as
transcendent unless He can be conceived of truly as
" living His own life " prior to and apart from creation.
Otherwise He becomes wholly dependent upon nature,
the soul of nature, and can only be said to become
conscious, in the sense that nature contains self-
conscious spirits in whose consciousness God may be
said to be conscious and in whose moral goodness
God may be said to be good.[2] Here we are back in

---

[1] This idea found support in John i. 3, according to the ancient
punctuation. "Without him [the eternal Word] was not anything
made. That which hath been made was life in Him," see R.V.
marg. and Westcott's Commentary. "That which was created . . .
represents to us what was beyond time in the divine mind."
The idea is expressed in Emily Brontë's lines :

> "Though earth and man were gone,
> And suns and universe ceased to be,
> And Thou wert left alone,
> Every existence would exist in Thee."

[2] See above, pp. 69 ff.

pantheism with all its fatal moral and intellectual weaknesses.   For if God is only the soul of nature, we seem to have no security as to which tendency in nature—the morally purposeful or the morally indifferent, which seems far the vaster—is going to prevail. God must be all that nature is.   If we are to vindicate, what our moral consciousness so imperatively requires, the existence of right and of a supreme moral will over the whole creation, personally willing the right and condemning the wrong, we must be able to believe in a God who prior to creation and apart from creation has will and character—that is, is transcendent—a God who has His life and being in Himself.   I am persuaded that the only refuge from pantheism—which of course takes us back behind Christianity, and all that it has won for the world, upon the old Pagan ground—is to maintain that in some real sense—which we at least can only express in temporal language—God is prior to creation, and exists eternally complete in Himself in the full blessedness of self-realizing being " before the world was."   I acknowledge that human reason could never, by its unassisted efforts, have arrived at this conception of God the Creator [1]; but granted, what we cannot doubt, that it is involved in the revelation of God, given through the prophets and in Christ, and lies indeed at its very heart, I should contend that reason must welcome it as its only refuge from the pantheism which reason itself, in that department especially which is called moral philosophy, is bound to declare unsatisfying and to seek to transcend.

I acknowledge indeed, with all competent theologians, that all human thought and language which

---

[1] So St. Thomas Aquinas.

ascribe to God priority in time to His creation [1] and
distinctive acts of choice between alternatives, is
inadequate thought and language, inadequate to the
eternal reality. The doctrine of the relativity of
knowledge in this sense we must heartily welcome.
The absolute truth we cannot know. But I suggest
that all this sort of language for which the Church
has contended, which is indeed the language of
revelation, is the only language which we can use
to express the transcendent truth, and the opposite
kind of language is fundamentally misleading and
false.

5. The idea of the immortality of human souls,
which was the outcome among the Jews of the
prophetic teaching, and which Jesus Christ so
solemnly confirmed,[2] has marked characteristics.
First, it was reached wholly under the pressure of their
belief in God.[3] There was first the belief in His
justice, which as regards individuals was plainly not
fulfilled in this world, and must needs have a larger
world for its exercise. The school of the Sadducees,
it is true, still clung to this world as the only known
scene of God's government, and sought to find satisfaction for their sense of justice in the idea of the
immortality of a good name handed down and an

[1] I suppose the best phrase is St. Augustine's—not that creation
was in time, but that it involved time. Time and creation are
correlative.

[2] Mark xii. 24 and parallel passages.

[3] As is well known, the Jews were sedulously prohibited by their
prophets from any attempt to get into direct touch with the spirits
of the dead. In our day we need not question the legitimacy of
enquiry by trained investigators into " spiritualistic " phenomena.
But we need continually to protest that no doctrine of survival
which has moral value can be based upon anything else except faith
in the justice and goodness of God—of which faith it seems to be
an inevitable consequence.

honourable family perpetuated.[1]   But the conscience
and heart of Israel as a whole demanded a real and
personal immortality.   Secondly, it was the sense of
personal communion with God, into which the soul
of man was admitted, which made it at last impossible
to doubt that this communion begun here would
be perpetuated and fulfilled beyond death.   Such was
the belief that Jesus Christ confirmed.   It was a
belief in immortality of so fully personal a kind that
it took shape in a doctrine not merely of the immortality
of the soul, but of the resurrection of the body.   This
particular form of the belief as it was perpetuated
in Christendom is so bound up with the belief in the
resurrection of Christ that we will defer its consideration till a later stage of our enquiry.[2]   Now we will
only ask whether philosophy has any valid objection
to urge against the belief in personal immortality.

No doubt philosophy is shy of it.   As has been
already noticed, speculative thought tends to depersonalize what it touches.   And the belief in personal
immortality is bound up with the emphasis on personality as a far more important category than any
abstraction such as thought or knowledge.   These
we believe to be functions or qualities of persons.
Fully rational being is only known to us as the being
of a person who feels and wills and thinks.   Philosophers like Dr. Bradley and Dr. Bosanquet are fond
of speaking of personality as " transcended," " dissolved in a higher unity," " merged," " blended,"
" fused," " absorbed."   I fear I must understand
Lord Haldane in a similar sense.   But I believe this

---

[1] See Ecclus. xl. 9–11, xliv. 10–15.

[2] The grounds of belief in Christ's resurrection are considered in
this volume in connexion with the discussion of miracles.   But
its full import as a part of the whole meaning of Christ's person and
work is reserved for the second volume.

tendency to depreciate the distinctive personal self, as if it were a merely temporary limitation on the large life of reason or spirit, to be wholly a mistaken tendency. I think the emphasis on personality both in God and in man as the highest category, an emphasis which we owe to Christianity, is one of the chief glories of that religion, and one chief clue to its power of being the religion of common men and not merely of an intellectual class. In fact, the deepening of the spiritual life, and spiritual vision in the best of men, tends on the whole conspicuously to make their personality more intense and more markedly individual. He that loseth his soul by utter unselfishness shall " save " it and " keep " it and " win " it. Personal character is a greater and deeper thing than any quality of a person such as the power of abstract thought. Moreover, the communion of souls in its most intimate form of friendship and love, though it proves that personalities can in wonderful ways interpenetrate one another, does not even tend to reduce the distinction of persons. It is, indeed, between those most different that personal intimacy is often most real and permanent. Finally, in their relation to God the souls of men whom we should describe as most absorbed in God are not so absorbed as to lose their proper and distinctive being. Paul and John the son of Zebedee and Augustine and Theresa of Avila do not in this life show any signs of becoming less individual by being united to God, nor do they ever lead us to suppose that when they pass the barrier of death it will be otherwise. They will see God, they believe—not become God.[1] In a sense,

---

[1] I know that some mystics have used language which suggests becoming God, but the conscience of Christendom has always been shocked.

the personality of God embraces all the world and all
finite personalities, but He has created finite personalities and given them the freedom to realize themselves *in* Him without losing themselves—to work
out their own salvation—surely not that the distinctive
personality so gradually and painfully won may lose
the supreme joy of offering to God its distinctive
contribution—its self. I think that our deepest moral
and spiritual experience—all the experience which
makes the belief that the spirit does not perish with
the death of the body a rational belief—leads us to
believe also that what survives death must be our
personal self, purified and deepened and enlarged,
but not merged or lost.

6. We remain now face to face with the only one
of the difficulties raised by philosophical or speculative enquiry which, to my mind, is really formidable
—that is, the question whether in view of the vast
area of seeming moral indifference which the universe
in its enormous spaces of time and extent presents,
and in view of the seeming cruelty of nature and of
the mysterious powers which control human destiny,
it is really reasonable to believe in a God who is both
the Creator and Sustainer of all that is, whose being in
some sort nature's laws must express, and who is at
the same time Perfect Goodness—Eternal Love.

This is a tremendous question indeed. I suppose
that in regard to it men in all ages have been differ-
ently disposed—some inclined towards optimism,
some towards pessimism. Seneca says in his day
that " the greater part of mankind complains of the
malignity of nature "; and certainly in our day the
effect of the war and its consequences has been to
strengthen the forces of pessimism among us. There
are very many among us who certainly have " the

will to believe," but who find the belief that God is love very difficult. The days seem to them far off when it was possible with any plausibility to contrast the " simple doctrine " that God is love with the " elaborate and difficult dogmas " of the Church. For they feel that it is only the dogmas that Jesus Christ is God, and His mind God's mind, and that God, the God of nature, really vindicated Him by raising Him from the dead, that do in fact sustain their tottering faith and hope in God.[1] With these dogmas, however, we are not yet concerned—only with the positive content of the prophetic revelation reaching its culmination in Jesus Christ; and as to the content of this there is no question.

These prophets and this Jesus, " the prophet mighty in word and in deed," proclaim with unhesitating assurance and emphasis the goodness of the one God who made and rules all things. And further, there will be no question that this assurance is conveyed to us—quite without arguments about apparently adverse facts, but at least in full view of all the facts in nature and in the world of man which appear to contradict it. It was not the sort of truth which their experience would have suggested to the prophets when the world was being trampled by remorseless and blood-stained powers, or to the rejected and crucified Christ. If they believed it and affirmed it as they did, it was as an assurance imparted to them by God Himself in spite of experience.

It is not then an " easy " doctrine. But is it really consistent with candid reflection upon experience, or as we say, consistent with the facts ?

First, we must open our eyes wide to take in all that is implied in the belief that God has created

[1] Cf. 1 Pet. i. 21.

hosts of free beings and made them his vicegerents in the world, in spite of the fact that their freedom involved the possibility of their rebellion, and that, in fact, such rebellion or sin on the widest scale has disordered the world and distorted its history. That is, we are bound to say, a fact, and a fact the full meaning of which we do not readily realize. It carries the vastest consequences. It is only with great difficulty that we can represent to our imagination what the world would have been as God meant it to be—that is, if sin and rebellion had not been, or had been but a rare and intermittent tendency. Even to-day, if the mass of men would repent or change their minds, and would set themselves to serve God and do His will, in a very few years we should have even in the dark places of the earth a paradise instead of a hell. And it is not only over human life that the influence of human perversity or ignorance extends. A distinguished professor of biology, who is not an apologist for Christian doctrine, Sir E. Ray Lankester, assures us that not only the mass of human diseases is due to sin, but that " every disease to which animals (and probably plants also) are liable, excepting as a transient and very exceptional occurrence, is due to man's interference." [1] Certainly thoughtless piety has constantly misused the phrase " it pleased God to order," or " to do " so and so, with regard to orderings and doings which we have the best reason to know are flat contrary to His will—of which we can only say,

---

[1] *The Kingdom of Man* (Constable, 1907), pp. 33 f. : " It is a remarkable thing—which possibly may be less generally true than our present knowledge seems to suggest—that the adjustment of organisms to their surroundings is so severely complete in Nature apart from Man, that diseases are unknown as constant and normal phenomena under these conditions."

with our Lord, " An enemy—some hostile will or
other—hath done this."[1]   Now, we certainly have no
faculties adequate to answer the question whether
the gift of freedom might not have been given with
less disastrous results.   It is a merely foolish question.
All we can do is to recognize that correlative with
freedom is the possibility of sin, and that the world
as God made it and would have had it be would
have been, as we can see, a wholly different world
from the world as it has in fact been.   Also we must
note that the deeply impressive voices that have so
continuously assured us that God is good, in face
of all their torturing experience of the world as it
is, have finally assured us also that His love has
eternity to work in, and is bound in the long issue of
things to do the utmost that love can do for every
single conscious human soul.   At the last, we can
easily conceive, every still conscious human soul
may be found saying, There is nothing that I
have experienced, however bitter and unjust and
humiliating at the time, which has not been for
good.[2]   We are never entitled to forget the warning

[1] Cf. Jas. iv. 1 : " Whence come wars and fightings among
you ? Come they not hence, even of your pleasures that war in
your members ? "   There is nothing in Shakespeare's presentation of
human nature more impressive than the sense which he gives us in
his great tragedies of the almost boundless havoc in human societies
which a single will, obsessed with some violent passion or wilfulness,
can work.

[2] Finally lost souls—only so by their own persistence in refusing
the known good and choosing the evil—I feel bound to believe there
may be.   To believe that it may be so is, I think, bound up with
accepting the reality of moral freedom.   But I conceive that the
lost also will recognize that the mind of God towards them was only
good.   And though their awakening must be awful indeed, and the
figures under which it is described are so, I do not think an orthodox
Christian is precluded from hoping that the issue of hell, which is
the state of the lost, will be extinction of personal consciousness or
dissolution of personality.

of Bishop Butler—that from the point of view of our present experience the world presents to us, at the best, " a scheme imperfectly comprehended."

Next, we must steadily contemplate how much of the progress of the world—not only the moral progress of the individual soul, but also the progress of the race, where progress has been—has been due to suffering and to vicarious suffering. We have no faculties capable of answering the question, What place would suffering have held in the world if there had been no sin ? But in the world as it is there is almost nothing worth having which can be won or maintained except at the cost of pain. As Pamela's parents said to her : "O, my child ! Trials are sore things ; and yet without them, we know not our-selves, nor what we are able to do."

I think that the rational result of these considera-tions, faithfully and thoughtfully entertained, is to remove a great part of the " heavy and the weary weight."

But there remains the oppressive feeling due to the inconceivably vast spaces of nature which seem to have no moral meaning or significance, and to the awful consideration of the pain of animals. But we need to restrain our imagination by attending to our almost boundless ignorance in these directions. For all we know there may be no fact or force in the vast universe which has not some attendant spirit whose destiny is as much conditioned by it as ours is by the world we inhabit. Truly we have not in our possible knowledge any, even the slightest, reason to deny rather than to affirm such a suggestion. We know nothing whatever about it. With regard, again, to the conscious pain of animals, though it remains to my mind that part of the whole " burden of the mystery " which is hardest to bear, we cannot really estimate their joys or pains, or the proportion of one to the other. The great naturalists appear to have been mostly, like Darwin, optimists in their estimate of the happiness of animals. And so far as animals attain to consciousness, have we any real grounds for denying that their painful contribution to the process of nature may have some recompense in some kind of life beyond ? We have indeed, here again, nothing approaching to knowledge. But I confess that the glint of pain in an animal's eye remains, if not a valid argument against belief in God's goodness, yet, as often as my mind dwells on it, a source of unrelieved discomfort. Of course, in regard to natural processes as a whole, we are bound to take note that the estimate of nature as a " gladiator's show," which was fashionable in Huxley's day, has been greatly modified, and almost reversed, by the emphasis which recent biology lays on the capacity for sociality, co-operation, and " unselfishness," as chief among the conditions which throughout the animal kingdom make for success. Indeed, Thomson and Geddes, in their recent manual,[1] dare to conclude their brief summary of scientific reflection on the subject with the words : " It is much for our pure natural history to see no longer struggle, but love, ' as creation's final law.' "

On the whole, I seem to myself to stand in this position. What I am conscious of is not a struggle between faith and reason. No ; it is reason in me which demands goodness in God. If I am rationally sure of anything, it is that I find impressed upon my inmost conscious being the obligation of goodness—

[1] *Evolution*, pp. 246–7.

12

the sense that I exist in order to be good. And I am
wholly unable to interpret this purpose of goodness,
which I cannot doubt to be real, except in terms of
the goodness of God. Thus it is reason in men which
makes them cry out for some sign of divine justice
and mercy. It is reason in Prometheus which, beyond
the cruelty of Zeus, cries out to some fundamental
justice at the roots of being. It is reason in Hecuba
which, above the vain gods of Olympus and deeper
than the powers of Hades, invokes some eternal
justice, by whatever name called, which punishes the
wrongdoer.[1] It is reason in Antigone which, behind
and above the state law, adores a moral law which
is divine, and in obedience to which she is prepared
to die. Reason, then, welcomes the revelation
which proclaims with such assurance the only word
which can make sense of the universe. And within
the region of human experience the truth of this
word of God, verified as it has been in the consciences
of thousands of the best of men, for whom it has
passed from faith into knowledge or assured conviction, presents on reflection no real difficulty. In the
remaining region of the non-human universe I am
rationally bound to lay great stress on my inevitable
ignorance. I have no faculties enabling me to
judge how much suffering is inevitably incident to
physical evolution, or whether any system less full
of pain could have been created. There remain,
however, in this region of the world, certain elements
in reality which it is certainly hard to reconcile with

---

[1] Euripides, *Troades*, l. 884. " O foundation of the earth and on
the earth having thy seat, whosoever thou art, hard for knowledge
to find, Zeus or Necessity of nature or Mind of men—thee I addressed
in prayer : for moving in thy silent path thou guidest mortal
destinies according to justice."

divine goodness ; but I am sure they cannot reasonably be held to justify rejection of the assurance, which so convinces me of its divine origin, as to the goodness of God, and which, on the ground of human nature, where alone anything like adequate knowledge is possible for me, has justified itself so fundamentally to the best men. If I stand before Christ and listen to His assurance and reject it, I seem to be self-convicted of wilfulness.

III

Comparative Religion.—Among the comparatively new sciences which have disturbed old-standing religious positions, we reckoned the science of comparative religions. As against the crude, old-fashioned view of heathen religions as simply false, this new science has been sympathetically investigating the various forms which the religious faculty or instinct has taken among various races and in various periods ; it has sought to observe religion as a whole among men, to study its origins, its processes of development, its moments of special illumination, its deteriorations, its similarities and differences, and all its apparatus of priesthoods, sacraments, *mana*, tabus, rituals, and sacred books—all with an impartial mind as so many manifestations of one common spirit and tendency. Then the question arises : Is this sort of impartial study and appreciation of the various religions of the world compatible with the belief that one race, Israel, was chosen by God to be the organ of His special self-disclosure—a self-disclosure which had its culmination in Jesus Christ, and through Him was destined to become the catholic and universal religion—the one all-embracing faith for mankind ?

We may answer, surely, that there is no incompatibility. I cannot understand why this belief should make us in any way desire to minimize or regard with grudging eyes the truth and excellence which appear in other religions. When Christianity came out into the world of Greek culture, though it combated vigorously what it regarded as the errors and corruptions of Hellenism, yet, at least through many of its greatest teachers, it acknowledged its large element of truth and it assimilated its treasures, appreciating it as having been, in some sense like the religion of Israel, a preparation for Christ. It did this because it believed that God left not Himself without witness in any nation, and that the divine Word or Reason and the Divine Spirit were everywhere in the world at work. This is the temper in which we would approach all forms of religion. If we find high thoughts in Babylonian psalms, or in the psalm of the Egyptian heretic king Akhnaton, or in the sacred books of Persia, if we find a wonderful ethical beauty in the wisdom of the Buddha or of Laotze or of Confucius, or again a divine power in the dramatists and philosophers of Greece, we ought not to be in any kind of way scandalized. If marked similarities to the ideas and institutions of Judaism and Christianity present themselves in the sacramental cults and rituals of many nations, we should be delighted to note and appreciate them. All this will be no more bar to our believing that Israel had a special vocation to be " the sacred school of the knowledge of God and of the spiritual life for all mankind," than a sympathetic interest in the art of all the world will hinder a perception of the special vocation of Greece. We have already examined our reasons for believing that Israel had this special vocation.

We contend that no religion can, as a school of spiritual truth, be set alongside of Israel's. That is a matter of evidence. At a later stage of our enquiry we shall seek to estimate the claim of Christianity to be the catholic and final religion, and its ethical standard the perfect standard. That, again, will be a matter for candid consideration. But granted that those claims are true, they should generate in our minds no kind of grudging jealousy towards other religions. If Christianity is destined in the providence of God to supersede them all, this, we conceive, would be not by excluding, but by including and assimilating to the fuller truth, all the elements of value which each religion is found to contain.

It is, of course, quite as possible to over-estimate the merits of a non-Christian religion as to depreciate them unduly—to under-estimate the corruptions which it has nourished as to magnify them.

For instance, it has become the fashion in many quarters even ludicrously to assimilate Buddhism to Christianity. But, as a matter of fact, they embody radically different principles. Thus the root principle of Christianity is that life in all its forms is good as the gift of the good God, and that, the closer our union with God, the more intense and full will our personal life become : as our Lord said, " I am come that they might have life, and have it abundantly " ; " I am the Life " ; while the root principle of Buddhism is " that life is the greatest of evils," and Sakya Muni " devoted all the strength of his soul to free himself from it, and to free others ; and to do this so that, even after death, life shall not be renewed any more, but be completely destroyed at

of Chronicles a partly imaginative history—history written, not as it was, but as it should have been from the point of view of the later priests and scribes. And besides this, we have in the Old Testament all kinds of literature : devotional poetry, as in the Psalms; moral stories, like Esther and Jonah, and the stories of Daniel, written on a rather remote historical basis; dramas, like the book of Job and the Canticles ; philosophy of a special kind, as in the Wisdom literature and Ecclesiastes, and (what is peculiar to Judaism) the later Apocalypses—much of this literature being pseudonymous, as the latter part of the book of Daniel, dating from the second century, is written as in the person of Daniel, who lived four centuries before, or Ecclesiastes in the person of Solomon. And in some of the Prophets there is, besides their genuine work, the work of later prophets, such as " the second Isaiah " (chapter xl. and onward), incorporated with it.

When such results are pressed upon believers in the Old Testament, they are apt angrily to ask, " Then what remains of our faith ? " and I have tried to convey the answer in chapters iii and iv. We must start from the solid historical ground of the period of the written prophets. We must reassure ourselves, on this solid ground, of the reality of God's self-revelation. Then we shall find ourselves believers of a surety that God did " in many parts and in many manners speak in old times unto the fathers by the prophets "—that the Spirit, who is God, really " spake by the prophets." That is the essential thing. Then we shall recognize how the prophetic spirit gradually purged and reinterpreted the folk-lore and traditions of Israel to express moral and religious truth instead of empty falsehood, and how there were different grades and kinds of inspiration, as in psalmists and wise men and codifiers of law and compilers of stories for moral edification, all in different degrees inspired by the Divine Spirit. So viewed, the Old Testament not only becomes much more interesting, but also holds its unique spiritual value not in opposition to, but in harmony with, historical criticism. It is in recognition of the legitimacy of such considerations that our Anglican Convocations have remodelled the question and answer which, in the Anglican service for the Ordination of Deacons, is to be put to those entering the ministry and is by them solemnly to be answered. The question used to run simply, " Do you unfeignedly believe all the canonical scriptures of the Old and New Testament? " This question remains, but the sense in which it is asked is defined by additional words, " as conveying to us in divers manners the Revelation of God which is consummated in Jesus Christ." And the answer, which hitherto has been " I do believe them," becomes " I do so believe them."

•　　　•　　　•　　　•　　　•

Now, I have tried to set out very briefly the result in my own mind of bringing the intellectual contents of the Biblical revelation to the bar of the various sciences and of philosophy, acknowledging the jurisdiction of the courts in one sense and denying it in another—denying their right to exclude *a priori* the possibility or credibility of divine self-disclosure, but acknowledging their right to test its contents by their own sciences, seeing that, at bottom, the acknowledgement of the validity of our reason is the only basis of any kind of certitude. But we have not found that the sciences or philosophy provide any

valid bar to the belief in the divine revelation, the
reality of which impressed us so deeply. Accepting
the revelation whole-heartedly as of God, we find
ourselves still free men with free minds in the worlds
of philosophy and science, more free, we dare to say,
than the unbeliever and the sceptic.

Additional note to p. 144. I cannot understand how Dr. Rashdall
(*Theory of Good and Evil,* p. 317) can contend that to accept determin-
ism, as he finally does, which certainly at the last analysis makes
the sense of freedom, responsibility and guilt an illusion, makes no
serious difference to morality and religion. He admits that this is
" the most important question." He admits that " our knowledge
of the empirical facts is far too small to enable us to say that . . .
the hypothesis [of indeterminism] would be indefensible " if
" any demand of the moral or religious consciousness really necessi-
tates, or even strongly recommends " it. But he proceeds to argue
that it does not. This, I say, I find amazing. It is to me quite
certain that if I had believed myself at the last resort necessarily
determined to do whatever I do, the spring of moral effort would
have been quenched in me. It is only the conviction of real freedom
and real reponsibility which makes resistance to evil imperative and
possible.

CHAPTER VII

THE HISTORICAL RELIGION

I⊤ is true in a sense of the Old Testament religion that it is an historical religion—in the sense, that is, that it depends upon the belief that God revealed Himself, not merely in the order of the world as a whole, but particularly and more fully in an historical process in a particular race and period, extending from Moses to Christ. But this conviction rests upon no single event or group of events which is open in any degree to reasonable doubt. We have been able to study its grounds without having to discuss whether anything actually happened which critics deny or any document is authentic which critics doubt. But the case is quite different when we advance upon the ground of the New Testament. The faith which is presented to us in the New Testament indisputably centres upon a single person, in a sense in which it would not be true of any other great religion. Thus Buddhism centres upon Sakya Muni, in that it regards him as the discoverer of a method of escape from the will to live with all its desires and illusions—that was " the way " or " the path." The Buddha is a very moving historical character about whom we know a good deal. But nothing depends upon the verdict which criticism may pass upon the recorded incidents of the life of the Buddha. " The way " remains none the less to be followed by disciples all the world over, who accept the principle that life and the desire for life is an evil and the root of all evil. " The way " would remain if the personal leader were proved a myth. Mohammed, again, is believed in as a prophet, but no more. His existence and substantially the character of his teaching no one can doubt. I think myself that no believer in the reality of the inspiration of the prophets will be likely to doubt that he was originally really inspired to restore, as he professed to do, the religion of Abraham, that is the basis of the true religion ; and that his rejection of Christianity, so far as he rejected it, is to be attributed in great measure to the exceedingly debased form in which it was presented to him. But there was nothing original or unique in his teaching about God or man ; and whatever the estimate we form of this wonderful man, at the beginning of his career or in its subsequent stages, nothing much depends on any particular incident which criticism is concerned to doubt or deny.

But it is quite different when we come to consider the religion of Jesus Christ as it appears in the New Testament, and (let us say) in the Apostles' Creed, which expresses its doctrine about God in a summary form. Everything there centres upon the person of Jesus, and the functions and aspects of His person, and (in the Creed almost exclusively) upon particular incidents of His life—His birth, His death, His resurrection, His ascension into Heaven, His mission of the Spirit with its consequences. These events enter into the substance of the belief. It is a belief that God has taken action for man's redemption in such and such historical events.

Not, of course, that the Christian Church has ever been content with a merely historical witness. Christ

Himself was plainly aware that not the most miraculous external events by themselves would change the heart of man. "If they hear not Moses and the prophets, neither will they be persuaded though one rose from the dead." Thus the Christian appeal to certain events in history has always been balanced by the appeal to a continuous spiritual experience of need and satisfaction. It has expected the Spirit of God, working in the hearts of men, to generate such an inward disposition and experience as to make the testimony to past events credible and certain to their minds. And it has, in fact, been the witness of the corporate life of the Church, or of the lives of genuine Christians—the saints, which has made, as it was intended to make, the message of their creed intelligible and credible to others. Thus no one can reasonably accuse Christianity of merely appealing to past events. Nevertheless the whole continuous spiritual appeal of Christianity to the hearts and consciences of men rests upon, or is bound up with, a specific witness borne by certain original eye-witnesses to certain events. The inward assurance is made to rest upon facts—as St. Paul said at Athens, "God has given assurance to us (concerning his purpose in Christ) in that he hath raised him from the dead."

It is because the asserted facts are largely supernatural or miraculous, and because so much of spiritual consequence is made to turn upon them—the whole question, in fact, of God's redemptive purpose—that the Christian records have been, especially in recent times, the subjects of sharply critical examination and many very radical and very different reconstructions, through at least two generations of critics. No doubt the existence of Jesus of Nazareth as a teacher, and certain ideas as to the character of His teaching, may be said to be undisputed by any sane critic. Nevertheless, the positive residuum left by the criticism of, let us say, Harnack, or Schweitzer, or Kirsopp Lake, is in each case disputed by other critics; and the residuum which can be even approximately called undisputed seems to most of us very meagre. In any case, it stands in very marked contrast to the robust and confident religion of the New Testament or the Creeds.

Its dependence on historical events, or events declared to have actually happened, is constantly spoken of as the disadvantage of Christianity, because it is thereby rendered constantly liable to attack by that singularly nervous and subtle and solvent influence, modern criticism. And thus many people, from Ritschl to Inge, have been anxious to disembarrass Christianity from the elements which make it obnoxious to this sort of attack. But the question is whether they do not thereby disembarrass it of its essential worth; or even whether anything is gained by calling the residuum Christianity. The strength of Christianity—its power of appeal to men of different ages and classes and educations—lies, as seems to me indisputable, in its being rooted in a person of whom we have adequate, trustworthy knowledge, or, in other words, upon the substantial historical truth of the Gospels—not their critical infallibility, but their substantial trustworthiness. If this is a position impossible to maintain, or if the destructive criticism which has been so long prevalent in the intellectual world has its way, I do not doubt that " something will remain," but it will be a residuum so intellectually uncertain in outline that it will result in diverse " schools of thought " for studious men—which will not make much appeal to the common man, hard pressed by life, and not inclined to subtle thought—side by side with different sorts of superstitions for the vulgar, or blankly dogmatic creeds for those who at all costs must have a definite religion and are prepared not to think for themselves. No one can contemplate such a return to the conditions which preceded the advent of Christianity into the world without a sense of disaster.

The Christianity, then, of the New Testament or of the Creeds, the Christianity which at its best has proved itself a power of such incomparable force for the redemption of common human life, is a distinctively historical religion—rooted in an historical person presumed to be adequately known, and in particular crucial incidents concerning Him, notably His death upon the Cross and His resurrection the third day from the dead. And, because we are determined to give our reason its full claim of unrestricted freedom, we will not be guilty of the folly of ascribing too much authority, or final authority, to the intellectuals of a particular epoch. The " intellectuals " in history, even when they seemed to wield in their generation an almost incontestable authority, have too often proved mistaken, and their confident positions have too often been abandoned. Thus at least their authority must not restrain us from thinking and judging for ourselves. So we will, with all the openmindedness of which we are capable, examine the claims made on behalf of the Christ of tradition to be the Christ of legitimate history, to see whether they fall, or perchance can stand.

That this enquiry may be freely made we need to have in mind three considerations.

1. The first concerns the nature of God. Many of our philosophers, like Dr. Pringle Pattison, appear

to deprecate any attribution to God of particular
action along particular channels, as if that derogated
from His universal presence and action in the world.
This plainly prejudices their minds against the
" particularity " of the Christian religion.   But our
newly recovered or newly acquired belief in the
self-disclosure of God through the Hebrew prophets
will not admit of our entertaining this abstract
philosophical scruple.   Here, we are convinced, is an
instance of God's acting along a particular line by
way of inspiration, much more continuously and
intensely than in the world at large.   His universal
action is found not to exclude particular intention
and particular action.   And surely this is the verdict
of nature as a whole.   God acts more intensely in
man's mind and personality than in rocks or beasts.
He shows more of Himself in the free moral conscience
than in the automatic action of plants.   Again, the
spirit of beauty—which is God in one aspect—was
more intensely present in the Greeks than in the
Romans or the rest of the races.   It is a fact to which
all belief in God must accommodate itself, that God's
general presence and action is compatible with His
fuller and intenser presence and action here and there.
And there is no *a priori* reason why His fuller and
intenser self-revelation of Himself through the
Hebrew prophets should not have had its culmination
in the particular historical person of Jesus.

2. We shall not for a moment be so foolish as to
entertain the idea of exempting the sacred documents
of Christianity from the severest and freest criticism.
Reason essentially demands that historical criticism
shall apply itself with equal and full freedom to every
document.   But obviously historical criticism reaches
different results when it applies itself to different

epochs and to different kinds of documents. It reaches different results when it applies itself to the legend of Arthur, the story of Alfred and the history of Henry VIII, or when it applies itself in the Old Testament to Adam, to Abraham, to Elijah, and to Isaiah. We must apply criticism to all records with the varying results which the records warrant. But we must be very careful in each case that what we are applying is really historical criticism, and not what may be more properly called intellectual prejudice. No doubt all historical criticism implies, more or less, intellectual presuppositions—it must come to its examination of documents with certain canons of probability. But these canons of probability must be very carefully examined and themselves criticized. All good historical criticism must be very submissive to the real evidence in each particular case; and while it cannot do without *praejudicia*— that is, general presuppositions, based upon its general philosophy of experience—it must be very careful that these *praejudicia* are not arbitrary " prejudices "—whether ecclesiastical prejudices or rationalistic. And to secure this, it is necessary that the *praejudicia* of any current school of critics should be exposed to the light and carefully scrutinized, so that nothing should intervene between our judgement and the evidence, which prevents the latter from having its due force.

3. Thirdly, we had better seek to estimate, in the light of the general experience of mankind, the relative value for religion of myths or symbols on the one hand—that is, statements or stories which cannot make any serious claims to be literally true—and serious statements of fact on the other. It is necessary to consider this question, because recent " modernists "

13

in religion, convinced that the miraculous narratives of the New Testament cannot be historically true, have been consoling themselves, and seeking to console others, with the reflection that the creed and scriptures contain confessedly many apparent statements of fact which are only symbolic and not literally true statements, and that no serious harm to religion will occur if we are compelled to go a little further and to recognize that such phrases as " he was born of the Virgin," " he was raised the third day from the dead," " he ascended into heaven," are not literally historical, but have symbolical value, symbolizing the spiritual truths that the birth of Jesus was providential and His nature pure, that the apostles were convinced by spiritual visions that death had not triumphed over Him, and that His moral Lordship is a spiritual reality.

Now, we cannot doubt that "symbols" or "myths" (as Plato conceived them) have played a great and beneficent part in religion and must continue to do so. Thus (i) the Fathers of the Christian Church, following St. Paul, have always been forward to assert that all our statements about the being of God as He is in Himself—the transcendental reality—are symbolical, in the sense that they are the expression in human language of a reality which we cannot really grasp with our present faculties or expound in human terms. " Man has no celestial language," and can only express eternal things in the best phrases that experience has provided him with, confessing their inadequacy. What they have contended is that such phrases as " Three persons in one substance " are the best phrases which human language can supply ; that they have divine authorization behind them ; and that to decline to use such phrases because they are inadequate would be to open the door to positively misleading denials or misconceptions.

(ii) There is a whole group of subjects which lie at present outside possible human experience—the beginnings of the world, the end of the world, heaven and hell and the state of the dead—with regard to which there would be to-day very general agreement to recognize that we know nothing except in symbols or myths, such as the stories of creation in Genesis—which there is every reason to believe inspired of God, but are none the less not historical—or the visions of the end of the world and the day of judgement and heaven and hell. It is commonly said that in early Christian days these stories or pictures were believed to be literally true, and that it is a great change to accept them as symbolic. Now, it is certainly the case that in the middle ages and under the Protestant Reformation an undue literalism prevailed ; but in the first four Christian centuries the principle of symbolic representation of all that lies outside present human experience was at least widely accepted, and applied to the story of creation and the visions of the end. About heaven and hell it is commonly said that till recent days everyone believed that heaven was a place above our heads and hell a pit beneath our feet. If, however, we consider how Platonism had influenced the educated world, with its doctrine of myths or symbolic stories about creation and heaven and hell, and how deep its influence was on the Christian Church, or at least on its educated members and especially the Greeks, we shall be inclined to doubt this. Certainly Church teachers frankly recognized that " he sitteth on the right hand of God " was a symbolic statement and not a literal truth. Certainly St. Paul, in his language

which were in reality quite different, and which might quite as well have been described as they were.[1]

We must approach, then, this question: Did the historical self-disclosure of God through the Hebrew prophets really culminate in the way which the New Testament represents—that is, in a person who passed the measure of mere humanity, and in a series of events connected with Him, some of which at least are conspicuously supernatural and miraculous? All questions, however, concerning the person of Christ are deferred to another volume. But the circle of ideas about Christ's person and functions in the New Testament is so closely bound up with the specific Old Testament doctrine of God, with which this volume is concerned, that we will devote ourselves at once to two questions, which must receive solution before questions about Christ's person can be profitably asked or answered. (1) Can we rely upon the New Testament documents as historical, when we treat them critically? (2) Can we regard the miraculous incidents recorded as credible, supposing the evidence appears to us to be cogent? Or in other words, is it fair to say that, if we believe the prophetic teaching about God, which Jesus Christ so certainly confirmed, to be really true, we shall find that no *a priori* reason remains in our minds constraining us to disbelieve the witness of the New Testament to miraculous occurrences; and conversely that what makes that witness incredible to so many intellectuals of our day is that in fact they do not believe in the God of the prophets and Christ, but have re-

[1] Mr. Clement Webb has dealt admirably, as it seems to me, with the relation of myth to history, both for Plato and for us (see *God and Personality*, pp. 168, 175, 177, 179), and has spoken true words on the value of a distinctively historical religion (*Studies in the History of Natural Theology*, p. 30).

verted to a conception of the purely immanent God, which does not essentially differ from the conception of God current in the Greek world which Christianity superseded ?

Let us seek, then, first of all, to obtain an estimate of the historical value of the New Testament documents in general and especially of those most important for our purpose.

CHAPTER VIII

THE HISTORICAL WORTH OF THE NEW TESTAMENT

I

CHRISTIANITY presents itself, then, to mankind as, in a special sense, an historical religion, that is as a Gospel and a life centred in and based upon a certain group of historical events—the life, death, resurrection, ascension of Jesus of Nazareth and the mission of His Spirit to perpetuate His activity in His Church. History has proved the manifest advantages of a religion which thus makes its appeal to facts of actual occurrence, and we have recognized also its equally manifest peril, supposing it should appear that historical criticism of a legitimate kind can invalidate the supposed facts. It is necessary, therefore, at this stage to look to our New Testament documents and to ascertain whether we can trust both the direct record of the Gospels and Acts as properly historical, and the rest of the documents as being in the main what they profess to be, and as supplying therefore abundant evidence of what the first generation of Christians believed and practised, and of their general outlook over the world.

Now, in respect of the documents of the New Testaments, the advanced critics of the Tübingen school, dominant half a century ago, and their followers, were accustomed to assign most of them to comparatively late dates and to unknown authors. This was the view which called itself critical a generation ago.

But of recent years there has been, on these questions of date and authorship, a marked reaction, of which Adolph Harnack—the greatest, I suppose, of contemporary scholars in the Christian literature of the first century—is representative. When he published in 1897 his *Chronology of Ancient Christian Literature*, the following passage produced a sensation :

" There was a time," he wrote, " and the general public is still at that date, when it was considered necessary to hold the most ancient Christian literature, including the New Testament, as a tissue of deception and falsehood. That time has now passed. For science it was an episode during which she learned much, and after which she has much to forget. The results of my investigations go in a reactionary sense far beyond what one might call the moderate position in the criticism of to-day. The most ancient literature of the Church is, on all chief points, and in the majority of details, veracious and worthy of belief from the point of view of literary history. In the whole New Testament there is probably only one work which can, in the strictest sense of the word, be called pseudonymous, it is II Peter. . . . I do not hesitate to use the word retrogression, for things should be called by their right names. In our criticism of the most ancient sources of Christianity, we are, without any doubt, in course of returning to tradition. The problems arising from the criticism of the sources . . . as well as the difficulties in the way of constructing true history will probably present themselves, in a few years, under an aspect essentially different from that they bear to-day, to the majority of competent critics."

This declaration is accompanied with a good deal of vituperation of critics as men " fixing their attention on all kinds of details in order to argue against clear and decisive conclusions." [1] This lan-

---

[1] Harnack, *Chronologie* (Leipzig, 1897), vol. i, pp. viii–x. This was followed by Harnack's works on St. Luke and the Acts, entirely reversing his previous opinions. See Sanday's *Life of Christ*

guage, I say, created a sensation as coming from one who had shared the more destructive opinions, and who still in his beliefs about Christ remained as far removed from orthodoxy as ever. We in England who had watched the struggle between the destructive German school of critics and our own conservative scholars, amongst whom Dr. Lightfoot was the greatest, saw in such language the recognition of the fact that, on the main questions of date and authorship, the conservatives had gained a solid victory—not a victory over criticism, but a victory of sane criticism against those who were really misusing it for ulterior purposes.

1. Let us then see how matters stand about our Gospels. The canonization of four Gospels—that is, their selection by the Church as the four authoritative records of the Master's life—goes back to the middle of the second century.[1] Let us now proceed to examine their credentials, or at least the credentials of two of them—St. Mark and St. Luke.

As to St. Mark we have the famous statement contained in one of the fragments from the lost work of Papias, the Bishop of Hierapolis in Phrygia— " Expositions of the Oracles of the Lord "—written not later than about A.D. 130. This Papias, we ought to say, gloried in not depending upon written documents, but upon competent witnesses, and relates how he had taken his opportunities of intercourse with those who had been companions of the first disciples of Jesus, or " the elders," as he

in Recent Research, p. 76, note 1. Sir William Ramsay, the distinguished traveller, scholar, and historian of New Testament times, is another example of a man who began with the Tübingen view, and was converted by the evidence of facts and documents.

[1] See Burkitt, *The Gospel History and its Transmission* (Clarke), p. 257.

calls them. "If ever anyone came who had been a follower of the elders, I would enquire as to the discourses of the elders, what was said by Andrew, or what by Peter, or what by Philip, or what by Thomas or James, or what by John or Matthew or any other of the disciples of the Lord; and the things which Aristion and the elder John say.[1] For I did not think that I could get so much profit from the contents of books as from the utterances of a living and abiding voice." This, then, is his statement about Mark and his Gospel.

"This also the elder said: Mark, having become the interpreter of Peter, wrote down accurately everything that he remembered of the things that were either said or done by Christ; but, however, not in order. For he neither heard the Lord, nor had been a follower of His; but afterwards, as I said, he was a follower of Peter, who framed his teaching according to the needs [of his hearers], but not with the design of giving a connected account of the Lord's words. Thus Mark committed no error in thus writing down some things as he remembered them. For he took heed to one thing: not to omit any of the things he had heard, or to set down anything falsely therein."[2]

This account of the origin of St. Mark's Gospel we can accept as historical, unless it were so rigorously interpreted as to mean that there is nothing in St. Mark's Gospel which is not derived from Peter's teaching. Anyone who reads the Gospel, and notes how much of it consists of scenes in which St. Peter figures, will feel its probability.[3] Taking it, as is now generally done, for true, we have to consider who this John

---

[1] Aristion and John are regarded as still living at the time of his enquiries.

[2] Salmon's trans. (in the main), *Dict. of Chr. Biog.*, iv, p. 186.

[3] See Batiffol's *Credibility of the Gospels* (Longmans), p. 126.

Mark who wrote the Gospel was. We find him in the Acts,[1] about fifteen years after Pentecost, in his mother's house at Jerusalem, and this house we find a place of resort for the first Christians. It must have been a fairly large house, to hold the " many " who were gathered together and praying. It had an outer gate and a portress, like the gate and portress at the high priest's house (John xviii. 16). There Mark must have enjoyed the fullest opportunities of seeing and hearing the apostles and first disciples, both men and women. He drank constantly at the fountain head of that oral tradition which lies behind all the written Gospels, that witness of the apostolic company to what they had seen and heard " all the time that the Lord Jesus went in and went out among us, beginning from the baptism of John unto the day that He was received up from us." [2] He was among the men (and women) whose special privilege it was to treasure this witness. In his Gospel[3] there is introduced the incident of the young man in a linen cloth who was a spectator of our Lord's arrest. It is so singular, and so irrelevant to what goes before and after, that I do not think it can have any meaning but one. It is like an irrelevant figure in a sacred picture of the Renaissance which has in its mouth the label with the words *Iste perfecit opus*. The young man must have been the author of the Gospel. So we should suppose that his familiarity with the apostolic company was of long standing. Thus when Barnabas and Paul returned to Antioch from their visit to Jerusalem, which had been undertaken to

[1] xii. 12, 25.   [2] Acts i. 21-2.
[3] xiv. 51-2. Whether his mother's house contained the *cenaculum* is matter of pure conjecture. That St. Mark was the " young man " is something near to certainty : see Salmon's *Human Element in Gospels* (Murray), pp. 499–500.

carry assistance to the Church of Judaea under the threat of famine, John Mark, Barnabas's cousin, was a natural person for them to take back with them to help in their work. He was closely associated with them in the early stages of the first missionary journey.[1] But he left them before they went inland from Perga to the Pisidian Antioch—it is conjectured because his training at Jerusalem left him still unwilling to commit himself to St. Paul's " liberal " platform in respect of the welcome to be given to the Gentiles. A few years later he is still at Antioch, when Paul and Barnabas had their sharp contention as to whether he was a fit person to be a second time their companion. As it was, Paul and Barnabas separated in consequence of the dispute, and Mark went with his cousin Barnabas alone. There follows a gap in our knowledge about Mark of some ten or twelve years. Then we find him with St. Paul in his prison at Rome,[2] a trusted friend, but apparently just about to start for Asia. Then later again in St. Paul's second captivity,[3] we find him writing to Timothy in Ephesus and begging him to take Mark and bring him with him (to Rome), for " he is profitable to me for ministry." [4] This was no doubt Mark's function—not originality, but ministry to those greater than himself. A year or so later, after St. Paul's death, Peter writes from Rome, in his first epistle,[5] of Sylvanus, " a faith-

---

[1] Acts xiii. 5.   [2] Col. iv. 10.

[3] That St. Paul was liberated from his first captivity in Rome, which is described in the Acts, is rendered certain by the fact that Clement of Rome, writing towards the end of the first century, asserts (cap. v) that St. Paul went to " the limit of the West" before he was put to death. No one writing in Rome could mean by this phrase anything but Spain : see Lightfoot's note. Granted this, it seems to me that it is unreasonable to doubt the historical *data* of 2 Timothy.

[2] 2 Tim. iv. 11.   [5] 1 Pet. v. 13.

ful brother," who is to carry his letter, and of "Mark my son," who is with him. This reminds us of the statement of Papias's elder—that he was "Peter's interpreter." The relationship indicated suggests a prolonged connexion between the two men; and presumably we may fill up the ten or twelve years' blank space in Mark's life with the picture of him as Peter's companion, wherever he may have been, hearing his often-repeated teaching about the earlier experiences of the twelve with their Lord, and either noting it down at the time or preparing to write by storing it in his memory.

Well, now, after all these experiences, who—outside the twelve apostles—could be better qualified than Mark to write an account of the ministry of Jesus? He had lived so long in the atmosphere of the apostolic witness. And when, without overburdening ourselves with commentaries, we set ourselves to the study of his Gospel—how does it strike us? I speak for myself: it produces upon me an irresistible impression that I am in the presence of reality. I do not know how often, after reading some "critical" work having for its aim to prove that even Mark's account is two or three removes off the original facts, I have gone back to read the little book itself without note or comment, and received afresh this irresistible impression. I am sure that I am here, again and again, listening to one who records what he himself saw and heard—the look of the face of Jesus, the tones of His voice, His gestures, the movement and feelings of the crowd. No doubt you have that feeling sometimes when you read the best novelists. But this sort of realistic power did not exist in the literary circles out of which the Gospels came. And this particular Gospel is singularly destitute of literary skill or grace. Besides, the modern novelists describe for us ordinary human nature. It may be safely conjectured that even they would not have succeeded in producing out of their imagination a life-like image of so supernaturally conceived a person as Jesus. The Gospel, we feel assured, is not the work of either the crude popular imagination which fashions a legend, such as we get in the apocryphal Gospels, or the individual imagination which produces an historical romance or adorns a tradition. Here is the real Man in his real surroundings, as one saw and heard and bare witness.[1] And this one, on internal indications, we believe to be, as tradition tells us he was, Simon Peter.

I do not mean that it is all Peter. Suppose that beside Peter's story of the feeding of the five thousand, Mark heard another story of a miraculous feeding, in which the numbers were four thousand instead of five thousand, and seven loaves instead of five, and mistook it for a different incident, and so gave us an account of two events where really there was but one, this would make no material difference to us. We are asking not for infallibility, but for quite trustworthy history.

It cannot be pleaded that Mark, even if he often heard Peter tell the same incident, could not have remembered his words so minutely. On the contrary, that was the special faculty of the Jewish disciple.

---

[1] See Hawkins, *Horae Synopticae*, pp. 95–105. He quotes from A. B. Bruce on this Gospel : " These marks [in the Gospel] are such as to suggest an eye and ear witness as the source of many narratives, and a narrator unembarrassed by reverence. This feeling, we know, does come into play in biographical delineations of men whose characters have become invested with sacredness, and its influence grows with time. The high esteem in which they are held more or less controls biographers, and begets a tendency to leave out humble facts, etc."

Mark had been trained in Jerusalem presumably, in the Jewish schools, where exact verbal memory was the very faculty especially cultivated. He would have been trained to be an adept in this very thing. " The good disciple," said the Jews, " is like a cistern built of concrete, which does not lose one drop." [1] Our modern education is on quite different lines. Also the Synoptic records are even for us singularly easy to remember, not only our Lord's words, but the records as a whole. What we should suppose is that Peter gave regular instructions, in whatever church he was temporarily abiding, and selected a group of incidents and sayings such as he considered best adapted to his hearers, and that these were frequently repeated, so that St. Mark could well reproduce them quite accurately. This is exactly what Papias's " elder " suggests to us.

It is often asked how it can be that there is no indication, or so little indication, in Mark of a Jerusalem ministry such as the Fourth Gospel records, if this were really historical. But I think this question is based upon a mistake. What gives the scope to Mark's narrative is mainly the selection of incidents for the first instruction of converts made by Peter. There was no intention of making a complete record.

We take note that, though St. Mark must have been very familiar with Paul's mind and Peter's mind as we find it reflected in their epistles, the narrative of his Gospel is extraordinarily free from any influence of a doctrinal kind derived from such experience. All the atmosphere of the record is the atmosphere of the first discipleship with its ignorance and slowness of spiritual perception; and the phraseology and

[1] See Batiffol, pp. 162 f.

manner of teaching is that of Jesus and no one else—
even when, as in the case of the title " Son of Man "
or the method of teaching by parables, the phraseology
and manner had been quite abandoned in the churches
of apostolic foundation.

On the exact date of Mark's Gospel, and on the
question of there having been more than one edition,
we need not dwell. The elder's information suggests
certainly that Mark wrote when he was no longer a
hearer of Peter, that is, when Peter was dead, and so
Irenaeus tells us. We may suppose the Gospel to
have been written, as it now stands, just after Peter's
death, say in A.D. 65–7. The suggestions which were
abundantly made in Tübingen days of a second-century
date have now been abandoned.

My contention is, then, that in John Mark you
have a man admirably qualified to give us an exact
account of the story of the apostles about their
experiences with our Lord, and especially of St. Peter's
story, and that we have every reason to believe that
he has reproduced it with the most faithful and simple
diligence. St. Mark's Gospel, then, has every claim
to count for good history.

2. Now let us pass from St. Mark to St. Luke and
the two books ascribed to him—the third Gospel and
the Acts of the Apostles. There does not appear to
have been any question raised in early days as to the
authorship of either of these books. In the preface to
what is (I am not alone in thinking) one of the best
and most interesting commentaries on any book of
the Bible, Mr. Rackham's Commentary on the Acts,[1]
will be found a summary of the reasons for believing
the tradition to be true as regards the Acts and
incidentally as regards the Gospel. The following

[1] In the *Westminster Commentaries* (Methuen).

points may be regarded as certain, in my opinion. (1) That the Acts is the work of one author, that is, that St. Paul's travelling companion, who often implies his presence at the scenes he records by the use of the pronoun " we," was the author of the whole book.[1] (2) That the Gospel and the Acts are by the same author. (3) That no one of St. Paul's travelling companions can be put in plausible rivalry with St. Luke " the beloved physician," to whom tradition ascribes the books. (4) That the language of the books themselves supplies the evidence that the author was a well-educated man and most probably a physician, owing to his use of careful medical language.[2] Granted the authorship, a very interesting question arises as to the date. The Acts takes us up to the end of the second year of St. Paul's imprisonment at Rome. Then it closes, as we feel abruptly, with an adverb. Is it conceivable that if, as has been commonly supposed, the Acts was written some fifteen years or more later, the author could have given no indication of the result of St. Paul's trial or of the manner of his death ; or that he could have given so favourable an impression of the policy of the Empire towards the Church, without the least hint that it was so soon to pass into a policy of deliberate persecution, under which Peter and Paul would be martyred with many others ? Is it likely that no hint would have been given that Paul was mistaken when he assured the sorrowing Ephesians that he would " see their

[1] This was proved by Sir John Hawkins, *Horae Synopticae*, pp. 148 ff. Harnack has not recently added much to the cogency of the proofs : see Headlam's *Miracles*, p. 166 n.

[2] This was the argument of Hobart, *Medical Language of St. Luke*. He overpressed his argument. But I think that, after all deductions, enough solid ground remains for his argument to stand upon firmly.

face no more " ? [1] Are not all the probabilities of the case met by the theory that the Acts was written up to date, i.e. about A.D. 63, while St. Paul was still awaiting his trial, and that if the author had intended to continue his narrative, his intention was frustrated, perhaps by his own death ? This has been very ably argued by Rackham—not for the first time. When he wrote (1901) he had to reckon among his opponents the famous Professor Harnack. But since then Harnack has changed his mind and, reproducing and reinforcing the arguments of Hawkins, Hobart, and Rackham as to authorship, has finally claimed it as almost certain [2] that St. Luke wrote the Acts up to date, and that the Gospel, the first of St. Luke's two volumes, must therefore have been written earlier, and as the Gospel is based upon Mark's Gospel, that again must have been accessible in A.D. 60 at the latest.[3]

On the whole, I think those who argue for this position have the best of the argument. But I do not want to lay stress on anything that is disputable. Sir William Ramsay—who is unrivalled as an independent investigator of the history and conditions of the early Christian Church, by means not only of the study of all available documents, but by constant travelling, especially in Asia Minor, where he has had great success as a discover of inscriptions— prefers a later date for the Acts ; but he has been the most eager and strenuous advocate both for St. Luke's authorship of Gospel and Acts and for his character as an entirely trustworthy historian.

[1] Acts xx. 25 and 33. In fact St. Paul returned to Asia and to Miletus, where this scene took place, if not actually to Ephesus (2 Tim. iv. 20).

[2] *Date of the Acts and Synoptic Gospels* (Williams & Norgate).

[3] But St. Luke had intercourse with St. Mark at Rome, and may very well have seen his material before it was published.

Indeed, the vindication, by inscriptions and otherwise, of St. Luke's trustworthiness on all that touches the Roman Empire has been startling.

"The ground covered by St. Luke," writes Mr. Rackham, "reached from Jerusalem to Rome, taking in Syria, Asia Minor, Greece, and Italy. In that field were comprised all manner of populations, civilizations, administrations—Jewish and Oriental life, Western civilization, great capitals like Antioch and Ephesus, Roman colonies, independent towns, Greek cities, 'barbarous' country districts. The history covers a period of thirty years, which witnessed in many parts great political changes. Provinces like Cyprus and Antioch were being exchanged between the Emperor and the Senate; parts of Asia Minor, e.g. Pisidia and Lycaonia, were undergoing a process of annexation and latinization; Judaea itself was now a Roman province under a procurator, now an independent state under an Herodian king. Yet in all this intricacy of political arrangement St. Luke is never found tripping. . . . St. Luke is equally at home with the Sanhedrin and its parties, the priests and temple guard, and the Herodian princes at Jerusalem, with the proconsul of Cyprus and Achaia, the *rulers of the Synagogue* and *first men* of Antioch in Pisidia, the *priest of Zeus* at Lystra, the *praetors, lictors,* and *jailer* of Philippi, the *politarchs* of Thessalonica, the *Areopagus* of Athens, the *Asiarchs* with the *people, assembly,* and *secretary* of Ephesus, the *centurions, tribune,* and *procurator* of Judaea, the *first man* of Malta, and the *captain of the camp* at Rome. Such accuracy would have been almost impossible for a writer compiling the history fifty years later. In some cases where his statements had been impugned, St. Luke has been signally vindicated by the discovery of inscriptions, as in the case of the politarch of Thessalonica and the proconsul of Cyprus." [1]

The chief stumbling-block in the way of a high estimate of St. Luke's accuracy as regards the secular details of his story used to be his statement about the first enrolment under Quirinius.[2] But Ramsay has

[1] Rackham, *Acts,* p. xlv. [2] Luke ii. 1.

made the reality of such an enrolment remarkably probable; and inscriptions tend to connect it with Quirinius. At the worst, if Tertullian is right in putting it under Saturninus and not under Quirinius, the mistake is only a slight misdating, and Ramsay does not admit even this. The method of enrolment by "every man going up to his own city," which St. Luke affirms, was derided as absurd forty years ago, but has been amazingly supported by the discovery of an Egyptian papyrus on which is a census order of a Roman governor (of A.D. 104) which precisely orders everyone to go for enrolment to his own city. And this is now recognized as a method of the imperial administration in the provinces.[1]

Granted, then, St. Luke's authorship, and bearing in mind the vindication of his accuracy as an historian in general, let us read his Preface to the Gospel. It is in St. Luke's own Greek, the Greek of a cultivated man, quite unlike the Hebraic style of the first part of his narrative, where he is obviously relying on some already-existing Aramaic narrative. Well, this preface gives us a singularly convincing account of St. Luke's intentions and qualifications. He notes that the Roman gentleman, for whose benefit he writes, had received instruction,[2] presumably such as was imparted to all Christians orally, in the matters of his story; he notes that there had been already

[1] The whole matter can be seen summarized in Box's *Virgin Birth of Jesus* (Pitman), pp. 51–66, and in Ramsay, *Was Christ born in Bethlehem?* (1898) and *Bearings of Recent Discovery on the Trustworthiness of the N.T.* (1915), ch. xix–xxi. Ramsay, I admit, often gives the impression of pressing his points a little further than they will legitimately carry. In Pelham's *Outlines of Roman History*, p. 385, "Luke ii. 1" is cited as historical evidence.

[2] See "Those things whereon thou *wast instructed*." The instruction was presumably *oral*. But the word used does not imply this.

many attempts to put the narrative of the first apostolic witnesses into writing, but he is not apparently satisfied with these attempts. He has had the opportunity of tracing the events of our Lord's history accurately from the beginning, and he is determined to give an orderly and trustworthy account of them, for Theophilus's benefit, and doubtless for the general benefit also, as writers do to-day when they write an "open letter" addressed to an individual, but intended for the general public. There is no claim made by Luke to special inspiration, but only a claim to have had the fullest opportunity of gathering information and to have taken advantage of it so as to be able to produce an accurate narrative. Not that he is careful about verbal or minute accuracy, as is shown by the apparent difference between the summary narrative of our Lord's last appearance and disappearance at the end of his Gospel and the more exact account given in the beginning of the Acts, or by the three accounts which he gives, differing in detail, of St. Paul's conversion: plainly it satisfies him to give a truthful account without troubling about minute accuracy.

And we can discern in great measure his sources of information. He was St. Paul's constant companion from the time of his second or (perhaps) his first missionary journey. In his captivity at Rome, St. Paul bore witness that "Luke the beloved physician" was with him, and under these circumstances he must have had intercourse with St. Mark, from whom he took the main substance of his Petrine narrative to incorporate in his own book.[1] Besides this, there is

[1] It is very likely that when Papias or his informant described St. Mark as not having written what he wrote about our Lord "in order" (see above, p. 187), he meant that St. Mark's Gospel was un-

a large part of St. Luke's narrative, consisting especially, but not exclusively, of our Lord's sayings, which is common to him with St. Matthew. Here, also, it is commonly supposed they were drawing upon a document or documents consisting in the main of our Lord's discourses, which is commonly known among critics as Q.[1] That there was such a document or documents I do not think we can doubt, and criticism ascribes to it a very early date; but the scope of the document remains quite uncertain. Besides St. Mark and Q, St. Luke gives us probable indications of other sources of information. He mentions two individuals connected with Herod's court—" Joanna the wife of Chuza Herod's steward " and " Menaen the foster-brother of Herod the Tetrarch "—and these persons probably account for the special information which he obviously had about matters connected with the Herods. Besides, he mentions repeatedly a group of women who accompanied our Lord and ministered of their substance to Him and His disciples, who were present in Jerusalem at the Passion, and who were in the apostolic company after the Ascension, Mary the mother of Jesus being amongst them.[2] From this group we should suppose Luke to have derived the narrative with which his Gospel opens, after his preface—a narrative which shows evident marks of coming from the mouth or hand of a woman. The special mention of Rhoda in the household of Mark's mother probably indicates whence he got his account of Peter's release; Philip

systematic and incomplete, and was contrasting it with the more systematic and complete narrative of St. Luke. But we have lost the context.

[1] The first letter of the German word *Quelle*, " the source."

[2] See viii. 2–3, xxiii. 49, 55, xxiv. 10, 22; Acts i. 14.

the Evangelist, with whom " we " stayed at Caesarea,[1]
and Mnason, the " original disciple," who accompanied Paul and his company, including Luke, to
Jerusalem, and was to give them lodging there,[2]
would be good sources for all the earlier narratives of
the Acts. On the whole, it is obvious that St. Luke
had very good opportunities of " tracing accurately
from the first " the incidents of our Lord's life from
His birth to His Ascension, and the beginnings of
the Church before he himself became an eye-witness
of its expansion. We do not claim infallibility for
him in detail. But we have the best reason to
claim for him that he is a careful and well-informed
historian in direct access to those " who from the
first were eye-witnesses and ministers of the word "
—which is the claim of his preface.

His narrative is coloured by his disposition, which
is apparent. He loves to emphasize the humility and
poverty of Christ and His companions, and our
Lord's insistence on the blessing of poverty and the
danger of wealth ; he loves to bring out the mercy
of Jesus and the readiness of the divine forgiveness,
which He proclaimed and ministered ; he loves to
recall all that dignifies womanhood ; he hates controversy, we should suppose, and loves peace ; and
probably he minimizes the amount of division of
opinion, as between Judaizers and Paulinists, that
there was in the first Church. But after all it was
the peace party which prevailed. And an historian
like Tacitus is not supposed to be a better historian
because he retails the scandals of an earlier generation. In fact, the special characteristics of our Lord
which he brings to the front were, we have reason to

---

[1] Acts xxi. 8.   [2] Acts xxi. 16.

believe,[1] really His characteristics—humility, meekness, and gentleness. It is James the Lord's brother, who would have been claimed by the Judaizers as their leader, who speaks of " the wisdom that is from above " as " first pure, then peaceable, concessive, easy to be entreated, without partiality, and without hypocrisy," and declares that " the fruit of righteousness is sown in peace by them that make peace." He suggests that the peaceable spirit in the early Church was the prevailing spirit, and would win the day, and that the violence of party, which he contrasts with it, was destined to fail. Thus we shall not call St. Luke a less good historian because he preferred to stress this spirit of peace at work, and to throw somewhat into the shade the acrimony of partisans.

There is one other matter, which concerns the Gospels generally, to which attention must be called. The destruction of Jerusalem, like, for instance, the French Revolution, created a chasm in national history between what went before and what came after. All the whole apparatus of the national life of Israel—its parties, its proceedings, its temple-worship, its interests, its centralization—was destroyed with the destruction of the city and temple by the Romans in A.D. 70. A later writer who had not lived in the old order would never have recovered its atmosphere. But all the Gospels reflect that atmosphere faithfully. The conclusion, emphasized by Sanday, Harnack, and many others, is that the materials of the Gospels were practically all in being before the destruction of Jerusalem, and that the after-time had no serious effect upon them. This conclusion we may, I think, take for certain.

[1] See 2 Cor. x. 1.

I should advise a student to proceed at this point to review the status of the Epistles, and to leave the question of the First and Last Gospels. But a word may be said in explanation of this course.

As to our St. Matthew, it appears to have been taken by the Church from the first as the premier Gospel, and there is no sign of disparagement. The well-known fragment of Papias tells us that " Matthew compiled the *Logia* in the Hebrew speech, and each man interpreted them according to his ability." I think Lightfoot proved that the word *Logia* (oracles) [1] might refer to a Gospel containing incidents and discourses alike, like our First Gospel. Also Papias appears to mean by his use of the past tense " interpreted "—that by his time there was an authoritative Greek version. But our version does not seem to be a translation from a Hebrew original ; nor does it seem to be likely that one of the Apostles would have been content to rely for the scheme and incidents of his Gospel upon St. Mark's confessedly very imperfect selection of incidents, as fully as our First Gospel does. What appears to be most probable, on the whole, is that St. Matthew really composed in Aramaic a collection of our Lord's discourses with some connecting narrative, and that someone unknown, not long after A.D. 70, used this collection, in combination with St. Mark's narrative, and some other material which came to him, to produce our first Gospel " according to Matthew." We can rely with great confidence on the bulk of the discourses of our Lord in St. Matthew ; but where there are

[1] There is another interpretation of this word which would make St. Matthew's work a compilation of O.T. " oracles " which were believed to have been fulfilled in Christ. But I think it more probable that Eusebius's interpretation was correct.

important differences in discourse or narrative between St. Matthew and St. Mark on the one hand, and St. Matthew and St. Luke on the other, and where we have independent narratives in " St. Matthew " without other support, we want to know, and can find no answer to our question, whether we are dealing with the Apostle or with some unknown Palestinian disciple.[1] In some three cases we have to admit that prophecies from the Old Testament have been allowed to modify the details of the narrative of the First Gospel,[2] and in connexion with our Lord's death and burial the author introduces material which it is difficult to believe to be historical. On the whole, it must be admitted that our St. Matthew presents in some aspects an unknown factor and an unsolved question, and (though it affects a very small area of the whole) we had better rest content at starting with St. Mark and St. Luke ; though even so it must be said that the whole of the Sermon on the Mount and the parables in chapter xiii and elsewhere, and the famous ending of chapter xi, " Come unto me," even though they are unsupported in the other Gospels, are self-evidencing and unquestionable.

I have recently elsewhere expressed my reasons for believing that St. John, the son of Zebedee, is really the author of the Fourth Gospel, and that his scheme of the history must be taken as true and used to supplement the account given in the Synoptic narratives, with which he was plainly acquainted, and

---

[1] In the case of the story of the Birth of our Lord (Matt. i., ii.) and of His reported sayings about the Church (Matt. xvi.) we shall have occasion to examine the trustworthiness of our first Gospel later on.

[2] Matt. xxi. 2 (the introduction of the ass beside the colt) ; Matt. xxvi.15, cf. xxvii. 3–10 (the specification of thirty pieces of silver) ; Matt. xxvii. 34 (the gall).

which he intended to supplement and occasionally
correct, and that the discourses of the Fourth
Gospel must be taken as recovering from oblivion
very real and important features in our Lord's
teaching. To this last point we shall have to return
later, when we are considering the nature of our
Lord's person. Nevertheless, inasmuch as a student
would find himself " up against " the great mass of
critical opinion in holding this position, I should
advise him to defer the question till he has felt the
ground secure under him on the basis of the two
Gospels of St. Mark and St. Luke.

Thus, then, we may take it for granted that in
these two Gospels we have narratives by known men,
whose opportunities for knowing what the " eye-
witnesses " recorded were as good as could be desired,
and whose narratives as we read them are, in the
highest degree, convincing. We do well to saturate
our minds in these two documents. We shall find
ourselves on the most solid historical ground. Nothing,
I think, could resist this conviction, except a dogmatic presupposition that the supernatural things
there recorded cannot have actually happened.
This dogmatic presupposition we shall have to
investigate carefully. For the present let us leave it
out of account, and let the Gospels make their full
impression upon us.

From time to time we may meet people who are
moved by the consideration that if the astonishing
things recorded in the Gospels and Acts had really
happened, we should have heard more about it in
contemporary secular historians, especially the
Jewish historian Josephus. But in fact this
argument, so far as concerns the historians of the
Empire, has no force. " Miracles," such as are com-

monly recorded in the Gospels and Acts, were also
reported in the Roman Empire in connexion with
sacred shrines and persons.[1] And though, as will
appear, the miracles connected with our Lord have
a very distinctive character, the mere report of them
would not have stirred the sort of excitement which
it would excite in the modern world. The common
people of the pagan world would have said that such
things had often happened, and the intellectual
sceptics that such things had always been believed
by the vulgar. Moreover, it was not the habit of
the literary classes to pay any attention to popular
religions. We are led to believe that the mystery
religions, with their rituals and sacraments, were
among the most important features of the society
of the Empire in the period coinciding with the spread
of Christianity, but the allusions to them in general
literature are very meagre.[2]

Thus what Tacitus, the only serious historian of the
early Empire who remains to us (writing A.D. 115–17),
tells us about the origin of Christianity is as much as
we should expect. The name Christian, he says [3]—
he is writing to account for Nero's treatment of them
—comes from Christ, who was sent to execution,

[1] E.g. The miracles of Vespasian recorded by Tacitus and
Suetonius, see below, p. 258.

[2] "No Roman historian, from Tacitus to the scandal-mongers of
the third and fourth centuries, ever wrote imperially. Their outlook
was strictly confined within the walls of Rome" (Platnauer,
Septimius Severus, Oxford, 1918, p. 25). "Of the manner in which
the Empire was ruled, of the condition of the provinces, they [the
Roman aristocratic writers] tell us little, and probably did not care
to know much" (Pelham, *Outline of Roman History*, Rivington,
p. 436).

[3] *Annals*, xv. 44. It is possible that Tacitus borrowed what he
said about Christianity, as well as what he said about the Jews,
from the *Historiae* of Pliny the Elder (A.D. 23–79). See Batiffol,
The Credibility of the Gospel (Eng. trans., Longmans), p. 36.

under Tiberius, by the procurator Pontius Pilate ; " but the execrable superstition, repressed for the moment, broke out again not only in Judaea, the home of this plague, but also in Rome, where all horrible and shameful things flow together and maintain themselves." But more, no doubt, might be expected from the Jewish historian Josephus, who wrote in the last quarter of the first century. He gives us a brief but interesting account of John the Baptist and of Herod's reason for putting him to death. He also gives an account of the putting to death by the high priest of James " the brother of Jesus who is called Christ." As the text stands, there is also some account of Jesus Christ Himself. As it stands, however, it bears obvious marks of a Christian hand.[1] It is disputed whether it is merely interpolated by a Christian or whether it is a forgery. Whichever be the case, we have evidence enough that Josephus knew something about Christ. But when he wrote, Christianity was dreaded by the imperial authorities. Josephus wrote to make them favourable to the Jews. His motive for silence about Christianity was obvious enough. And if he was almost wholly silent, it cannot reasonably be suggested that it was from ignorance.[2]

II

The Second and Third Gospels, then, and the Acts of the Apostles are by known men—John Mark, a member of the original apostolic company in Jerusalem, where he lived in his mother's home, and then the trusted companion of Barnabas, Paul, and Peter,

[1] Dr. W. E. Barnes, Hulsean Professor of Divinity at Cambridge, denies this : see *Testimony of Josephus to J. C.* (S.P.C.K.).

[2] The whole matter is discussed by Batiffol, *op. cit.*, lect. i.

and Luke " the beloved physician," the companion of St. Paul ; and these men had the best opportunities of intercourse with those " who from the beginning were eye-witnesses and ministers of the word," and their narratives are found extraordinarily convincing. We have, then, here documents which, judged by the standards of history, are fully trustworthy, and they would have been, no doubt, unhesitatingly received were it not for the supernatural features of which they are full and the tremendous claim upon men's lives and thought which they involve. Whether these features and this claim constitute any good reason for disputing their trustworthiness we shall have very carefully to consider. We leave the matter now and proceed to consider the rest of the documents of the New Testament—especially the Epistles.

But first something must be said about the presuppositions of the Epistles and about their relation to the Gospels.

The Epistles, like St. Luke's Gospel,[1] were not written to convey to the converts their first instruction. This they presuppose. And it is very instructive to observe exactly what is presupposed. Thus (i) there is constant mention of the holy names of the Father, the Son—the Lord Jesus, the Christ—and the Holy Spirit, as of familiar persons, and of our Lord's atoning and saving work, and of angels and evil spirits. On these subjects instruction is plainly presupposed. (ii) The disorders arising in the Church at Corinth at the Lord's Supper and a particular phase of opinion about resurrection lead St. Paul to restate precisely what

---

[1] Luke i. 4, " That thou mightest know the certainty (or accuracy) concerning the things wherein *thou wast instructed* "—doubtless when Theophilus became a Christian. The instruction was oral, no doubt. But the word is quite general.

he had delivered to them at his first coming in the form of a narrative about the institution of the Eucharist and the death, burial, resurrection, and appearances after the resurrection of Jesus Christ.[1] In the latter case he specifies that what he communicated to them was the same message as the other apostles delivered. St. Paul elsewhere alludes to our Lord's being of the seed of David, and to the moral characteristics of his life, " meekness and gentleness " and humility, and to specific words of the Lord,[2] as to familiar things. How much teaching about the life of Jesus on earth was given to St. Paul's converts we cannot exactly say. But the apparently quite accidental disclosures of his first teaching about the Eucharist and the Resurrection lead us to feel that the amount may have been considerable. St. Peter's converts received, no doubt, the substance of St. Mark's Gospel, so far as that comes from St. Peter. (iii) There was definite instruction in moral duties and in the Day of the Lord and the judgement to come.[3] (iv) The Epistles presuppose rudimentary instruction in the meaning of the sacraments.[4] (v) An acquaintance with and acceptance of the Old Testament as inspired of God is always assumed. All these elements constituted *the tradition* (paradosis)—the teaching which was first delivered by the Apostles and which it was the primary business of the Church to hand on [5]—this was the " sound doctrine," the " faith once for all delivered." This oral instruction, then, given to the first converts, was the basis on which the super-

---

[1] 1 Cor. xi. 23 ff., xv. 1 ff.
[2] Rom. i. 3; 2 Cor. x. 1; Phil. ii. 8; 1 Cor. vii. 10; 1 Thess. iv. 15.
[3] 1 Thess. iv. 1-3; 2 Thess. iii. 6; 1 Cor. xi. 2; Heb. vi. 2.
[4] Rom. vi. 3; 1 Cor. xi. 23; Heb. vi. 2.
[5] 1 Tim. vi. 20; 2 Tim. i. 13, 14, ii. 2; Jude 2.

structure of all the written documents of the New Testament was reared.

Next to this in order of time came, not the written Gospels as we have them, but the Epistles or most of them. St. Paul's Epistles disclose how manifold and diverse were the special difficulties and dangers of his different Churches, at Thessalonica, in Galatia, at Corinth, at Colossae :—hence different occasional letters dealing with these difficulties, and emphasizing and expounding the meaning of the Gospel in different aspects according to local needs. Some of the Epistles, indeed, have more of the nature of formal treatises, e.g. the Epistles to the Romans, Ephesians, and Hebrews ; but most of them are markedly occasional, and need to be read in the light of their circumstances.

Then, as time went on, the need of written accounts of the Lord's life, of the most authoritative character obtainable, became evident, and the Synoptic Gospels were written, all, I think, before or just after the date of the destruction of Jerusalem.   The wonderful thing about them is that, though St. Mark and St. Luke, at least, had been living in the atmosphere of St. Paul's preaching, yet their record of the Lord's life is almost wholly free from anything which suggests later controversies or developments. They have been microscopically examined for " Paulinisms," but almost nothing suggestive of perversion, in the interests of later controversies or tendencies, is to be discovered —in spite of the fact that the tendencies of the time were full of danger, and that " words of the Lord " adapted to the needs of the Church would have been found very useful.   Nevertheless, these two Gospels remain, as far as we can see, strictly within the limits of the history as it was, though the authors

15

which it seems to me the evidence shows to be pseudonymous is the Second Epistle of Peter. That, indeed, claims to have been written by an apostle; and it was as being Peter's that it was at last and after much hesitation accepted by the Church into the canon. But we have no reason to claim infallibility for the literary judgment of the Church, and the evidence against it seems to me to be cogent. Nothing remains to consider but the Apocalypse. Whether this book belongs to the period following the persecution of Nero, i.e. whether it was written just before A.D. 70, or whether it belongs to the persecution of Domitian at the end of the century, or whether different parts of it must be assigned to each period, is a very difficult question. Whether, again, it can be ascribed to the same author as the Fourth Gospel and the three Epistles is also an open question. The external evidence is exceedingly strong for ascribing it to St. John the Apostle. But, at any rate, it was written at one of the two dates named above, by a prophet called John, who claims both direct inspiration and authority such as seems apostolic, and it discloses how he interpreted the conflict between the Church and the now persecuting Empire, and what issue of the conflict he foresaw, with a passion and a power which belong to no other Apocalypse.

Enough has, I hope, been said to satisfy one who is beginning the study of the origins of the Christian Church and its real character and claim that he could use the documents of the New Testament as a whole with confidence in their authenticity and trustworthiness, if they were records of ordinary events or of an ordinary human person. It is, as we shall see reason to believe, not historical criticism properly so called, but something quite different which has led to their being disputed.

APPENDED NOTE

The following facts seem to me to constitute a valid ground for accepting their authenticity.

1. St. Paul's deliverance from his first captivity must be accepted as a fact, on the ground that Clement indisputably implies that he fulfilled his intention of going to Spain (see above, p. 189 n. 3). This leaves room for the movements of the apostle referred to in the Pastorals.

2. The ecclesiastical situation disclosed in the Pastorals harmonizes with that described by Clement as arising *before the death of the apostles*—and by the apostles he means especially St. Peter and St. Paul. He is writing to the Corinthians about the authority of the presbyters or "bishops." He describes their origin : how Christ was sent forth from God and the Apostles from Christ—how they preached in country and towns and "appointed their first fruits, then they had tested them in the Spirit, for bishops and deacons" of the future converts. Later he describes how "the Apostles knew through our Lord Jesus Christ that there would be strife about the title of the bishop. Therefore for this reason, having received perfect foreknowledge, they appointed the aforesaid, and afterwards they gave an additional injunction that, if they (the aforesaid presbyter-bishops and deacons) should fall asleep, other approved men should succeed to their ministry." What this additional injunction was is implied in the following sentence : "Those then appointed by them [the apostles] or afterwards by other distinguished men, with the consent of the whole Church, etc." [1] Here it appears that the additional provision made by the apostles was that there should be, after they were gone, "distinguished men" with an authority like theirs to appoint presbyter-bishops and deacons. This provision for the future was made, Clement asserts,

[1] Clement, cc. 42 and 44.

while the apostles were alive, but doubtless in view
of their death. And I think this assertion exactly corresponds with the situation of the Pastoral Epistles.
Timothy and Titus were such distinguished men, clothed
with an authority like that of the apostles, and especially
to appoint presbyters.

3. The personal relations of St. Paul to Timothy and
Titus and other persons, but especially to Timothy, disclosed in the Epistles, and the accurate delineations of
character involved, constitute an unmistakable evidence
of authenticity. The Second Epistle to Timothy is from
this point of view especially marked as authentic, but
there are similar marks in the other Epistles, and they are
all unmistakably bound together by unity of style and
subject.

4. The special features of these Epistles are such as
belong to their purpose or circumstances. For instance,
the moment is just such as would bring to the fore the
conservative and disciplinary side of St. Paul's mind. No
one can read the First Epistle to the Corinthians without
seeing that this side of his character was always there
and often in evidence.

5. The only real difficulty is in the phraseology. That
is in certain respects markedly different from the other
Epistles of St. Paul. I should be disposed to find the
best explanation of this in the supposition that St. Paul
used for these Epistles an amanuensis, to whom (perhaps
because he did not write shorthand) he left much dis-
cretion in wording the sentences—content that they should
express the idea which he had no doubt carefully made
plain : on this, I would refer to Jones, *op. cit.*, pp. 280–91.

CHAPTER IX

THE PREJUDICE OF CRITICISM

OUR survey of the Gospels of St. Mark and St. Luke—for we left the First and Fourth Gospels aside for the moment—has disposed us to believe them. We found that the writers must have had the freest access to original witnesses of the events which they describe. Their intentions were conspicuously simple and honest. They appear to have no design except to record things as they happened. It is true that in their narratives we are presented with a person and with events quite unparalleled in the history of the world. But we have found ourselves, as we have read and re-read these records, quite unable to believe that we have here a work of imagination. The portrait is convincing. The elements in the narrative—the things done and the things said—cohere in a wonderful unity. Moreover, when we read the Epistles, while we were struck with the vivid picture which they give us of the life and interests of the earliest Christian Churches, we made this note: that these interests and controversies of the apostolic Churches, though St. Mark and St. Luke must have been intimately acquainted with them, do not appear to have discoloured the narratives of the first experiences of the apostles while our Lord was still on earth. Neither in the phraseology nor in the substance of the books could we discover any appreciable trace of these later interests. Thus we find ourselves disposed to take the Gospels for what they profess to be, and to give them an open-minded hearing.

But we find that this is exactly what the intellect of Europe for the last seventy years has, as a whole— so far as it has paid attention to the origins of Christianity—been steadily refusing to do. It has been occupied in substantially rewriting the Gospels. It has been producing an " historical Jesus," markedly unlike the original in the Gospels, or rather several discordant pictures all unlike the original in many most important respects. Now, when we set ourselves to examine the cause of this undoubted fact, I think we shall find it to be that the intellect of Europe has been in rebellion against the miraculous and generally the supernatural, of which the Gospels are confessedly full. This presupposition, which is strictly philosophical rather than historical—that miraculous and supernatural events cannot really have occurred—has made necessary that radical reconstruction of " the Jesus of history," which presents Him in a form so unlike that which the Gospels present in so many ways.

The grounds of this rebellion against the Gospels as they stand is very vividly presented in Renan's *Souvenirs d'enfance et de jeunesse,* in which he discloses to us the intellectual motives which led to his repudiation of the principles of his education in Catholic seminaries, and account for the version of the history of Christ which he gave the world in his *Vie de Jésus.* He speaks contemptuously of historical criticism as a science. It can claim no real authority. It can never really reconstruct the past. " The regret of my life is to have chosen for my studies a class of researches which can never become authoritative [*qui ne s'imposera jamais*], and which will remain always in the stage of interesting considerations about a reality which has for ever vanished." [1] What really came to control his imagination and his mind was the majestic certitude of the physical sciences. The spirit of the physical sciences repudiates the miraculous, and can find no such evidence of miracles having ever occurred as its canons of proof would require; and with the miraculous it repudiates the whole category of the supernatural. "The affirmation that everything in the world is of the same colour, that there is no particular supernatural nor special revelation [*révélation momentanée*) presented itself as authoritative in an absolute manner over our spirit. The clear scientific view of a universe, where no free will superior to that of man is at work in any appreciable manner, became since the beginning of 1846 the immovable anchor whence we have never departed." [2] "People who are in accord with positive science do not admit the special supernatural, the miracle," though they are capable of idealism.[3] So far the brilliant Frenchman. The prejudice with which he reapproached the Gospel story is made quite plain. But the Frenchman had already got his inspiration from Germany.[4]

Of German Biblical criticism in its application to the New Testament, and especially to the Gospels, we have recently had a brilliant survey by Albert Schweitzer in a book which he called *Von Reimarus zu Wrede*,[5] which means the history of the criticism of the Gospels since Lessing published (in 1774–9) the famous *Wolfenbüttel fragments* (the fragments of his

---

[1] *Souvenirs*, p. 263.
[2] pp. 337–8, 282.
[3] *Vie de Jésus*, Pref.
[4] *Souvenirs*, p. 291.
[5] In the English trans., *The Quest of the Historical Jesus*.

friend Reimarus, issued by him after Reimarus's death from Wolfenbüttel in Brunswick, where he was librarian), down to Wrede's publication of *The Messianic Secret in the Gospels* in 1901.   It is a brilliantly written history of a process which, as far as the study of documents is concerned, can be said to tend towards agreement in results, but as far as concerns the picture presented of the " Jesus of history," shows an astonishing divergence, which remains unreconciled. There is the " Jesus of Liberal Theology," who preaches the Fatherhood of God and the Brotherhood of man—all that is most attractive to the modern humanitarian spirit. This is the theology represented in Harnack's famous lectures, *What is Christianity?* and it is familiar enough in this country ; and there is the less familiar " Jesus " of the apocalyptic school, represented by Schweitzer himself, who is an apocalyptic prophet or visionary enthusiast, of a fanatical type, deluded by the conviction of the immediate arrival of the world catastrophe and the Kingdom of God, in which he himself is to be the predestined Messiah or Son of Man.   The differences between these two presentations of the " historical Jesus " is sufficiently startling. It is not now the time to dwell on them.   But any student of Schweitzer's pages can perceive that what enables critics to form such strangely different estimates of an historical figure is that both schools are agreed in repudiating such large elements in the records as they stand—not on grounds of criticism, but on grounds of *a priori* assumption—that the question of what is to be allowed to remain becomes largely a question to be decided by arbitrary choice. The fundamental assumption of all the critics whom Schweitzer takes seriously is the assumption that the miraculous did not occur, and that the theological beliefs associated with the acceptance of miracles have vanished with them. Jesus, as Reimarus said, must have remained " within the limits of humanity." That He did certain cures which seemed to the people miraculous is not to be denied, and is quite explicable. But other miracles, such as must really involve a supernatural power, have no basis in fact.[1] Reimarus's thorough-going denials were not immediately acceptable. But they were revived by David Strauss, the first edition of whose *Life of Jesus* appeared to shock Europe in 1835. From him Schweitzer dates the final abandonment of the miraculous by German theology. Many things remain quite unsettled. "What has been gained is only that the exclusion of miracle from our view of history has been universally recognized as a principle of criticism, so that miracle no longer concerns the theologians either positively or negatively."[2]

According to Schweitzer, there have been three great alternatives concerning Christ presented to criticism, of which the first was finally decided by Strauss, "either purely historical or purely supernatural."[3] The historical and the supernatural are to be regarded, we observe, as incompatible alternatives.

So it still appears to Harnack. If, as we have said, he now dates the documents very early, he is only the more sure that myths, such as the ascension of Jesus or His birth of a virgin, can form themselves very quickly.[4]

[1] Schweitzer, pp. 17 ff.   [2] p. 111.

[3] The second alternative was " either Synoptic or Johannine." This was decided by Tübingen and Holtzmann. The third, clearly propounded afresh by Johann Weiss, is " either eschatological or non-eschatological." This remains still undecided.

[4] See Harnack, *Acts of the Apostles*, pp. 158 f.; *The Date of the Synoptic Gospels*, p. 161.

Now, Schweitzer makes game of the "Liberal" Jesus and of that of Renan the Frenchman. "This professedly historical Jesus is not a purely historical figure, but one which has been artificially transplanted into history. . . . What is admitted as historical is just what the spirit of our time can take out of the records in order to assimilate it to itself." But we seem to see the same arbitrariness in the apocalyptic Jesus of Schweitzer. All these schools of critics start with an invincible, dominant prejudice. It may not indeed be so boldly expressed as with Strauss, whose (almost) sole consideration is declared to be that " in the person and acts of Jesus no supernaturalism shall be suffered to remain." [1] "He who would banish priests from the Church, must first banish miracles from religion." "Christianity is so living a power, and the problem as to its origin so rife in important consequences to the immediate present, that the student must be literally stupid whose interest in the determination of such a question can be strictly confined to the historical." The bias here is plain indeed! But though the bias is not so gross and palpable in other leaders of criticism as in Strauss, yet they have all of them in their minds a dominant pre-supposition, derived not really from historical science properly so-called, but from a certain philosophy of the universe, which we shall have to examine carefully—the presupposition that miracles are incredible, and are the expression of a supernaturalism which they reject. What this impossible supernatur-

---

[1] *New Life of Jesus*, i, p. xii. "This negation is for our object, which is prospective, and not merely retrospective and historical, a principal, if not the sole consideration. It consists in this : that in the person and acts of Jesus no supernaturalism shall be suffered to remain ; nothing that can press upon the souls of men with the leaden weight of arbitrary, inscrutable authority." Cf. p. x.

alism exactly is, differs from critic to critic no doubt. Thus the limits of what can be rationally believed differ in different cases, but, as will be indicated directly, not only miracles, but the real incarnation of the Divine Son in human nature falls apparently for all these schools of critics outside the limits of the rationally credible.[1]

This spirit of continental criticism—which for want of a better name we call rationalistic—is, I believe, logical in thus recognizing that what it is rejecting is not merely miraculous facts, but the whole conception of a supernatural incoming of God into human life which had sought to extrude Him, and into nature where men had sought to forget Him. And this spirit of continental criticism has had not a few representatives in England. It found expression in that strange anonymous book *Supernatural Religion*, which forty-six years ago began its meteoric and short-lived career, hailed triumphantly as the very expression of the best mind of the age, but passing rapidly under a cloud, owing chiefly to the critical exposure to which it was subjected at the hands of Lightfoot. To-day, a much better scholar and more competent thinker, Dr. Kirsopp Lake, is giving it powerful expression, in a much less malevolent but in a not much less trenchant form than was given it by Strauss.

But in England—perhaps only in England or the British Isles—we also find a group of scholars who are prepared to declare, or who strongly suspect, that

---

[1] As to miracles, the healings of the sick are admitted to have occurred in some sense, i.e. the recorded healings are not more than exaggerations of what actually occurred. But what are excluded are the "nature miracles"—e.g. the raisings of the dead, or the feeding of the five thousand, or the walking on the water, or the birth of the Virgin, or the corporal resurrection of Christ.

miracles are, if not strictly impossible, yet in fact
incredible, but who at the same time themselves hold
the full supernatural faith in the incarnation of God
the Son in the person of Jesus Christ, and who even
profess some indignation that the orthodox faith of
those who cannot accept the miraculous should be
impugned. Of this group Dr. Sanday was the most
conspicuous example. As is well known, that eminent
scholar in the last years of his life, if he did not
certainly deny the real occurrence of miracles, did
at least seriously doubt it. But he was strenuous
in maintaining that such doubt or positive rejection
was quite compatible with Christian orthodoxy. He
was indignant that anyone should question the right of
those who repudiate miracles still to recite in good faith
the Catholic creeds, because the essence of those creeds
lies not in certain specific miraculous facts, but in a
certain specific and supernatural faith. We are not at
the moment concerned to discuss questions connected
with the person of Christ. We are only concerned to
get clearly into our minds Dr. Sanday's opinion. He
wrote [1]: " The central truth which it is most
important to guarantee is the true Godhead of Father,
Son, and Holy Ghost ; that our Lord Jesus Christ is
truly God and truly Lord, very God and at the same
time very man. I imagine that, if we were to cross-
question ourselves as to what we mean when we recite
the Creeds, it would be something like that in its
simplest form. . . . We should all agree that anything
really less than this would be hypocritical. The man
who, in his heart of hearts, really believed less ought
not to stay where he is " (i.e. a minister of the Church

---

[1] *Bishop Gore's Challenge to Criticism* (Longmans, 1914), p. 9.
Some later words of Dr. Sanday lead me to doubt if he held to the
position so clearly defined above.

of England). I read these words when they were first
published with not a little astonishment—as for other
reasons with which we are now not concerned, so
because they imply so naïve a confidence that
miracles can be discarded and the old conviction of
faith about the person of Christ retained in all its sim-
plicity. I was the more surprised because in the same
pamphlet [1] Dr. Sanday speaks in highly complimentary
terms of Dr. Loofs " as one of the best and most
cautious of the Germans," and refers us to his little
book *What is the Truth about Jesus Christ ?* [2] For what
is the point of this book ? It is to declare that the
ancient orthodox doctrine of the Trinity and the
Incarnation is out of the question for the modern
critical scholar. Dr. Loofs holds what in technical
terminology would be called an Adoptionist doctrine
of Christ and a Sabellian view of God—that is, he
holds that Christ was a man possessed in some
undefinable and unique manner with the Divine
Spirit so as to make Him the revealer of God and the
beginning of a new manhood. But that " the historical
Jesus is the pre-existent Son of God " he not only
repudiates, but declares that all learned theologians
repudiate and must repudiate. " Those who are
impartial enough," he writes, to see certain points
of his argument, " are thereby convinced that the
orthodox Christology cannot give us the correct
interpretation of the historical person of Jesus. And
there is hardly a single learned theologian—I know of
none in Germany—who defends the orthodox Christology in its unaltered form."

But we need not go to Germany in order to convince
ourselves that the repudiation of miracles is based on
a state of mind which will have much wider effect

[1] p. 29.   [2] English trans. (Scribners), 1913.

than the repudiation of certain supposed events.
How indeed should it be otherwise? For the repudiation of miracles cuts very deep into the Gospel
narratives. Thus Dr. Sanday thinks that the miracles
of feeding had a basis in fact. Our Lord did really
organize and preside at a quasi-sacramental meal.
Some small portion of food, such as was available, was
distributed so that, as at a sacramental table, all
should feel they had been sharing together. The
narrative, he says, is all true except that they were
not " filled." It was not a case of a satisfying meal.
Afterwards the tendency among the disciples to fashion
miracles for their master on the analogy of the Old
Testament miracles brought it about that the reputed
miracle of Elisha, when he fed the hundred men with
the twenty loaves of barley and the fresh ears of corn,[1]
was reproduced on a much larger scale and attached
to our Lord, on the basis of what has really been not a
satisfying of their appetites with food but a piece of
sacramental symbolism. But this manipulation of
the narrative cuts very deep. Not only the word
" filled," and (it should be added) the collection of the
fragments after the meal, must vanish, but the whole
motive and setting of the story is altered. For in the
story there is not the suggestion of anything else,
except that Jesus was determined to " satisfy " a
crowd with food, when His resources were manifestly
much too small. It is only His compassion for men's
physical needs that is in view (Mark vi. 24), and then
the miraculous power that was in His pity. There

---

[1] 2 Kings iv. 42. This interpretation of our Lord's miracle as an
imaginative exaggeration of Elisha's is due first to Reimarus. It is
curious that the miracle of Elisha as recorded in the book of Kings
appears to be hardly miraculous. Twenty loaves and an undefined
quantity of ears of corn could really supply something worthy to be
called a meal to a hundred men.

is also no suggestion of any incident in the Old
Testament as a modifying force. If what really
happened was only the sacramental distribution of
minute fragments, then plainly our narrative in Mark,
although the context indicates that Peter must have
been present, is not Peter's story, nor the story of
any eye-witness, but only a reflection several degrees
removed, upon which so much imagination has been
expended that its original character is quite obliterated. An eye-witness might be wrong in the
figures. The seven loaves might become five or the
four thousand persons five thousand. But the whole
character of the incident could not be altered in his
memory.

To take another instance from the critical reconstruction of the Gospel story—if the tomb of Jesus
was not really found empty on the morning of the
Sunday after the crucifixion, the story in the Gospel
of Mark must be far removed from the original experience. Once more, if the " naturalists' " prejudice is
to prevail, the miracles of healing must in most cases
have been at least greatly exaggerated before they
reached their Gospel form. No one could give a
naturalistic interpretation of ten lepers (in popular
estimation) all simultaneously suddenly healed,[1] or
even of one. How then, if the story has been so
fundamentally transformed, can it be plausibly
pleaded that the words of Jesus Christ (on which the
theological creed is built) have escaped similar distor-
tion and exaggeration ? Do men exaggerate the
actions, or do they in fact become exaggerated, more
than the words of great leaders and heroes ?

It will not, then, surprise us to discover that English
critics, like those of France and Germany, plainly

---

[1] See Luke xvii. 14 and v. 12 ; cf. Mark i. 40.

regard the record of the teaching of our Lord as open
to as much suspicion and requiring as much revision,
before it can be accepted as historical, as the record of
the miracles. Thus we are assured by Dr. Glover that
Jesus did not call Himself the Son of God,[1] though
there is no fact better certified in our foundation
documents than that He did; and by Dr. Rashdall
that He probably did not proclaim Himself the final
judge of all men,[2] and that He never spoke of His death
as to have an atoning or ransoming value for the souls
of men [3]—again in spite of the fundamental records;
and by Dr. Inge and others that He founded no Church
and instituted no sacraments.[4] Dr. Kirsopp Lake
will not allow it to be probable that He even called
Himself the Christ (in the specific sense) or the Son
of Man, or was so called during His lifetime,[5] though
here, I think, most of the other critics whom I have
named would dissent from him. But Dr. Glover,
again, assures us that St. Paul was the first to call
Him "the Lord." [6] More than this, though He is
represented so plainly as speaking with infallible
authority, we are constantly warned that He was
plainly under a delusion about the immediate coming
of the kingdom, and shared the popular superstition
about devils and their possession of men [7]; and others

[1] *Conflict of Religions*, p. 138: "terms which Jesus did not use."
[2] *Conscience and Christ*, p. 48.
[3] *Idea of Atonement*, pp. 27 ff.
[4] *Outspoken Essays*, pp. 227, 249, and elsewhere.
[5] *Landmarks*, pp. 48–52.
[6] *Conflict*, p. 156.
[7] All these points enumerated above will come up for discussion
in due course in the next volume. It is worth noting that the
popular rejection of the belief in the devil, as a mere superstition, is
not so modern as people suppose. Fielding's landlady in *Tom
Jones* cries, "But as the parson told us last Sunday, nobody believes
in the devil nowadays."

of the left wing warn us that we cannot rely upon His sinlessness in any strict sense.

Now, the noticeable thing about these multiplied denials is that they are based on no critical grounds— that is, they all contradict our foundation documents —St. Mark and Q. Thus in these documents our Lord again and again calls Himself Son of God, and is so called, in a sense clearly not applicable to other men.[1] In the Sermon on the Mount[2] and in several—surely indisputable—parables His position as final judge, even of men's secret motives, is clearly implied. In two passages of St. Mark the atoning or ransoming value of His death is apparent, and His identification of Himself with the suffering servant of Isaiah is elsewhere evident.[3] That He founded a Church and instituted sacraments intended to be permanent is not only asserted or implied in the Gospels, but is necessary to explain the action of the Church as recorded in the opening of the Acts, and presupposed in the Epistles; and so far as concerns the Eucharist, it is declared by St. Paul as part of the tradition which he delivered.[4] So, again, Jesus is called Lord in the Acts[5] in the supreme sense some time before St. Paul was converted; and the title must have been so familiar to the Aramaic-speaking Church of Judaea that it passed into St. Paul's Greek Churches in its Aramaic form, *Maranatha*, " Come, O Lord ! " But over this ground we shall have to go again when we face the question, What think ye of Christ ? All that

[1] See Mark xiii. 32 and xii. 6, xiv. 61–2; Matt. xi. 27=Luke x. 22. If these words can be eliminated, anything can.
[2] Matt. vii. 22–3.
[3] This will be argued later.
[4] 1 Cor. xi. 24–5.
[5] Acts i. 36; cf. x 36

I want now to indicate, and what I have, I think, made evident, is (1) that neither in the case of our scholars nor in that of the Germans is it anything that can be legitimately called criticism of the documents which is at the root of the denials which I have been enumerating : it is a certain intellectual presupposition about the miraculous and generally the supernatural; and (2) that Dr. Sanday's assumption, that the miraculous could be dropped out of the record without affecting the traditional belief in the teaching and person of Jesus, is not only wholly improbable in itself, but also contradicted by our experience at home as well as among continental scholars.

We must take it for granted, then, that the elimination of the miraculous cuts so deep into our documents as to render the whole foundation of fact insecure. The interval between the facts as they are assumed to have occurred without miracle and our earliest records, so full of miracle and the assumption of miracle, becomes so great that the historical Figure as He must have been becomes dim.   How He is to be represented seems to depend on the arbitrary judgement of the particular critic, who may be of the Liberal Humanitarian school or of the Apocalyptic school or of some other.   But, though some of the critics who repudiate the miraculous are more conservative than others, I cannot myself doubt that there is among such critics an inevitable trend towards a purely humanitarian estimate of the personality of Christ, that is, a repudiation of the conception of Jesus Christ, as the eternal Son of God for us men and for our salvation made flesh, which has possessed Christendom. It is quite plain, then, that what has to be freely and deeply scrutinized is the intellectual ground for the repudiation of the miraculous and the supernatural *a priori*. If this should turn out to be invalid, then, and only then, shall we have a chance of being able to apply real or free historical criticism to the Gospels.[1]

[1] I wish to recall to mind some remarkable words of Bp. Creighton in a letter to Mrs. J. R. Green : see his *Life*, p. 330–1 : " Historical criticism is not a science : it is only an investigation of the value of evidence. It rests on presuppositions which are derived from experience. I am disposed to believe what is analogous to my experience : my criticism is awakened by what is not analogous. The destructive criticism of the N.T. rests on the presupposition that miracles do not happen. As the writers of the N.T. record miracles, it is necessary to explain how these records came into being. A number of ingenious and plausible theories about their nature and authorship and gradual growth have consequently been formed. Their number and persistency seem to add to their force. You say, ' Why are they not refuted ? ' The only possible refutation of them is to show that, apart from the presuppositions on which they rest, their conclusions are not capable of positive proof. . . . The miracles connected with the person of Jesus are analogous to the spiritual experience of the believing Christian. Therefore he is not moved by the presupposition that they are contrary to nature. The real question in dispute is the conception of nature. Biblical criticism will not solve that question."

CHAPTER X

THE PREJUDICE EXAMINED

The Synoptic Gospels, on grounds of external and internal evidence, claim acceptance as trustworthy historical documents. But the picture they present of the Christ is that of a " supernatural " person, and they are full of miraculous incidents. Any exclusion of the supernatural and miraculous from the narratives cuts so deep into their substance as to leave the residue incoherent, and the person described so dim and uncertain that the most diverse representations of Him have been given. Take the Gospels as they stand, on the other hand, and the picture has been felt over long ages to be in a high degree coherent and impressive. Nothing, it would seem, can justify the elimination of the elements objected to, except an *a priori* conviction that miracles either absolutely cannot have happened or at least are in fact incredible. The actual evidence, however, we shall have to consider very carefully. But undoubtedly the mind of the critical world for two generations has been that miracles, however apparently well certified, cannot in fact have happened, or at least that even very good evidence cannot persuade us to believe that they have happened. And inasmuch as historical evidence never can be really compulsory, there is an unreality about a good deal of the recent discussion of it. We must go back upon the presupposition. Is this presupposition that " nature " is a system closed and complete in itself, so that the idea of an " intrusion " into it of anything " from beyond," or the idea of any " interruption " of its regular law or order, is unthinkable—is this presupposition rational and tenable ?

To justify this way of putting the question, we must seek to define with sufficient exactness what is meant by the supernatural and the miraculous. Let it be granted, then, that there is a cosmos, or world of order and law, with which experience familiarizes men, and which science investigates with ever-increasing confidence that nothing will be found there disconnected or arbitrary. Let it be granted also that (say) the physical resurrection of Christ from the dead, or His feeding of the five thousand with the five barley loaves and the two fishes (or further the personality of Christ as a whole) does present itself in this *cosmos* as something which it cannot account for—postulating some power at work of which it knows nothing. Let it be granted, finally, that these events are supposed to occur for this very reason—because instinctively and inevitably men cannot attribute them to " nature," but will be driven to see in them signs that the power behind nature, the power of God the Creator, is through them giving signs to men of a special purpose to which their attention is thereby effectively called. Then we seem to have got a sort of definition of a miracle. It is an occurrence in the process of nature of something which nature, that is, the experienced order, cannot account for, and which constrains men to recognize a special or extraordinary action of God calling attention to a special purpose. And the supernatural is all that constrains men to believe that nature with its customary order is not closed or complete in itself, but part of a larger and higher world of existence from which it is not separated by any unsurmountable barrier.

That will suffice for the moment.   Obviously the word supernatural is a word which raises scruples in the mind of the believer in God.   It suggests a nature which goes of itself and seems to relegate God to a sphere beyond, from which He " intervenes " in nature, as if He were not there all along, the doer of all that is done.   The believer in God would feel, quite truly, that the enlightened imagination always sees the visible order on the background of the invisible—sees God in all things and all things in God.   The word " nature," he would say, should suggest the whole [1]; and should not ascribe a sort of completeness to what is only a dependent portion. This must be granted.   Nevertheless, the visible world and its order and law has so impressed itself on the imagination of men, and moulded their language as a thing in itself, that we need the word nature to describe it, and the word supernatural to suggest whatever may lie in the unknown beyond. In the same way the idea of miracle may be objected to as suggesting that God is there most evident when something happens which is disconnected and disorderly.   This impression we shall seek to remove. But to start with, I think we may accept the account of the miraculous and the supernatural given above as, even if roughly, giving the right impression and raising the right question—Is " nature " such a system, so self-complete and closed, whether demon-

[1] Cf. a famous passage in Bp. Butler's *Analogy*, Part I, cap. i: " Persons' notions of what is natural will be enlarged in proportion to their greater knowledge," etc.

strably so or so found in experience, as that we may pronounce incredible events in nature which its observed order cannot account for, and which can only be interpreted as special acts of God forcibly calling attention to a special purpose ? Is there such a closed system ? Is it the postulate of science ? Or is it the impression so strongly conveyed by experience that we cannot get beyond it ?

I

The conception of nature as a closed system appears first, I believe, formulated with sufficient distinctness by the Stoics.

"Everything that happens is followed by something else, which is necessarily linked to it as to its cause, and is preceded by something to which it is linked as its cause. For nothing in the world exists or happens without a cause, since there is nothing in it which is detached and separated from the whole sum of preceding events. For if any uncaused movement were introduced, the world would be pulled asunder and dissevered, and would no longer remain for ever one, ruled according to a single order and arrangement." [1]

But the idea was reintroduced into the modern world by Spinoza. His God—the object of his intense intellectual passion—was simply great nature with its invariable laws, existing under the double mode of mind and extension or matter. This awful, impersonal being is the only substance which the intellect in man can legitimately recognize and legitimately worship. And the sway of its law is absolute. It excludes all possibility of any such

[1] This is from Alexander of Aphrodisias (c. A.D. 200), called "the exegete of Aristotle," but giving the Stoic idea of nature; cf. Ueberweg's *History of Philosophy*, i. 184, and J. Wendland, *Miracles and Christianity* (Hodder & Stoughton), p. 252.

freedom of wills as would admit of the occurrence of anything contingent—anything which full knowledge could not have certainly predicted—in the universe. Freedom in this sense belongs neither to man nor to God. And there is nothing knowable beyond nature or above its laws.[1]

It is this kind of conception of a self-complete and closed system of nature which appears as lying behind the denials of the miraculous in Strauss and Renan and in the German rationalists. And the question is—is it valid? It is no doubt the postulate of the physicist and the chemist. But is it simply a working postulate, which is found true and necessary in a group of sciences which take certain aspects or parts of nature in abstraction from the whole, but which cannot be taken as valid for the whole of experienced reality?

Let us test it by its applicability to the freedom of the will — the moral freedom of man — which, we contend, is a fact in experienced " nature." I think we shall find that the question of the reality of moral freedom, which has been already discussed, and the question of the credibility of miracles are at bottom one and the same question.

The idea of moral freedom is not in itself antagonistic to the idea of perfect law. A world of free beings can be conceived whose willing obedience to divine law would have resulted in a free world as completely dominated by or expressive of law as inanimate or irrational nature could be. So Dante magnificently conceives Paradise. There " God's will is our peace," and the slightest desire of departure

---

[1] There are no doubt expressions in Spinoza's writings which suggest a more personal conception of God. But the above represents, I think, his final mind as he quite clearly expresses it.

from His will has become inconceivable. Law, as a
burden, is transcended, but it is not abolished in a
world where perfectly free love expresses itself as
perfect order. But freedom of choice, though it
need not involve any actual departure from order,
involves the possibility of it, and has, in fact, resulted
in world-wide lawlessness. Here, I say, we get to
the crux of the whole question. No doubt the free
will of men has been absurdly exaggerated. As a
fact, it is strictly limited. There is no such thing
as human independence. All the forces which any
man employs, in choosing or carrying out his choice,
are drawn from beyond himself. It need not be
claimed that he can add to the sum of energy. His
conditions again determine the channels along which
he must use the powers which are available. Nevertheless, in the heart of this world of determinate and
determined forces and laws there lies this mysterious
and unique thing—free choice. As has been already
argued, the choice of the will at the last analysis
decides in which direction—in the form of which kind
of action—the energy stored in the human organism
is liberated. Something has happened which
mechanism cannot explain. Nothing can explain it
except the frank recognition of moral will as here
directive of physical force.

Moreover, here, in the region of moral choice, we
are conscious of what Kant has called the categorical
imperative of duty. This again has been argued
already. The soul of man is conscious of a moral
purpose above him claiming to control his action.
The purpose of nature, or the God of nature, appears
to be that he should be " good," as he can be only
by the free choice of his will. We are thus bound to
think of the great power, within the grasp of which

we live and move and are, as not mere unconscious force, but also as conscious moral will and purpose—as willing righteousness. Here we feel ourselves planted on ground from which our reason cannot suffer us to be dislodged. Nature has behind it and within it a Being of whom the moral will in us and the moral personality is a better image than either mechanical force or unconscious life. Thus to think of God is not " anthropomorphism "—that is, the reducing of God into the image of man. It is more truly described as " theomorphism "—that is, the recognition that the human personality, which is the highest form of life known in nature, is a better " image of God " than physical forces or chemical combinations. Call God, if you will, superpersonal, but at any rate you must think of Him as not inferior to man—as at least rationally willing and choosing in accordance with a purpose of righteousness in the whole universe of things. This tentative conclusion, to which our reason pointed us, receives the strongest possible confirmation in the self-disclosure of God given through the prophets and Christ, which we have decided to accept as real.

Now, then, we have a conception of God which is in no way antagonistic to the " universal reign of law " in nature, but which gives it a new meaning. The very being of God is law and order. Nothing arbitrary or disorderly or disconnected in action can be conceived in connexion with Him. The " uniformity of nature " is the exhibition of His perfect orderliness.[1]   But the principle of the order

[1] It is only as the exhibition of God s will that the word "law" was first applied to nature: "Thou hast given it a *law* which shall not be broken " ; and it is only in this sense that the use of the word is really legitimate. It always suggests something more than mere regularity. It suggests some authority behind the regularity.

of nature is now seen to be not blind mechanism, but the perfect reason and perfectly free will of the supreme God the Creator.

This sort of conception of God no doubt received its most forceful expression within the race of Israel. The Jehovah of the Old Testament is, as we have seen, presented as most intensely personal, holy and free, the Creator and Governor of all that is. He is represented as having made man his vicegerent in the government of the world. Man is to "have dominion" over all the lower orders of creation. But on the vastest scale he has misused this stewardship, and his misuse of it has disordered not only his own nature and life, but the whole superficial order of the world. It has raised huge structures of insolence and cruelty and lust. And the blindness and wilfulness of sin have obliterated or monstrously perverted man's *thought* of God on the vastest scale. This is the burden of the Old Testament. And God has not seen fit to annihilate either man or his freedom. He tolerates the vast disorder. But He counterworks it. He enters into the struggle. He sets redemptive forces to work. He chooses His human instruments in the race of Israel, which are, if they will consent, to fulfil His special purpose. He bears with their obstinacy and wilfulness and ignorance. He perseveres. Through infinite difficulties and seeming failures He brings His redemptive purpose to its climax or critical moment. It is the coming of the Christ. And it is in this critical moment that God is specially—not then only, but then specially—represented as "baring His arm" in miraculous—that is, abnormal—action. And the point is: Is not the credibility of such action, at such a crisis, bound up with the belief in a God who is personal, rational, and

free—in the world, but also beyond it and over it ?
The point of a divine miracle, as the Bible conceives
it, is not to be a mere portent, but a sure indication to
men's minds that the moral will of God is supreme in
the world. It is just this sense that the wide and age-
long prevalence of sin has dissolved. The very order
of nature with its apparent moral indifference—God
" making His sun to shine on the evil and on the good
[indiscriminately], and sending rain upon the just and
on the unjust "—has helped this moral blindness.
The mind of mankind has utterly misconceived God.
" Thou thoughtest wickedly that I am even such a
one as thyself." Man's pride has left Him out of
account, and despised Him. The rejection and
crucifixion of Christ is, of course, the supreme example
of such moral blindness. The " weakness of God " is
there shown at its supreme point.[1] Is it not at least
conceivable that at such a supreme crisis—and indeed
at the like crises—God should have " bared His arm "
and given mankind, or such portion of mankind as
have " eyes to see," assurance—such assurance as is
given by Christ's resurrection from the dead—that
at the last issue the power which rules in the physical
world is on the side of righteousness—that it is the
same God who commands in conscience and speaks
through prophets ?   It is true that the testing of faith
lies in enduring and seeing Him who is invisible. This
is the normal task of faith. But surely the Father
of spirits may see that this testing ordeal must be
tempered. Frequent miracles would destroy the
reality of this probation, as they would destroy the
sense of the divine order. But on the supreme
occasions, can the human reason have the audacity

[1] Cf. Ps. lxxviii. 61 : " He [God] delivered his strength into
captivity, and his glory into the adversary's hand."

to say they may not be necessary? Can it have the audacity to say that, on practically no evidence such as will leave to the will of man any responsibility for choice or faith, will it accept the fact of their occurrence? Certainly my reason cannot approach this point. Can I conceive that the reinforcement of the moral conscience, the sense of the supremacy of right, which we identify with Christianity, could have occurred without the resurrection? There is great reserve in the exhibition of the miraculous in the Bible, Old Testament and New; there is great limitation in the evidential function assigned to it. To this attention will be called. The Bible records are no encouragement to any childish love of the marvellous. But is it not to deny reason to God to deny the possibility or credibility of miracle? Is it not the very mark of rational power, as compared to blind force or animal instinct (which may be intelligence in a sense, but is petrified or dead), that, under exceptional circumstances, it is not tied to the uniformity of custom? It can act exceptionally under exceptional circumstances. What God is doing from this point of view when He works a miracle is not to violate the order of the world in the deeper sense. He innovates, it is true, upon the normal physical order, but solely in the interest of the deeper moral order and purpose of the world. Miracle is, from this point of view, God's protest against the monstrous disorder of sin. It is God the Creator recreating what man has defaced. At the last God is to come into His own—that is the day of the Lord. But He from time to time gives some foretastes of this final self-vindication, and they are "miracles." This is in effect Augustine's famous vindication of the miraculous.

" Not unreasonably we say that God does something contrary to nature which He does contrary to what we know in nature. For this is what we call nature—the customary course of nature as known to us, against which, when God does anything, they are called marvels or miracles. But as to that supreme law of nature, which is hidden from our knowledge either because we are impious or because we are still deficient in power to understand, God can no more act contrary to it than He can act contrary to Himself. . . ." [1]

And to admit the credibility or the actual occurrence of miracles in effect lays no fresh burden upon science. The sciences of physics and chemistry—and we may include biology—cannot account for all that is in nature. They cannot account for the action of free wills or for the consequent disorder of sin, any more than they can account for miracles. But neither the actions of free wills, nor the very rarely occurring miracles, hinder their effective investigation of nature on the level that lies below freedom. When a materialist philosophy has attempted to ignore freedom and still to take all human life into its province—as the old political economy attempted to deal with industrial life on the basis of a mechanistic philosophy of human motives—it has always conspicuously failed. Mechanism can give no account of

[1] This passage, which has been quoted in all modern treatises on the subject, beginning with Trench, is from *Con. Faust.* xxvi. 3, cf. also : " God, the maker of all natures, does nothing contrary to nature, for what is natural to anything is what He does, from whom is all the law and number and order of nature." When Lord Haldane (*Reign of Relativity*, p. 414) defines the miraculous as " what violates the principles of the order to which it belongs," he seems to be postulating in nature a complete separation of its "orders" which does not really exist. The intellectual demoralization which a too facile belief in miracles might occasion (see Pratt's *The Religious Consciousness*, pp. 27, 446) is not a temptation to which we are very liable to-day.

miracles.   But also it can give no account of freedom
or sin—that is, of human nature.

II

The above argument views miracles on the background of sin—as God's protest against the false
imagination or moral blindness which sin begets in
the minds of men.   This is, on the whole, the Bible
view of miracles.   And, different as their basis in
evidence is, it applies to the Old Testament miracles
as well as those of the New.   But there is another line
of argument which applies only to the miracles of
Jesus Christ, and it starts from the belief that in
Christ we see something new to human experience—
a new level reached in creation—such as it may be
supposed would have occurred in any case, even if sin
had never been.   The argument runs thus : If Christ
truly was, what His disciples came to believe Him to
be, the eternal Word or Son of God, Himself very God,
made man or " flesh," there was thereby constituted
a new thing in nature, a new relation of the Creator
Spirit, the Spirit of Life, to matter, a new level in the
evolution of life, such as would naturally exhibit new
phenomena.   From this point of view " the works "
of Christ are natural in His case—the natural out-
flowings of the power which He alone, or He first,
possessed.   It was " natural " that He, being what
He was, should so heal the sick, should so control
nature, should so be raised from the dead, as is related
in the Gospels.   In a phrase of Athanasius's, it is all
" in rational sequence "—it is what would be expected
in the case of such a person.

There are signs in the New Testament of this sort
of conception of Christ's miracles as His natural
" works," the natural expression of a hitherto un-

17

exampled nature. So the centurion, whose faith Jesus so strongly commended,[1] sees in Him one doubtless subordinate to God, but nevertheless, within God's world, holding so lofty a position that nature must obey His commands, even as in the world of the Roman Empire he himself, as centurion, though he was a man " under authority," the authority of his imperator, was yet able to command—to say to this man Go, and he goeth, and to that man Come, and he cometh. Such a command over the forces of nature he instinctively feels to belong to Christ. Miracles of control over nature are what he would expect in the case of such a person. So elsewhere in the Gospel there is attributed to Christ a certain kind of inherent " power " which, apparently like a natural force, faith in the sick can draw out to heal them, and only faith can draw out. When the woman with an issue of blood touched the garment of Jesus, He perceived that virtue or healing power—the " power that was in Him "—had gone forth.[2] And on another occasion, where faith was lacking, it is said that He could do no mighty works.[3] Such phrases suggest a " natural " faculty which could heal the sick and raise the dead— a " natural " outpouring of inherent life-giving power, which a certain lack of response could restrain or inhibit. So in the case of our Lord's own death, Peter, after he has recovered from his moral blindness, sees in the resurrection of Jesus nothing astonishing. As the prophet had foreseen, in the case of such an one, the very idea of the corruption of death was impossible to entertain—" it was not possible that he should be holden of death." [4]

In the face of the actual evolution of the universe,

---

[1] Matt. viii. 9.   [2] Mark v. 30.   [3] Mark vi. 5.
[4] Acts ii. 24; cf. John x. 18.

such an argument is quite legitimate. For from the point of view of evolution it is untrue that the future must always resemble or has always resembled the past. Nature has not been in this sense uniform. We are bound to think of it as disclosing successive layers or stages, each successive layer or stage exhibiting laws or phenomena of its own, which from the point of view of the lower level would appear miraculous.[1]

Thus, however life emerged out of a merely mechanical universe, it emerged as a new thing with new laws. Plants growing and beasts moving are miraculous from the point of view of inanimate nature. Inanimate nature and its laws cannot explain these growths and motions. So human, rational beings, when first they builded and planted, however they emerged upon the world's surface, were doing a new thing, exhibiting a quite new power of moulding nature to their purposes. Their mastery of nature was miraculous from the point of view of merely animal life. A new level had been attained, and it exhibited new marks of activity. The future, in which they were the prominent feature, did not resemble the past. In the same way, when Christ came, in His person was a new relation of life and mind to matter, and He would naturally, as a " new creation," exhibit a new kind of control over nature.

It must be recognized that the old objection to miracles as urged by Spinoza, and still by Renan and

---

[1] Cf. Pringle Pattison, *Idea of God*, pp. 97, 104–5 : " a new plane or level of existence, qualitatively different, and, through that difference, opening up a new range of possibilities "; " actual 'increments' or 'lifts' in the process, where quantity may be said to pass into quality, differences of degree into differences of kind." " Each new fact in turn must be sheerly unintelligible if we take our stand at the stage below." Cf. Haldane, *op. cit.*, pp. 125 ff.

his contemporaries, represented the dominance in the domain of science of the mathematical sciences. The norm of science was physical mechanism. Recently the normative influence of biology has become dominant. And biology demands new categories which physics and chemistry cannot supply. They cannot account for the behaviour of living things. Thus the argument is quite valid that—granted (what in fact we are not considering in this volume) that Christ cannot be reasonably accounted merely as man, but must be interpreted as God incarnate— He must be expected to exhibit actions natural to Him, which would be " miraculous " from the point of view of the nature which lies below Him.

Some apologists [1] for miracles have laid their main stress on this kind of argument. They have insisted that Christ's miracles are natural to His person. Nevertheless, it must be admitted that this separation of the miracles of Christ from all other miracles is not what the New Testament as a whole suggests. It seems to demand an explanation of the miracles of Christ which (apart from all question of evidence [2]) would assimilate them to those of the Old Testament as acts of God. In the Old Testament they are represented as acts of God wrought to show His purpose for Israel and to ensure that purpose. So in the New Testament the miracles done by Christ, or in His case, are represented as the acts of God who sent Him bearing witness to Him.[3] They are attributed to the Divine Spirit who indwelt Him,[4] and (often) are pictured as done by God in answer to the prayer of

---

[1] Including myself in *Bampton Lectures*, lect. ii.

[2] See later, p. 248.

[3] E.g. Acts ii. 22, 24, x. 38, 40, xvii. 31. This is the constant mode of expression.

[4] Matt. xii. 28 ; Acts x. 38.

Jesus.[1] In a word, they are abnormal acts of God done to call attention to His Christ. So specially the resurrection is the act of God marking out and finally designating Jesus as His Son and as His authorized representative through whom He is to judge the world. That is to say, our thoughts are in the main directed by the miracles not to the special nature of Christ but to the nature of God as transcendent Creator, under whose hands nature is plastic and must fulfil all His will.

Thus we come back to the sole question which really occupies us in this chapter. There can be no doubt that one who holds the prophetic doctrine of God the Creator can find no *a priori* difficulty about the miracles of the Bible. They are not unworthy of God. They are not arbitrary acts. They are the exhibition from time to time of His special purpose in the world in connexion with Israel or with Christ, an exhibition given as it were in protest against the blindness of a sin-perverted world. They are not perversions of the real order of the world, but acts done to wrench back a sin-perverted world into its proper order. They are part of a redemptive process which seeks the restoration of the divine order in nature, not its overthrow. Thus we come back at last to our original question—Is the invincible repugnance to entertaining the reality of miracles, bred in the mind by physical science, a legitimate repugnance ? Is the practically prohibitive prejudice against miracles which it generates really rational ? Or, in other words, is the scientific view of nature legitimately exclusive of any other view ?

There can be no question—as has been already noticed—that any study exclusively pursued tends to narrow the mind. " No man having drunk old

Matt. xxvi. 53 ; John xi. 42.

wine desireth new. He saith the old is good." No man having become through long years exclusively absorbed in the scientific conception of nature as the scene of invariable law can fail to resent the occurrence of miracles. But we contend science is not the only legitimate avenue to reality. The moralistic approach is at least as real. From that point of view the moral will of God and the fact of moral freedom in man and the vast portent of universal sin become the prominent facts, and the philosophy of divine redemption, and with it of miracles, becomes intelligible and acceptable.

The two points of view are practically not the least incompatible. Miracles, it must be remembered, are on all showing very rare occurrences. That is of their essence. They do not occur as a hindrance in the path of the scientific investigator. His postulated world of fixed laws is before him all the same, whether personally he believes in certain miracles or no. All that is asked of him as a scientific man is that he should recognize the abstraction of his sciences, and seek to impose no dogmatic or *a priori* barrier against the conception of the possibility or credibility of miracles—a possibility and credibility which are, as has been shown, really bound up with faith in the God of the prophets and of Jesus Christ.

III

But there are many—historians and students of history—who might read this sort of argument which we have been advancing and feel that it does not in any sense meet their case ; but who at the same time would be unaffected by any exhibition of the strength of the historical evidence for (let us say) the corporal resurrection of Christ from the dead. What closes

their minds *a priori* to evidence is not any abstract
conception of nature, but what they would describe
as a general deduction from history. " Religious
history," they would say, " is full of reported miracles,
some of them reported by eye-witnesses or on what
appears to be very strong evidence. But we have
ceased to believe them. We either regard them as
the influence of certain powerful personalities upon
other men's minds and bodies, which is a fact of
nature such as is described under the general head
of ' suggestion,' or of ' auto-suggestion,' which is
akin to it. Or we believe that under certain conditions men's minds are so obsessed with the demand
for miracle that they ' see ' what they desire to
see and their reports have no objective value. We
notice that the more reasonable apologists for Bible
miracles have given up the attempt to maintain
almost all the nature-miracles of the Bible, i.e. those
that defy any naturalistic interpretation—for the
miracles of healing as recorded can be interpreted
as not more than exaggerations of actual facts. No
one now maintains that Balaam's ass really spoke
or that the sun really ' stood still ' at Joshua's
behest. Nor is any claim put in for the ecclesiastical
miracles. They only claim the real occurrence of the
nature miracles of the New Testament or some of
them, especially the miraculous birth and corporal
resurrection of Jesus Christ. By this process of
gradual withdrawal they show that they are fighting
a losing battle. And the sooner they cease to fight
it, the better in the interests of religion." [1]

But such an argument is full of misrepresentation.
For my own part, though I am not disposed to think

[1] Such an argument I have seen proceeding from Dr. Sanday's pen,
but unpublished.

spread tendency among not unintelligent people to believe that miracles are even to-day of fairly frequent occurrence—such, I mean, as are reported from Lourdes, or are ascribed to spiritual healers or to the contemporary Christian Sadhu,[1] or are said to be worked under the influence of " Christian science," or, what may perhaps turn out to be very important, such as are recorded by spiritists—that is, the movements of furniture or other material objects, which apparently, if they are truly reported, must be ascribed to the action of beings—discarnate spirits—from another world.[2] If, as a distinguished man of science asserts,[3] a table in a modern drawing-room " made most caressing movements to and fro, and seemed as if it could not get close enough " to his wife, with motions expressive of affection, because moving at the will of his departed son, and expressing his feelings—then certainly our physical world is not a closed world, but is open to influences from the beyond which can materially affect its phenomena. The intrusion of unseen forces (the wills of spirits) can cause that to occur which " in the course of nature " could not have occurred at all. I imagine that if intelligent people in general come to believe such events really to occur, they will not be likely to disbelieve the miracles of the Gospel to have really occurred. I express no opinion, and indeed I am not qualified to express an opinion, on the reality of such occurrences. I confess an intense mental repugnance to the admission of their reality. But I seem to

[1] *The Sadhu*, Streeter and Appasamy : cf. above, p. 36.
[2] These would come under the head of miracles or signs, as the words are used in the N.T. to describe events in nature due, not to the will and action of God or of Christ, but cf other spirits (Mark xiii. 22 ; 2 Thess. ii. 9).
[3] Sir Oliver Lodge : see *Raymond*, pp. 216 and 263.

myself to be becoming more and more merely old-fashioned with regard to them. It seems to me quite likely that the next generation will find themselves in an intellectual world the attitude of which towards miracles will be not unlike the attitude of the Roman Empire, but quite unlike the attitude of the educated world of the last generation ; and by the attitude of the Roman Empire, I mean a disposition to accept such occurrences, without generally attributing very much importance to them.

. . . . .

However, enough has perhaps been said on the *a priori* credibility of miracles. My contention is threefold. *First,* that the evidence of the strictly miraculous in the New Testament is such that, as will appear, nothing can resist it but a predetermined mind possessed with the conviction that it is, if not impossible, yet incredible. *Secondly,* that it is neither impossible nor incredible, if the God of the prophets and of Jesus is the real God, if the world is what the Bible represents it as being, disturbed and distorted by the rebellion of free wills, and if the redemptive or recreative purpose of God needs such a manifestation of His power in the physical world to make it effective. *Thirdly,* that there is no ground for the assumption—the only assumption which can really arm our minds against the evidence—that the physical world which science investigates, the world of constant physical sequence and invariable law, is a self-complete and closed world, which can admit no influence from any other world. The evidence is against this theory of a self-complete enclosure, which cannot account for the action of human wills.

CHAPTER XI

WE have sought to set aside the *a priori* prejudice against miracles which, regarding them as impossible, or at least incredible, is bound to find some way of disposing of the historical evidence however cogent. This *a priori* dogmatism, we have argued, both is in itself unjustifiable, as being based upon an untenable view of nature and natural laws, and also, in eliminating the large miraculous element from the Gospel narrative, leaves the whole residual picture presented by the Gospels incoherent, unconvincing, and so uncertain as to be capable of any kind of arbitrary interpretation. If our imaginations are purged of this prejudice and we approach the Gospels with open minds, we find ourselves presented in the Synoptists with a picture of Jesus of extraordinary impressiveness, such as we cannot conceive to have been an imaginative invention.

Let us consider, first of all, the Gospel of St. Mark. We have already taken note of its characteristics, and have seen reason to believe that in its main bulk it represents, as the subapostolic tradition tells us, the teaching of Peter written down, after repeated hearing, by the perfectly simple-minded disciple John Mark. It bears all the marks of the eye-witness's story. It is extraordinarily lifelike. Also it is full of miracles. Of these the most are miracles of healing which, as they are recorded, go quite beyond

anything which admits of naturalistic interpretation.[1]
But amongst them are "nature miracles"—the
stilling of the storm and the feeding of the multitude
with the few loaves and fishes.[2] This last, as we
have already observed, is quite plainly an account of
a miracle wrought to appease natural appetite ; and
to transform it into a quasi-sacramental communion,
as Dr. Sanday would have us do, in which each par-
ticipant received but a tiny fragment, does violence
to the whole context.

We note again and again how the miracles give
occasion for unmistakably genuine sayings or gestures
of Christ, such as : " That ye may know that the Son
of Man hath power on earth to forgive sins."[3] " Go
thy way, show thyself to the priest . . . for a testimony
unto them."[4] " Is it lawful on the Sabbath day to
do good or to do harm? To save a life or to kill ? . . .
And he looked round about on them with anger,
being grieved at the hardening of their hearts."[5]
" How can Satan cast out Satan ? "[6] " And he
himself was in the stern, asleep on the cushion. . . .
Why are ye fearful ? Have ye not yet faith ? "[7]
" And straightway Jesus, perceiving in himself that
the power proceeding from him had gone forth,
turned about. . . . Thy faith hath made thee whole ;
go in peace."[8] "*Talitha cumi*"[9] (the actual Aramaic

---

[1] See Dr. Reginald Ryle in *Hibbert Journal*, April 1907, " The
Neurotic Theory of the Miracles of Healing."

[2] As has been explained, it is not at all unlikely that the "feeding
of the four thousand " is really an account of the same incident as
the " feeding of the five thousand "—an independent account, which
St. Mark received from some other source than St. Peter, and mistook for a separate event.   The two accounts differ in nothing except
the figures.

[3] Mark ii. 10.

[4] Mark i. 44.

[5] Mark iii. 4–5.

[6] Mark iii. 23.

[7] Mark iv. 38–40.

[8] Mark v. 30–4.

[9] Mark v. 41.

words given). " Give *ye* them to eat." [1] " Be of
good cheer : it is I ; be not afraid." [2] " It is not
meet to take the children's bread and to cast it
to dogs." [3] " If thou canst ! All things are
possible to him that believeth." [4] We note how
lack of faith in the people limits the power of the
Healer, [5] and how the blind man at Bethsaida is
gradually healed. [6] In a word, the whole picture,
full as it is of miracles, overwhelms us with the sense
of reality.

Next let us turn to the material in the Synoptic
Gospels which is common to St. Matthew and St.
Luke, and not derived from St. Mark. This is generally supposed to represent the earliest of the
written " Gospels," which is regarded as having
consisted mainly, though not exclusively, of an
account of our Lord's teaching, and is commonly
designated as " the Source," or Q. About the nature
and scope of such a document it is not possible to
speak with any certainty, but at least there lies
behind the First and Third Gospels a mass of common
material which is probably the earliest record we have
of Jesus, earlier than the Gospel of Mark. Though
it seems to have been in the main a record of His
teaching, yet the implications of miracle are both
abundant and exceptionally convincing. First we
should note the account of the Temptation of our
Lord, which we cannot hesitate to ascribe to our

---

[1] Mark vi. 37.   [2] Mark vi. 50   [3] Mark vii. 27.
[4] Mark ix. 23. I may add that in one of the miracles recorded
only by St. Luke—the healing of the ten lepers—we notice the same
convincing association with the miracle of a self-evidencing saying :
" Were there not ten cleansed, but where are the nine ? " etc.
(Luke xvii. 12–19). See also the characteristic action and speech
of Peter given only by St. Luke in the story of the miraculous
draught of fishes (Luke v. 8).
[5] Mark vi. 5.   [6] Mark viii. 22 ff.

Lord Himself. It is the account of a spiritual temptation given in material forms—a temptation, or series of temptations, strikingly unlike those of ordinary men, but profoundly suggestive of genuineness in connexion with the person of Jesus. The temptations are plainly those of a man starting on a great spiritual enterprise—the bringing in of the Kingdom of God—and fully conscious of extraordinary powers over nature. They have no meaning save for one who could, if He would, turn stones into bread, and amaze the people by alighting in the midst of them from the temple pinnacle. But He refuses to exercise His miraculous power for the satisfaction of His physical appetite or the astonishment of the people.[1] Then we have the healing of the centurion's servant,[2] where this observant Gentile recognizes in Jesus one—doubtless not supreme in nature, for He is under God—but holding in the economy of the world of nature a power like that which an officer holds in the Roman army over the men subject to him. He can surely command the services of nature with an unquestioned authority. And our Lord blesses the discerning faith of the Roman officer with the strongest commendation, and proves the truth of his discernment by exhibiting His power. Again, the habitual miraculousness of Christ's action is disclosed in His answer to the messengers of John the Baptist, who bring the question of his doubting spirit.[3] He bade them report to John the wonderful works which they had seen; " The blind receive their sight, and the lame walk, the lepers are cleansed, and the deaf hear, and the

[1] Matt. iv. 1 ff. ; Luke iv. 1 ff.
[2] Matt. viii. 5–10; Luke vii. 1–10.
[3] Matt. xi. 2 ff. ; Luke vii. 18 ff.

dead are raised up "; and the saying is noteworthy because among the wonderful works insisted upon is " the preaching the good tidings to the poor," and the insufficiency of miracles to generate faith is suggested by the warning, " Blessed is he whosoever shall not be offended in me." Once more, we have the denunciation by Jesus of Chorazin and Bethsaida and Capernaum for not giving heed to the powers He had wrought among them, which implies a great multitude of unrecorded miracles.[1]

Occasionally we seem to note a greater courage in St. Mark (or in St. Peter) in recording things exactly as they were, e.g. the limitation on the power of Jesus to heal where faith was lacking in those around Him—" He could do no mighty works, because of their unbelief "—which is not reproduced by St. Matthew or St. Luke. Again, in one passage of St. Matthew, where Jesus is represented, as in the other Synoptists, as transmitting to his disciples the power to work miracles of healing, we notice a heightening of the picture : " Heal the sick, raise the dead, cleanse the leper, cast out devils. Freely ye have received, freely give "[2]; where Mark refers only to healing generally and mentions particularly the method of anointing.[3] But this heightening of the miraculous colouring is not discoverable generally or to any considerable extent. The picture is substantially identical in all the Synoptic Gospels. Owing indeed to the fewness of the discourses of Jesus recorded by Mark, the picture of the miraculous worker is in higher relief in his narrative than in any of the other Gospels. But in all of them the authority to work

---

[1] Matt. xi. 21 ff.; Luke x. 13 ff. On all these elements in Q, see Headlam, *The Miracles of the Gospels*, p. 182.
[2] Matt. x. 8.   [3] Mark vi. 13.

miracles and the spiritual authority to teach and to forgive are represented as inseparable the one from the other. Here is a real man, but a real man endowed with the authority of God morally and physically. This is the irresistible impression.

In all the Gospels we note the relatively subordinate evidential position assigned to the wonderful works of Jesus. He was no mere wonder-worker, though He worked wonders. This is made evident in the account of His temptation. He would not obtain belief by dazzling men. He knew the worthlessness of such belief. " If they hear not Moses and the prophets, neither will they be persuaded," [1] in any really spiritual sense, by a supernatural occurrence. This appears to be the interpretation of our Lord's stern refusal to meet the demand of the scribes and Pharisees for a " sign " or a " sign from heaven." [2] This appears to mean some public demonstration of miraculous power on a great scale wrought to prove demonstratively His divine authority. And this He would not give. His miracles were incidental. They issued from a pity which knew that it had power to heal men's sicknesses and supply their physical needs, and could not refrain from using it ; but they were rather concealed than advertised ; or they were elements in the training of the disciples to trust Him utterly ; or if occasionally they were intended to serve, like the healing of the paralytic man, as proofs to the eye of the spiritual authority which He claimed, they were still incidental or unpremeditated, and in presence of a relatively small company. It is difficult to state with any accuracy exactly what function our

[1] Luke xvi. 31.
[2] Mark viii. 11 ; Matt. xvi. 1 ; cf. Matt. xii. 38–42, Luke xi, 16, 29 ff. ; cf. also 1 Cor. i. 22, " The Jews ask for signs."

Lord seems to desire His miracles to fulfil, but at least it is quite clear that he absolutely refused to astonish men into belief, knowing that such a belief would be of no spiritual value. " There shall no sign be given them but the sign of the prophet Jonah "—that is, the sign of the word of righteousness.[1]

There was in the Roman Empire at this date a widespread curiosity for the mere " wonder " divorced from any moral associations. This is very well exemplified in the account which Tacitus [2] gives us of the public "miracles" of healing wrought by Vespasian at Alexandria upon a blind man and a man with a dislocated hand, which he records as evidences of divine favour towards the Emperor. At the instigation of the god Serapis—that is, doubtless, the priests in his temple—these men urgently demand to be respectively touched by the Emperor's spittle and trodden upon by his foot. Vespasian's first impulse is to treat the idea as ridiculous. Then his vanity contends with his fear of ridicule. He becomes more and more impressed with the opportunity, as the men are urgent and flatterers encourage him. He seeks medical advice. The doctors' answers are various, but they declare that the blind man's faculty of sight is not extinguished and could be recovered " if obstacles were removed," and that the maimed man's dislocated joints could be restored to their proper functions if health-giving force were applied. They encourage Vespasian to believe that he has

---

[1] It is notable that the Greek word for " miracle " or " wonder " is never used in the Gospels, except for miracles of evil origin (Mark xiii. 22; Matt. xxiv. 24). " Powers " is the characteristic word in the Synoptists (cf. Mark vi. 5), and " signs " or " works " in St. John. These words carry moral and spiritual associations, as distinct from the mere marvel.

[2] *Hist.* iv. 81.

been chosen by the gods for this divine ministry.
They add that if he succeeds, it will be to the glory
of Caesar, and, if he fails, that the ridicule will
fall upon the two unfortunate men. So Vespasian,
in a burst of confidence in his fortunes, with a joyful
countenance makes the attempt, in presence of a
multitude watching intently, and with immediate
success. The one man got back the use of his hand,
the other the sight of his eyes. And surviving
witnesses still, Tacitus says, speak of the event,
though by his day lying could bring them no advantage.

Now, whatever interpretation we put upon this
narrative, we must recognize in it a very marked
contrast to the spirit of the Gospel narratives—in the
total absence of moral associations or conditions or
results attached to the working of the miracles. That
is the point insisted upon by Origen in his book
against Celsus.[1] He does not seem to deny the
occurrence of miracles in the pagan world, but he
points to the fact that the miracles of the Gospels
were wrought to make men morally better, and as
part of a great divine act of moral redemption for
mankind.

It is in accordance with this Christian tendency to
value miracles only as instruments of moral instruction
that, among the miracles of Jesus and his disciples,
those which made most impression—apart from the
central and all-important miracle of the resurrection—
were the castings-out of evil spirits of which we get
such graphic descriptions in the Gospels. They were
found specially impressive because the greater part
of the world lived in a terror of evil spirits, which was
paralysing and degrading, and these acts of redemp-

[1] See Origen, *c. Celsum*, iii. 28, 29.

tion manifested the power of Jesus to emancipate
men from the slavery of this terror and enable them
to lift up their heads as free men, sons of an Almighty
Father.

Of the mere desire for the marvellous or the fear of
it, we have examples in the Gospels in the desire of
Herod Antipas to " see Jesus, for he hoped to have
seen some miracle done by him " ; and in his earlier
belief (if it was serious) that Jesus was John the
Baptist risen again. Perhaps there are passages in
the Acts which seem to suggest in the earliest Church
a demand for miracles not unlike that of the mediaeval
Church.[1]   But this is not the temper of the disciples
in the Gospels.   They accept miracles readily enough.
They create no difficulty in the mind of any New
Testament writer.   But there is no such demand for
them as would imagine them and ascribe reality to
the imagination.   A sign of this is the fact that no
miracles were ascribed to one who came " in the
spirit and power of Elijah " and whom all reverenced
as a great prophet—" John did no miracle."[2]   In fact,
the disciples appear in the Synoptic Gospels as very
unimaginative men, and the miracle-hunger is not
in them.   Indeed, for the first three centuries of
Christianity there was comparatively little stress
laid upon miracles as " evidences," except on the
great crucial miracle of the resurrection; and though
there is occasional mention of contemporary miracles,[3]
yet Chrysostom speaks plainly of " signs " or miracles
as no longer occurring, and explains that they were
needed as guarantees of the divine intention when
the new religion or manner of life had to be first

---

[1] Acts v. 15, xix. 11 ff.   [2] John x. 41.
[3] See Origen on the " traces " of the old power still found in the
Church, c. Cels. i. 2, iii. 24. Irenaeus uses more unequivocal language.

established among men, but are not needed now.[1]
Similar language occurs in other early writers.

After that—in the fourth century—the temper
begins to prevail which found it necessary to attach
miracles to saints, in the same way as later painters
attached a halo to the saint's head. This temper
has been admirably and courageously described in
its monotonous consequences by the Dean of the
Jesuit company of Bollandists, who have produced
and are producing the gigantic work of the *Acta
Sanctorum*. No one interested in mediaeval credulity
should fail to read Fr. Delehaye's *Légendes Hagio-
graphiques*.[2] It is the almost universal prevalence
of this temper in the mediaeval Churches which makes
one justly sceptical about the records of miracles,
even when they appear to rest on very good evidence,
though it is very far from justifying universal disbelief.[3]

There are, in fact, two opposite tempers in men
which are destructive of the kind of appeal which
the Gospel miracles make to reasonable men. One
is the temper of pure credulity, which demands
miracles and invents them in accordance with its
desire. The other is the temper of *a priori* disbelief,

[1] See *Hom. in Matt.* xiv. 3, *Hom in Epist. ad Col.* viii. 5. *In
Ep.* i. *ad Cor.* vi. 2, "Do not make the fact that signs do not occur
now an argument that they did not occur then [in New Testament
times]. They were useful then, but not now."

[2] Brussels, 1905; English trans. (Longmans), *Legends of the
Saints : an Introduction to Hagiography.*

[3] Thus when we read (Suspicius Severus, *Dial.* iii. 13) of St. Martin's
anguish of conscience over his consent to communicate with those
who had promoted the execution of Priscillian for heresy, and learn
how he knew himself weakened through this sin, if it was a sin, in
his power of healing the sick, we feel sure that Martin believed himself to have, as his contemporaries undoubtedly believed him to have,
such power. Some mediaeval miracles rest on evidence that seems
to be conclusive.

which is bred of the modern spirit of physical science, when it is misapplied, demanding for events claimed to be historical the sort of demonstration which history does not often supply. If there is anything certain, it is certain that Jesus Christ did not intend to *compel* men to believe in Him. Certainly, for instance, He did not " prove " His resurrection from the dead except to those who had already faith in Him, though a faith which had suffered eclipse. It would have been wholly contrary to His principle of action to have confuted His adversaries by physical demonstrations.

Now we will turn our attention away from the " powers " wrought by Jesus or His disciples which it is impossible to disbelieve, to the " powers " unhesitatingly believed by the first Christians to have been wrought by God upon Him or in His case—notably His resurrection the third day from the dead, His ascension, and His birth of a virgin mother.[1]   With regard to these three miracles it will be necessary to go into detail.

I. The Resurrection

The denial of the real occurrence of the corporal resurrection of Jesus is surely, from the point of view of historical criticism, a desperate paradox. The Gospels show us the disciples after the death of Jesus as a dispirited band of men, who had been gradually disheartened by the seeming failure of Jesus, and

[1] This distinction, however, between the miracles of Jesus and those wrought by God in His case must not be pressed too far. The miracles wrought by Jesus are in the New Testament commonly regarded as acts of God wrought through Him by the power of God's Spirit given to Him (see above, p. 244) ; and, on the other hand, in John x. 18 (perhaps only there) Jesus speaks of Himself as rising by His own inherent authority, though that authority comes from the Father.

finally utterly discouraged by His rejection and
execution. "We hoped that it was he which should
redeem Israel" [1] describes their state of mind. It
plainly appears that this sense of disappointment and
failure so possessed them and dominated them that
they could hardly be aroused from their lethargy.
Then the early chapters of the Acts present to us this
same body of men confident and courageous—with a
courage which no hostility could shake. They had
plainly been suddenly driven round a sharp corner
by the sort of impact which only some strong external
force can exercise. And though they were not
emotional men, but prosaic and slow of spiritual
apprehension, and men, it would appear, liable to
jealousies and misunderstandings among themselves,
they had been transformed all together. It was a
corporate transformation, which again suggests the
impact of some startling fact of common experience.
And to such a fact they manifestly appeal. Their
outlook has been changed by the grave of Jesus having
been found empty on "the third day" after His crucifixion and burial, and afterwards by repeated appearances of the risen Jesus to individuals among them
and to the assembled group, by which their doubts had
been at last wholly dispelled, and a new and glorious
conviction of the divinely certificated lordship of
Jesus had come to possess them all in common.

The fact of the empty tomb seems to me as indisputable as any fact of history. If we find it now
impossible to suggest a deliberate fraud on the part
of the apostles [2]—and such a suggestion is negatived

---

[1] Luke xxiv. 21.

[2] I suppose the currency among the Jews of the report of such
fraudulent action on their part must be assumed to account for
Matt. xxviii. 13, 15. "His disciples came by night and stole him

alike by their character and by the state of despondency and hopelessness in which they were—there is no plausible explanation of the empty tomb. As to their experiences of the risen Christ, our earliest written witness is that of St. Paul, which we must examine.

But we must remark that there can be no reasonable doubt that what the apostles understood on the evidence of the empty tomb and the appearances was a *corporal* resurrection—viz. that the body of Jesus had been rescued from corruption and raised to a new kind of life. Peter and Paul in the Acts are alike represented as expressing the conviction that " he saw no corruption." [1] Now we turn to St. Paul's witness.

He wrote his First Epistle to the Corinthians in the spring of A.D. 55. A current doubt among the Corinthian Christians, not about the resurrection of Jesus, but about the destiny of those of their number who had passed away since they believed, leads St. Paul to repeat with much precision what he had taught them on his first visit to them in A.D. 50 or 51. But what he then taught them was nothing of his own. It was the common matter of the apostolic testimony (" Therefore whether it be I or they [the other apostles], so we preach and so ye believed " [2])— it was what he had " received " when he first became a Christian—probably in precise form at his first return to Jerusalem to " visit Cephas," that is Peter, three years after his conversion, which had occurred at some date soon after A.D. 30. What he taught them then was, as we see, a sort of formulated record of

away. . . . This saying was spread abroad among the Jews until this day." But we cannot feel complete confidence in the story of the military guard.

[1] Acts ii. 31, xiii. 37.   [2] 1 Cor. xv. 11.

the appearances, to which obviously he adds the personal record of what he had himself seen on his conversion.

"Now I make known unto you, brethren, the gospel which I preached unto you, which also ye received. . . . I make known, I say, in what words [1] I preached it unto you. . . . For I delivered unto you first of all that which also I received, how that Christ died for our sins according to the Scriptures; and that he was buried; and that he hath been raised on the third day according to the Scriptures; and that he appeared to Cephas; then to the twelve; then he appeared to above five hundred brethren at once, of whom the greater part remain until now, but some are fallen asleep; then he appeared to James; then to all the apostles; and last of all, as unto one born out of due time [an abortion], he appeared to me also."

This enumeration squares very well with the appearances recorded in the Gospels, save that it is a record of appearances to the " chosen witnesses " and omits the appearances to the disciples on the way to Emmaus and, notably, those to the women. This is very natural in a formal record drawn up by Jews. Also no note is taken of some appearances, recorded in the Fourth Gospel only. This again is not surprising. The object of the Fourth Gospel was largely to supply real (or as some would say, imagined) incidents which the common traditions had left unnoticed. Granted these omissions, the summary record in St. Paul squares well with the records or intimations in the Gospels and Acts. There the appearance to Peter alone is mentioned as occurring first,[1]

[1] Or " with what purpose," " in what sense "; cf. Acts x. 29.
[2] Luke xxiv. 34.

followed by the appearance to the twelve.[1] The
appearance to the five hundred is necessarily an appearance in Galilee, where alone there were so many
persons who in some sense could be called disciples,
and it can be identified with the appearance recorded
in St. Matthew.[2] The appearance to James is suggested
by the position which James is found occupying in
the primitive community in the record of Acts. The
later appearance to all the Apostles is naturally
identified with that specified in Acts i. 4, where the
summary which concludes the author's earlier book,
the Gospel of Luke, is developed in more explicit
form. All this is very satisfying if the documents are
treated naturally as historical documents.

The attempts to evade the evidence of St. Paul
appear to me extraordinarily forced. Thus (1)
St. Paul's assertion that Christ both died and was
raised the third day " according to the Scriptures " is
supposed to carry with it the suspicion that the belief
in the resurrection the third day was due to the felt
necessity for interpreting Scripture prophecy. But
this is most improbable. There is no prophecy
which compelled any such belief. The particular
text of Hosea suggested (" After three days he will
raise us up and we shall live in his sight ") has no
natural reference to Christ and cannot be shown to
have carried any influence. It is most true, as our
Lord is recorded to have insisted, that there are passages in the Old Testament which present us with a
suffering servant of Jehovah who fails and dies and
yet is divinely vindicated, passages which suggest
the idea of a vindication of the Christ through or
in spite of failure and death. But there was nothing,
except the occurrences recorded in the Gospels, to

[1] Luke xxiv. 36 ff   [2] Matt. xxviii. 16 ff.

account for the definite assertion " The third day he was raised from the dead."

Nor, again, (2) is there any plausibility in the constantly made suggestion that as St. Paul's own experience on the road to Damascus was a vision of Christ in glory, and as from heaven, so presumably he imagined the earlier visions of the apostolic company, not at all as they are recorded in the Gospels. On the contrary, St. Paul treats his own appearance as abnormal in time—he uses the rather startling expression " an abortion "—and there is not the slightest reason to suppose that he thought of the earlier appearances as given under the same conditions.

(3) Nor, again, is there any plausibility in the suggestion that inasmuch as St. Paul contemplates a resurrection of the departed members of the Church, which is consistent with their having suffered dissolution of their physical bodies, and declares that " flesh and blood [i.e. humanity under the physical conditions of the present] shall not inherit the kingdom of God," so we may suppose that he can have laid no stress upon the resurrection of Christ's *body*, but only upon His appearance in another "spiritual" body. If we read the whole passage we see that St. Paul has in mind three different kinds of resurrection : (i) the resurrection of Christ on the third day after His death and burial ; (ii) the resurrection of the since departed Christians, whose bodies had been presumably subject to the natural process of dissolution, but who were to receive at the final coming of the Christ in glory spiritual bodies, which would be both different from the bodies which had seen corruption and yet in physical continuity with them, in the way suggested by the grains sowed in the ground and rotting there, but yet living again in the ears

which spring from their dissolution; and (iii) the sudden transformation of those who shall be actually alive at the second coming, who " in a moment," " in the twinkling of an eye at the last trump," shall be transformed from the state of present-day physical life to the condition of the spiritual and glorified bodies wherewith they shall be associated with those who were dead and are now raised and with Christ. In all these three classes of cases St. Paul conceives a transformation more or less gradual or sudden of the natural body into the spiritual—" we shall all be changed "—and quite plainly he finds the norm or pattern in the resurrection of Christ, in whose case he plainly conceives in the simplest manner that in respect of that body in which He died and *was buried*—in respect of that same body He was raised.

As to the condition of Christ's resurrection body, he says nothing. We can only presume that he modelled his conception of the resurrection body of those who are in Christ upon what he believed about Christ the first-fruits. On this hypothesis he would have conceived of Christ's resurrection body as what he calls spiritual ; and I think that the ideas suggested in the Gospels agree very well with this conception. The risen Christ is represented as having passed out of the grave clothes, leaving them to collapse,[1] and as having left the tomb empty before the stone was rolled away.[2] Henceforth He is not represented as living here or there—in Jerusalem or in Galilee, at this house or that, or moving hither or thither on foot. He is translated apparently into a higher sphere of being, out of which he manifests himself in one form

[1] John xx. 6, 7; cf. Latham's *Risen Master* (Cambridge Press, 1901), p. 29.   [2] Mark xvi. 6.

or another as suits His spiritual purpose, appearing
in a room " when the doors were shut " as one who
no longer felt physical obstacles, but who could still
submit, if His purpose so demanded, to physical
conditions ; as showing His wounded side and hands,
and even eating and drinking with His disciples.
His condition is one of which hitherto men had never
had experience. His spiritual body was material
indeed, but it was one in which matter was wholly
subservient to spiritual purpose, and no longer
in any way an impediment or a restraint. To me it
appears incredible that the evangelists could have
derived from any other source than the actual
experiences of the first disciples the subtle details
which suggest the complex picture of the " spiritual
body " of Jesus after the resurrection.

My contention is, then, that we must accept St.
Paul's record in the only sense that it legitimately
bears, and read in the light of it the fragmentary
records of the evangelists. The apostles had a serious
sense of what it meant to be witnesses before the world
of a fact of quite transcendent and crucial importance.
They drew up their record in such a form as that in
which St. Paul gives it as the unanimous witness of
the apostles. Then the evangelists, according to their
special purposes in writing and their special sources
of information, give us particular stories of this or
that appearance which can be woven into a continuous
and harmonious narrative, as is successfully done by
Dr. Swete,[1] but with regard to which I do not feel the
least anxiety to deny discrepancies of detail, such as
occur always in the unstudied narrative, of first-hand
witnesses. Certainly the evangelist St. Luke had no
very rigid conception of the accuracy required of a

[1] *Appearances of our Lord after His Passion* (Macmillan).

faithful recorder, as we see if we compare the three
accounts he gives us of St. Paul's conversion—one by
himself and the two others in reported speeches of
St. Paul, which differ in details ; or, again, if we compare his earlier account of our Lord's dealings with
His disciples after the resurrection, given in his
Gospel, where all appears as one single interview,
with the account by the same author at the beginning
of the Acts, where the sequence of events is made
much more explicit and clear. This unconstrained
naturalness of narrative is more convincing than
scrupulous accuracy.

There is only one serious apparent discrepancy in
the Synoptic narratives of the manifestations of Jesus
to His disciples after the resurrection. In St. Mark
and St. Matthew our Lord is represented as telling His
disciples on the eve of His passion that after He is
raised up He will go before them into Galilee.[1]   And
accordingly the message sent to them after the
resurrection through the women is that He is going
before them into Galilee, and that there they shall
see Him, as He said to them [2] ; and in St. Matthew
the only recorded appearance is in Galilee.[3]   But the
appearances recorded by St. Luke are all at Jerusalem,
and there is nothing to suggest any injunction to go
into Galilee or any appearance there. This apparent
discrepancy disappears, however, if we suppose that
our Lord intended His disciples, as St. Mark tells us,
to go at once into Galilee, but that delay occurred

[1] Mark xiv. 28; Matt. xxvi. 32.

[2] Mark xvi. 7; Matt. xxviii. 7.

[3] As is well known, the conclusion of St. Mark's Gospel, as we are
familiar with it (xvi. 9–20), appears to be a later addition by one
familiar with the First, Third, and Fourth Gospels.   We can only
conjecture that St. Matthew follows the course of St. Mark as it
originally stood.

owing to their unbelief and slowness of heart.[1] They
needed to be reassured and convinced in Jerusalem,
and, according to the Fourth Gospel, it was eight days
before this conviction was gained by all of them.[2]
This accounts for the earlier manifestations in Jerusalem. St. Luke had special information about these
which he gives us, and does not seem to have understood the original intention of Jesus or its tardy fulfilment. If this was so, we understand the relation of
the two sets of appearances, both of which, as we have
seen, are implied in St. Paul's earlier summary.
Then after the appearance recorded by St. Matthew
they must have returned to Jerusalem and received
the injunction to tarry there till they were endued
with power from on high.[3] The forty days specified
by St. Luke [4] gives time for this sequence of events.

My contention is, then, that the historical evidence
for the resurrection of our Lord the third day from the
dead and His subsequent manifestations of Himself to
His apostles is in the highest degree cogent. Nothing
can resist it, except the sort of treatment of the narratives which can render insecure almost any historical
evidence. No doubt what makes it convincing is the
sense that this act of God in vindication of His Christ
is no mere portent, but something which our reason
needs and welcomes. The Bible records a long-drawn-
out process of divine redemption culminating in Jesus
Christ. His rejection and execution upon the Cross
would, taken by itself, have laid upon human faith an
impossible strain. There is no reason to believe that
anything at all resembling what the Acts records could

[1] Luke xxiv. 11, 25.

[2] Even when they reached Galilee, the narrative of St. John xxi.
1–14 would suggest that they were still bewildered and did not
fully understand their mission.

[3] Luke xxiv. 49; Acts i. 4.   [4] Acts i. 3.

have happened except on the basis of a conviction which the resurrection alone could have generated in the minds of the disciples. What they needed and received in His corporal resurrection was the assurance that the power of God—the Creator and ruler of the whole world, material and moral—was, in spite of the seeming failure of the Cross, on the side of Jesus. In this supreme crisis nothing could reassure them but such an evidence of divine purpose undefeated—such a foretaste of the day of the Lord, the day when God is to come into His own. And for us still to-day the ultimate trial of faith lies in the seeming weakness of good in the conflict with evil. It is supremely hard to believe that the whole power of the universe really and ultimately serves a moral purpose. It is only a corporal miracle such as the resurrection of Jesus which gives us the needed reassurance that there is only one sovereignty in the universe, the sovereignty of the righteous God, the Father of our Lord Jesus Christ, and that in the full meaning of the term " Jesus is Lord."

II. The Ascension of Christ

The New Testament as a whole is full of the conviction that Christ who was crucified was not only raised from the dead, but also by the right hand of God exalted to the seat of supreme sovereignty in the heavens.[1] His " session at the right hand of God " is, as has always been recognized, a symbolical statement, for, on all showing, God has no right hand. But the language used implies that the assumption into glory was an historical event, something that happened

[1] See Acts ii. 33–4; Rom. viii. 34; Eph. iv. 9, 10; 1 Tim. iii. 16; Heb. i. 3, iv. 14, etc.; 1 Pet. iii. 22; John vi. 62.

at a particular date, and St. Luke gives us the story of what occurred at the beginning of the Acts. This story of the ascension, as it presented itself to the apostles' eyes, involved no fresh miracle. It was simply the last of a series of " manifestations," all of which postulate in the risen body of Christ superiority to the conditions of material bodies as we know them. This has been pointed out. All the appearances were, it seems, condescensions to conditions of space and material life to which the risen Christ was no longer subject. Each was a purposive " manifestation." The last, the ascension, as St. Luke records it, was of the same kind. It taught the lesson of Christ's exaltation under the material symbol of a physical rising. Very likely those whose minds were first impressed by this ascension believed, as we no longer believe, that there is a place called heaven above our heads, and that the path of the ascending Jesus was the way thither. But still to-day, with our superior knowledge of the cosmic system, there is no other symbolic action which can be imagined which could convey the desired impression. Nor can we imagine how, without some such impressive occurrence, bringing the appearances of Christ to a decisive end, the disciples could have reached the state of mind in which we find them in the opening of the Acts, in which they are wholly without expectation of any more " manifestations " of Christ and wholly set on what is promised them—spiritual equipment for a task of unknown magnitude.[1]

[1] Heavenly spirits appear as messengers both to convey the first information of Christ's resurrection and on the occasion of the ascension, appearing apparently as men, not with wings. If such spirits exist normally unseen, I do not see why their occasional materialization should be incredible.

III. The Virgin Birth of Jesus

A flood of controversy—both by way of attack and rejoinder—has been poured over this question within the last fifty years, and it has a bewildering effect upon a student. But it seems to me that certain points emerge sufficiently clearly, which I will endeavour to point out.[1]

1. Great stress was laid at the beginning of the apostolic mission upon personal witness. The personal witness of the apostles had extended " from the baptism of John unto the day that he [Jesus] was received up from us," and their preaching about Jesus did not accordingly go farther back than the beginning of the Lord's public ministry ; and it was solely on the ground of this witness, and especially on the ground of the resurrection, that faith in Jesus was demanded. Consequently nothing concerning His birth—except His descent from David, which was apparently un-disputed,[2] and that He belonged to the family of Joseph the carpenter of Nazareth, who apparently died before the public ministry began, and of Mary, who certainly survived into the early days of the Church—entered into the first preaching of the gospel or the first knowledge of the Church. Certainly nothing concerning the birth of Christ was part of that assurance on the basis of which faith in Jesus was claimed. I may add that it ought not to this day to form part of the basis of the claim. This limitation of the apostolic witness accounts for the silence of St.

---

[1] Accurate and full information will be found in Dr. Box's *Virgin Birth of Christ* (Pitman, 1916), and I may refer to my *Dissertations* (John Murray), Diss. i.

[2] Mark x. 47 ; Rom. i. 3 ; Heb. vii. 14.

Mark,[1] who gives us in the main the cycle of Peter's preaching, and the silence of St. Paul. If, however, Luke was Paul's companion, and had gathered the materials of his Gospel before Paul's first captivity was over, he must surely have known all that Luke knew and therefore the secret of the virgin birth. He may very well have known it earlier. His faith in the radical sinlessness of Christ—sinlessness, I mean, not in fact only but in principle, inasmuch as Christ was the new man, the sinless source of the new manhood—would have made the idea very agreeable to him. But in any case, that he does not mention it seems to me nothing more strange than that he does not mention other crucial events of our Lord's life, as the bestowal of the Holy Spirit at His baptism, or His transfiguration. This limitation of the apostolic preaching accounts also for there being no narrative of the birth in St. John's Gospel, which is essentially a record of personal experience, but in fact St. John's Gospel, written at the end of the first century, shows evident signs that the writer knew and believed the virgin birth.[2]

[1] We note, however, that St. Mark apparently shrinks from the phrase "the carpenter's son" : see Mark vi. 3, compared to Matt. xiii. 55. It is probable that the latter phrase was original. Phrases attributing paternity to Joseph recur in the other Evangelists, where their meaning is guarded by the opening narratives.

[2] There is a reading of John i. 13 witnessed to by a number of fathers beginning from the second century—" *who was born* not of bloods [i.e. not of the mixture of human seeds] nor of the will of the flesh, nor of the will of a man [a husband], but of God"—which directly describes our Lord's birth of a virgin, and not a few moderns, like Dean Inge, find it convincing. For myself, I am disposed to prefer the reading of the MSS. But I have no doubt that this common reading clearly presupposes the fact of the virgin birth. See my *St. John's Epistles*, p. 139. Also I think Dr. Chase (*Belief and Creed*, Macmillan, p. 67 ff.) has made quite evident that St. John's irony is apparent in vii. 42, and that the fact that Jesus was born at Bethlehem is in his mind. Also I think Rev. xii. 4 has the narrative of Matthew behind it.

2. But when the first disciples had settled down to their faith in Jesus, on the basis of His resurrection and His life and teaching and the mission of His Spirit, they must have enquired about His birth and early years and must have wanted to know everything that could be known—all the more that even during our Lord's ministry it would appear as if scandal about His birth was not unknown.   This appears to be suggested in the taunt of the Jews.[1]   Anyway, they must have wanted to know.   It may very well have been that during Mary's life nothing was said in public. But Joseph must have taken steps before his death to guard Mary's reputation, and Mary could not have failed to leave her experience on record.   So we look at the two accounts we have got.   The effect is somewhat overwhelming.   The account in Matthew is wholly from the side of Joseph—his perplexities—the divine guidance vouchsafed to him in dreams—how he became the guardian of the new-born child through strange perils—the further guidance which brought him back from Egypt [2] and to Nazareth.   This early narrative of Matthew exhibits the author's zeal to find fulfilments of prophecy, but it very strongly suggests a statement by Joseph underlying it.   On the other hand, the narrative in Luke i. and ii.—so plainly a woman's story—if it is true, must be Mary's story.

3. Now let us take Luke's narrative apart.   He claims in his preface accurate knowledge of the course of all things from the first, and then promptly begins with the narrative of the birth.   Luke is a very honest man and good historian.   (The historical statement of

---

[1] John viii. 41.

[2] That Jesus was taken to Egypt was the basis of a Jewish or heathen accusation that He had learned sorcery there: see Box, *The Virgin Birth of Christ* (Pitman), p. 205.

Luke ii. 1–2, so long supposed by its falsity to discredit these early chapters, is now no longer regarded as false, but is found erected into a " proof text " in learned works about the Roman method of provincial administration.[1]) It is obvious that when you pass from Luke's preface to his narrative you pass from very good literary Greek to a Greek which is Greek only in the words used. The spirit and method is quite Aramaic. St. Luke, then, is quoting an Aramaic document or story. It is a woman's narrative. It is intensely intimate. It is primeval—that is to say, it suggests, if read attentively, no idea of an Incarnation, only of the coming of the promised Christ,[2] and, though it gives a hint of a searching crisis and anxious trials to come,[3] it could not have had its origin after His rejection by the Jews. The new-born Child is to be the promised son of David to restore the position of His house. He is to " have the throne of his father David," and to "reign over the house of Jacob for ever." [4]

We may take it for certain that (to quote Harnack's words) " the conjecture . . . that the idea of a birth from a virgin is a heathen myth, which was received by Christians, contradicts the entire earliest developments of Christian tradition." The early chapters both of Matthew and Luke are profoundly and thoroughly Jewish : Jewish anticipation never included a birth from a virgin mother for the Messiah ; and the whole atmosphere of pagan legend was alien from the home of these narratives.[5]

[1] See above, p. 197.
[2] See my *Dissertation*, pp. 17–18.
[3] Luke ii. 34–5.   [4] Luke i. 32–3.
[5] See Box, chap. viii. and my *Dissertation*, pp. 55 ff. ; also Harnack, *History of Dogma* (E. T.), vol. i. 100 n., and *Luke the Physician*, pp. 102 ff.

I do not see why appearances of angelic spirits should be put aside as obviously false.[1] But I am not concerned to deny *any* influence of pious imagination upon the story—only that it rests upon a real experience of Mary, as to which she could not be mistaken, viz. that Jesus was not begotten of a human father, though He was truly conceived in her womb and nourished and born in normal fashion.

4. When we take St. Matthew's narrative we have to deal with a Gospel the history of which is obscure. It is almost certain, I think, that it rests upon the work of Matthew the apostle and the Gospel of Mark, but whether the first two chapters were contained in Matthew's Aramaic work or come from the unknown Jewish editor of the book as we have it, we cannot tell. Plainly the author, whoever he was, is deeply interested to find fulfilment of prophecy, but whatever is thought about some of these suggested fulfilments, it is improbable that the "prophecies" brought forward in evidence in these chapters suggested the "events" to the imagination of the writer. The two last are notoriously difficult to treat as prophecies. The prophecy from Micah might have suggested, and did suggest, Bethlehem as the place of Christ's birth, but in the light of recent vindication of St. Luke's statements, the fact that Jesus was born there cannot reasonably be impugned. There remains the Greek version of Isaiah's prophecy, "The virgin shall be with child," of which it must be said that it had not suggested to the Jews the idea that the Messiah was destined to be born of one still a virgin. It would appear as if it was only after the Christians had come to believe the facts as recorded by St. Luke that they discovered this proof text.

[1] See above, p. 273.

The strongest grounds for believing in its actual occurrence are the evidence of St. Luke, and the striking indications afforded by the narrative of St. Matthew that it has underlying it the experiences of Joseph.

5. If we take the two narratives together, we find them utterly independent, and the author of each one appears to be ignorant of the narrative of the other. They are not strictly discrepant, but independent. The events of each can be fitted into those of the other, but Luke plainly does not know of the event of St. Matthew ii., nor Matthew apparently of the previous residence at Nazareth. But this independence of course emphasizes their point of agreement, viz. that Jesus was born at Bethlehem of a virgin mother.

6. That two discrepant genealogies should have been admitted into the Gospels (which was felt as a grave difficulty from the earliest times) is an amazingly clear sign that the Church was not at all given to manipulate documents in order to produce harmony. I think we may be quite content here, without seeking explanations of the discrepancy, to recognize that the Jewish families of pure descent were given to constructing genealogies; that these genealogies would have affiliated Jesus to His "father" in whatever sense he was His father; and that all we are concerned to ask is that these two genealogies should be taken to represent two independent attempts to construct a genealogy for Jesus.[1]

7. Criticism of the destructive kind has for long years fastened on these early chapters of Matthew and Luke as upon the weakest point in the citadel of the Creeds. I think that those who believe that the

[1] See Box, pp. 12 ff. and 38 ff., and *Dissertations*, p. 38.

historical citadel can be maintained should insist
that the question of the birth is secondary and not
primary, viz. that the question of faith in Jesus must
rest still, where it was made to rest from the beginning, on the life, teaching, death, and resurrection
of Jesus. On these, quite apart from any questions
concerning His birth, the faith stood and still could
stand. Nevertheless, when that standing-ground
has been gained, and the question of the birth,
blackened as it has been with controversy, is
approached, the honest student must not confuse
the raising of every conceivable objection to the
stories with evidence that they are really insecure.
Many of the objections have been fundamentally
refuted. In result I claim that the fair student
cannot resist the conviction that Luke's story shows
every sign of coming from a trustworthy source—
one of the only two trustworthy sources—and
Matthew's narrative from the other; and their
agreement is emphasized by their exceedingly
obvious independence. He must also admit that in
these two narratives there is no later dogmatic
motive at work. The idea of Christ is simply the
Jewish idea of the Messiah. Nevertheless, when the
story of the birth of Jesus became known—I suppose
before the destruction of Jerusalem—it was eagerly
welcomed, no doubt because of its harmony with
the belief about Christ's person as more than human.
The fact of the virgin birth became at once, it would
appear, by the beginning of the second century, an
element of the creed of the Church, now being formulated.[1] This was in part no doubt because of its

[1] See *Dissertations*, p. 41.   The evidence of *The Odes of Solomon*
should now be added.

felt congruity both with the idea of the divine
incarnation and with the idea of Christ as the sinless
source of the new humanity, the second Adam.
Already I think in St. John i. 13 the connexion of the
virgin birth with the sinless source of the regenerated
life is apparent. For myself, I confess I feel this
connexion to be most intimate. I think we are
generally right to resent any attempt to base upon
supposed logical necessity the claim that such and
such an event did actually happen. We doubt the
power of man's reason to say how things must have
happened.[1] Thus we may be thankful that it is
demonstrable that neither the idea of the incarnation,
nor that of the second Adam, lies behind the narratives of the birth in Matthew and Luke. Moreover,
the course of our argument has not yet taken us to
the point where the doctrine of Christ's person comes
in question, nor the doctrine of original or racial
sin. Nevertheless, I must confess that I cannot
imagine how the birth of the really sinless man could
have occurred without some physical miracle, so sure
do I feel that sin has somehow affected the physical
stock ; and I once drew from Huxley the admission
that if he believed—what he did not—that Jesus
was strictly sinless, he would suppose that that
involved as well a physical as a moral miracle. Nor
can I conceive how the birth in the flesh of the divine
person of the Son could have been mediated by

[1] Historical Christianity owes a deep debt of ingratitude to the
Roman Church for having allowed the sense of what would be fitting
in the case of the Blessed Virgin to become the basis for affirming,
with different degrees of dogmatic assurance, as two facts of
history, the immaculate conception and the corporal assumption
into heaven of the Blessed Virgin, for which there is no historical
evidence worth any consideration.

purely natural means. But these are questions which we are not yet in a position to entertain.

.   .   .   .   .

What I have desired to do in this chapter is to let it appear that, if a person will approach the Gospels without a dogmatic prejudice that miracles are incredible, he will find himself convinced that they actually occurred, and in particular that Jesus Christ was really raised from the dead the third day, really gave to His disciples the symbolical assurance of an ascension heavenward, and was really born of a virgin mother.

CHAPTER XII

CONCLUSION

LET us review the course of our argument. After
analysing the causes of the existing collapse in the
religious tradition among Englishmen (chapter i),
we sought to make a fresh start and rebuild from its
foundation the fabric of a rational belief, laying
stress on the importance for everyone of seeking to
form decisions—at least such provisional decisions,
based on the balance of probabilities, as can be
" put to account " by faith, and being verified in
experience can become convictions, or what St.
John calls knowledge.[1]

Thus, after some consideration of the varied means
and methods of apprehending truth (chapter ii),
we examined the grounds which seem to make faith
in God in some sense a rational necessity. But this
sort of philosophical faith (what is called " the higher
Pantheism ") we found intellectually unsatisfactory
because of the seriousness and magnitude of the questions to which it supplies either no answer or a very
vacillating answer. The immanent God of philosophy,
whose transcendence the reason seems unable to
establish, appears on being cross-questioned to be no
more than nature in one of its aspects. His (or its)
personality and character seems uncertain, and the

---

[1] 1 John v. 18, 19, 20.

grounds for belief or disbelief in the ultimate
supremacy of moral purpose in the world deeply
conflicting. Thus the higher Pantheism is always
in danger of lapsing into the lower Pantheism, and
in result seems to leave us practically where the
Greeks were before the vast moral uplift of Jewish
and Christian Theism came into our world. Especially from the religious point of view this immanent
God who is to be found in all things, but cannot be
conceived of as entertaining any particular purpose,
or answering particular prayers, or loving or judging
individual men, is utterly unsatisfying. Our minds
turned longingly to the God of the Hebrew prophets
and the God and Father of our Lord Jesus Christ
(chapter iii).

We satisfied ourselves that reason has no right to
decide *a priori* that the old idea of a divine revelation
is rationally untenable, and very carefully we sought
to examine the grounds of this belief. Critically
scrutinized, we found them in a high degree convincing.
We found that it is very hard to resist the conviction
that the prophets and Jesus Christ (regarded at present
as simply one of the prophets) were in touch—as other
men were not—with Reality, with the real God ; and
that in a long and continuous process, more or less
gradual, He was really communicating to them the
truth by which men could live, both about the divine
nature and purpose and about human nature. The
indisputable access of moral power and capacity to
deal with life, which the faithful recipients of this
word of God are seen to have received of old and still
receive, appears to certificate the truth of the message
which is the source of this new power ; for the communicated power depends wholly on the revelation
being regarded as true, that is, as true for the intellect

—postulating propositions about God and man and the universe which must be truths for philosophy as well as " practical truths " (chapter iv).

Then we analysed the intellectual content of the Revelation and found that, while it needs and can assimilate, as it did in fact assimilate, the philosophical belief in the divine immanence in nature, yet it lays its stress on the Personality of God, His absoluteness, His transcendence as the creator of all that is, prior to the world and independent of it, and His essential goodness and love. And with regard to man, we found it emphasizing his freedom, created as he is for free correspondence with God and for immortal sonship, and also his sins and his sinfulness. This universal human sin has introduced into the world the most widespread havoc, and has made necessary a divine process of judgement and also of redemption, which, beginning through the Jews, shows itself universal in Jesus Christ, and expresses itself in a divine kingdom here and now at work in the world, and destined for final victory in the Day of the Lord, when God shall come into His own in His whole universe (chapter v).

These new *data* for philosophy we then brought back to the area of intellectual criticism. We did not find that (*a*) science, legitimately so called, could offer any valid objection to their acceptance, the reality of freedom in man with all its intellectual implications being a fact of experience which science cannot ignore. Then (*b*) in the region of philosophy, when we are frank with ourselves and candidly open-minded, we discover that the idea of God which Hebrew religion supplied to the world is infinitely more intelligible than the idea of the philosophers, inasmuch as personality rather than abstract intellect is its

dominant category, both in its estimate of God and
of man. In particular we seemed to see the intellectual
necessity for the belief in God the Creator.   There
remained, we found, a very real and serious difficulty
in interpreting the whole experience of the universe—
including the seemingly purely material and animal
world—in terms of divine goodness and love.   Nevertheless, in the region of human life, the doctrine of
God's goodness has been undoubtedly verified in the
deepest experience of the best of men, not least in
the greatest sufferers, and we could not feel justified
in refusing the act of faith which assents to it as true
for the whole universe in its final outcome.   Also we
satisfied ourselves that (c) neither the science of
comparative religion nor (d) that of historical criticism
offers, so far, any bar to the acceptance of the religion
of the prophets and of Christ as true in fact and for
all men.

Thus our acceptance of the reality of divine
revelation leaves us free men, intellectually, in the
regions of philosophy and the sciences (chapter vi).

This faith postulates God as entertaining and
carrying out a particular purpose of redemption,
which begins with the race of Israel and discloses
itself as universal in Jesus Christ.   As proceeding
through a particular race and expressing itself in its
history, the religion of the Old Testament is an historical
religion, but it depends upon no particular incident
which critical science is tempted to deny.   But when
we advance upon the New Testament, the situation
is quite different.   There the divine self-disclosure
culminates in a particular person, Jesus Christ, who
comes to be believed in as the personal incarnation
of God (though with this special belief about the
person of Christ we are not concerned in this volume),

and whose recorded life is full of miraculous incidents, some of which—as His birth of a virgin, His resurrection, His ascension—appear as articles in the Christian Creed—essential elements of the self-disclosure of God. But criticism has been exhibiting now for some three generations an even violent aversion to miracle. Thus the attempt is made to disembarrass Christianity from the supposed disadvantages of the miraculous and (generally) of the supernatural. That an " historical religion " in the Christian sense has grave disadvantages in a critical age is obvious. On the other hand, we were forced to see how the strength of Christianity, especially as appealing to the common man, lay in its being a creed of facts. In particular we were led to stress the value of facts for religion by contrast to symbolic stories or Platonic myths (chapter vii).

Thus, to put the " historical religion " to the test, we took a preliminary survey of the Gospels and the rest of the New Testament documents, and we found ourselves on very sure grounds of history. The historicity of the New Testament on the whole appeared to be singularly convincing (chapter viii). We went back accordingly and examined the underlying spirit and motive of the destructive criticism of the last century, and we found that there could be no mistake about its strong, dogmatic prejudice against the miraculous and in great part the supernatural, such as has made the critics most arbitrary and uncritical in their treatment of the evidence. We examined the confident assertion of a few English scholars that the miracles could be eliminated from the Creed without touching the doctrinal foundation and found it singularly groundless (chapter ix). Then we sought to analyse the intellectual bases of this critical

prejudice against miracles and against the supernatural, and seemed to find in its bases a view of
nature, as both mechanical and self-complete, which is
without justification. It seemed to us that the fact
of freedom in nature, which inevitably extends itself
from man to God from whom it comes, opens the
door to the possibility of miraculous action, the
postulate of miracles being the real freedom of God
to " use means " for the redemption of a world that
sin has destroyed. We observed that miracles rightly
conceived, or as they are presented to us in the New
Testament, are not arbitrary violations of the world
order, but rather divine acts done for the restoration
of an order which sin had too grossly violated. Other
aspects of the miraculous were considered, and we
were left determined to investigate the question of
evidence without any obstinate and blinding prejudice
(chapter x). Thus we sought to estimate the evidence
for the reality of our Lord's miracles as a whole, both
" nature miracles " and miracles of healing, and then
in particular the evidence for the great miraculous
events in our Lord's story, which have been taken up
as elements in the Christian Creed, the resurrection
the third day from the dead the ascension, and the
birth of Mary the Virgin. It appeared to us that
the evidence of actual occurrence was so cogent that
nothing short of dogmatic *a priori* assertion of their
impossibility, or at least incredibility—an assertion
which we cannot make—could justify the refusal of it.
And accordingly we are bound to accept these
miracles as real occurrences (chapter xi).

Three points shall be made in conclusion :

1. My aim in this volume has been simply the
reconstruction of belief in God, and particularly of
such belief in God as is the background and pre-

supposition of the distinctively Christian beliefs, and such as is specially due to the prophets of Israel. But we have been driven upon the field of the New Testament for two reasons. Though we have considered Jesus of Nazareth only as a prophet, we cannot ignore the fact that, while He bases Himself upon the religion of the prophets, He yet advances upon it, and claims to have more to say with an authority which is altogether His own. Thus the prophetic doctrine of God is not complete except with the doctrine of Jesus included. But I have been driven more directly upon the ground of New Testament criticism by the question of miracles, and this because it is directly bound up with the fundamental question of the nature of God ; and before you can have satisfactory discussion of the specifically Christian questions—about Christ's person—about the atonement—about the Holy Trinity—you must have reached a stable position about this doctrine of God. Now if, as has been contended in this book, the prophets of Israel were the organs of a real self-disclosure of God, intended for the whole world but given in the first instance through them, then there can be to my mind no question at all but that miracles of God's working are possible and credible on adequate evidence. The evidence is there, cogent and, as it would seem, unanswerable. What hinders acceptance of the miraculous is the absence of belief that the God of the prophets is the real God. There will be no revival of specifically Christian belief except on the basis of, or accompanied with, a revived belief in the God of the prophets, and, conversely, granted the God of the prophets to be real, the claim for miracles will be at least no obstacle to belief in the Creeds. I go further and say that miracles, i.e.

20

actions of God in nature marking His special intention for the redemption of mankind, will seem, at the crucial moment of religious history, so natural as to be almost inevitable accompaniments of the revelation. On the other hand, the disbelief in miracles is not really based on historical criticism, but on a belief about God which is at bottom a rejection of the prophetic claim to reveal the real God, and a return to what is substantially the Greek philosophic theory of God, which Christianity in part assimilated, but in more important respects displaced. This higher Pantheism, both of the ancient Greeks and of the majority of modern philosophers, has so feeble a hold on the divine transcendence, and even personality, and at bottom is so deeply inclined to an identification of God and nature, like Spinoza's, that it can find no place for miracles and is bound to explain them away. But also the faith of the higher Pantheism is so uncertain of the moral character of the Ultimate Reality—so uncertain whether goodness is more than one element in a universe which is much greater than it—as to weaken profoundly, especially in the conscience of the " ordinary man," the sense of the final supremacy of moral purpose in the world. This is to say, in other words, that the higher Pantheism tends inevitably in common opinion to become the lower Pantheism, which merges God in nature and takes for inevitable all that is. I do not think it is open to doubt that the belief in the real occurrence of miracles and the belief in the God of the prophets are bound up with one another in an inevitable coherence. And, on the other hand, by a like inevitable coherence, the denial of the credibility of miracles is bound up with a disbelief in the prophetic God and a relapse upon a kind of Pantheism which substantially is that of the

Greek philosophers, especially in its effect or lack of effect upon the common conscience.

2. Secondly, I want to make this point. I think the decision in the great alternative, to which I have just called attention, turns, to an extent which it is hard to exaggerate, upon the question of the reality of freewill in man, not in any exaggerated sense, but in the restricted yet real sense which I have endeavoured to define above.[1] If man is really free, there is a real element of creativeness and spontaneity and contingency in the heart of nature, the conception of which may be extended indefinitely, but which is, at least, there where man is. The time process, the true meaning of which becomes first apparent in man, is then shown to have real meaning. God may, nay, as I have contended, must, be conceived of as prior to creation or nature, complete in Himself. But creation, or the process of nature, is a continuous process in which it is the purpose of God to reproduce in a gradual order, and finally, at least, by the co-operation of free spirits, an expression of His being and will. This is what we may reverently call an enterprise or an adventure on the part of God, because the element of freedom—freedom which may prove lawless—is something which God Himself will not overrule. The time series represents, with all its elements of contingency and uncertainty, a real and long-continued effort of God, though its end is certain. And this freedom allowed to man postulates a like and much deeper freedom in God, and supplies, as has been pointed out, the rationale for God's miraculous actions—that is, His occasional innovations upon normal method. On the other hand, if freedom is denied to man, it becomes natural to think of real

[1] See above, pp. 139 ff., 234 ff.

freedom as a vain imagination in the case of God also.
Nature becomes simply the necessary self-expression
of God.   Whatever is, could not have been otherwise.
The whole time series becomes inevitable, and, more
than inevitable, illusory.   All that, at the bottom, is
really there for the purified intellect to contemplate
is the absolute nature, the eternal and inevitable
" must have been."

3. Finally, I want to point out the modification
which belief in the reality of the self-disclosure of
God through the Hebrew prophets introduces into the
current doctrine of Relativity, of which Lord Haldane
has recently been the prophet.   No one, I think,
can dispute the truth of this doctrine, though whether
Einstein's discoveries and theories do more than show
it in a novel light I do not feel sure.   Anyway, the
postulates of each branch of human science are not
final and necessary truths, but are relative to the
particular science ;   and the absolute point of view,
from which all must be harmonized, is hard to come
by, and may be unattainable for ever by the finite
minds of men.   Certainly the mind of man is not
capable of discovering absolute truth.   This applies
to moral truth as much as to any other department
of reality.   The judgements of the conscience are not,
and never can be, absolutely the judgements of God.
It applies also (even on the postulate of revelation)
to theology.   The theologians have always emphasized
this.   " We see through a glass darkly " in our thought
about the ultimate things.   Nevertheless, this necessary doctrine of relativity does not supply any valid
ground for excluding the idea that behind the veil of
creation lies the Personal God.   Creation, as Dr.
Pringle Pattison and Lord Haldane say, appears in
"layers" : upon the merely physical or material

supervenes the vital, and upon the vital the rational and the personal. And the personal is, at least, a better image of God than the merely vital or merely mechanical. God, be it said, is superpersonal, but at least personal. Then also the supremely personal can act as a person. He can reveal Himself more intensely here than there. There is no legitimate ground for a dogmatic exclusion of this possibility. And on the surest grounds, as it seems to us, we have found this to be not only possible as a theory but actual as a fact. For those who accept revelation as a fact, in a particular line of history, mediated through the prophets of Israel and culminating in Christ, the doctrine of relativity is certainly not obliterated or negatived. The revelation of God in Christ may be spoken of as establishing " the absolute religion," in the sense that it is, for this world, final and universal, but it does not mean that " the absolute truth " is there unveiled. At least Christianity has never made any such claim. It has never claimed for us in our present condition the power to see God as He is. But, granted this, it does, none the less, introduce a limiting element into the doctrine of relativity. For here, given through the prophets and in Christ, we have not merely a judgement of human reason or conscience liable to all the uncertainties and relativities of such a judgement, but a real word of God. Such word of God is given through men and for men, as they now are, and must therefore be, as compared to absolute truth, relative and imperfect. But the truth which the self-disclosure of God enables us and requires us to put into human words is, as compared to all other human proposi-tions about God, necessarily of a higher quality and infinitely more trustworthy. Any real belief in a

divine self-disclosure carries with it the belief that
the word of God is trustworthy and has an infinitely
higher measure of truth than any merely human
judgement. Granted that it is gradually given, yet
it must be at each stage as close an expression of
absolute truth as human thought and words admit of.
It is for practical purposes absolute truth, because
it can be relied on utterly. This gradual revelation
in its earlier stages was always invested with divine
authority as far as it went. But in Christ it is
postulated for it that it attains completeness and
finality. That claim we have not yet sought to
estimate. Without assuming finality for Christ, let us
be content to recognize that if we believe the authority
behind the prophets and Jesus Christ really to be
the will of the Personal God revealing Himself to
man, the " word of God " proclaimed by them must
be admitted to be in such real sense *absolutely* true,
that it is true for all men and the highest kind of
truth about God which man can attain. It is absolutely true in the sense that any human propositions
which really ignore it or contradict it are misleading
and false.

TABLE OF SUBJECTS

INDEX OF NAMES

Back—" Belief in God "